Resistance and Psychoanalysis

Incitements

Series editors
Peg Birmingham, DePaul University
and Dimitris Vardoulakis, Western Sydney University

Available

Visit the series web page at: edinburghuniversitypress.com/series/incite

Resistance and Psychoanalysis

Impossible Divisions

Simon Morgan Wortham

EDINBURGH
University Press

Edinburgh University Press is one of the leading university presses in the UK. We publish academic books and journals in our selected subject areas across the humanities and social sciences, combining cutting-edge scholarship with high editorial and production values to produce academic works of lasting importance. For more information visit our website: edinburghuniversitypress.com

Edinburgh University Press Ltd
The Tun – Holyrood Road, 12(2f) Jackson's Entry, Edinburgh EH8 8PJ

Typeset in Bembo
by R. J. Footring Ltd, Derby, UK

A CIP record for this book is available from the British Library

ISBN 978 1 4744 2960 3 (hardback)
ISBN 978 1 4744 2962 7 (webready PDF)
ISBN 978 1 4744 2961 0 (paperback)
ISBN 978 1 4744 2963 4 (epub)

Contents

Acknowledgements

Parts of Chapter 1 previously appeared in 'Afterword: Impossible Divisions', *South Atlantic Quarterly* 112:1 (2013), 163–70. An earlier version of Chapter 3, 'What is a Complex?', was first made available in a pre-publication version by the *Journal for Cultural Research* in 2016. An earlier version of Chapter 4, 'Fleeced', was published in *Paragraph* 39:2 (2016), 149–64.

Preface

If nowadays political resistance is not merely embraced and encouraged but also suspected, at least in some quarters, of actually presenting an obstacle to radical political change – constituting, for those that mistrust it, a counter-revolutionary force that effectively arrests capitalism's, or neoliberalism's, trajectory of implosive decline – then resistance is, equally, a complex matter when it comes to psychoanalysis. Quite literally. As we will see in a later chapter, Freud in his 1914 paper 'On the History of the Psycho-Analytic Movement' refers to the theory of complexes which, for him, 'has neither itself produced a psychological theory, nor has it proved capable of easy incorporation into the context of psycho-analytic theory'. The word 'complex', in contrast 'had become naturalized, so to speak, in psycho-analytic language; it is a convenient and often indispensable term for summing up a psychological state descriptively'. For Freud, no other psychoanalytic term had achieved 'such widespread popularity or been so misapplied to the detriment of the construction of clearer concepts': 'Analysts began to speak among themselves of a "return of a complex" where they meant a "return of the repressed", or fell into the habit of saying "I have a complex against him", where the only correct expression would have been "a resistance against him".[1]

Reflecting on psychoanalysis's infancy during a time which marked a fundamental crisis in Europe's own history, Freud seems to waver a little concerning his attitude to the issue at hand. By attributing the term 'complex' almost entirely to Jung, he distances himself from responsibility for its entry into the psychoanalytic lexicon, and downplays its contribution to genuine psychoanalytic categories and forms of thought. For Freud, the word 'complex' has too frequently submitted to the errors and vulgarisations associated with popular psychology (albeit here, nonchalant misuse by analysts themselves is the cause of stern rebuke). Freud feels that habitual use of this word impedes more rigorous psychoanalytic terms, in particular 'repression' and 'resistance', which have greater interpretative power. Still, the word 'complex' is not utterly forsaken, but retains 'indispensable' value in its descriptive capacity. What damns the idea or discourse of the 'complex' – its catch-all quality, its ability to license appealing forms of generalisation – is thus also what partially recommends or redeems it (Freud is, of course, far from unwilling to use the term 'descriptively' on many occasions). Here, then, we find a telling ambivalence that surely prompts further investigation, not least since by *resisting* psychoanalytic theory in its proper form, the word 'complex' actually performs that for which it is purportedly an unfortunate misnomer: resistance itself. We should be wary of the word 'complex' since

---

1 Sigmund Freud, 'On the History of the Psycho-Analytic Movement' (1914), *The Standard Edition of the Complete Psychological Works of Sigmund Freud*, Vol. XIV, ed. and trans. James Strachey (London: The Hogarth Press and the Institute of Psycho-Analysis, 1957), pp. 7–66. For this particular passage, see pp. 29–30.

it is at risk of substituting itself as an *improper* name for more acute psychoanalytic categories. Yet the implication here is that the term itself *precisely* resists or represses that which it nevertheless improperly names: resistance, repression. Through the very act of misnaming, it enacts what it misnames. It performs what it also represses or resists. Resistance 'proper' is thus nowhere more evidently performed than by a term that improperly substitutes for resistance itself. Resistance, it seems, is indeed quite properly an improper business.

For Lacan, following Freud, psychoanalysis does not so much operate on the cause or origin of resistance, but rather on the discourse or speech through which it may be discerned. From this point of view, what is at stake is not what is repressed as such, but the *speaking* of the repressed. Therapeutic treatment therefore concerns itself with the integration of repressed material into a discourse or narrative that the subject can assume. Nevertheless, the speech of the patient is all the while marked and indeed constituted by this resistance. The discourse of the analysand is nothing but the site of resistances, the manifestation of its struggles. Moreover, resistance is far from just the effect of the patient's refusal to countenance or confront the repressed. As Lacan recognises, resistances in psychoanalysis are inherent to the composition of the ego itself. Resistance cannot therefore be ascribed merely to the intentional effort to thwart the analytic impulse. Indeed, rather than being seen as a defence, resistance should be viewed as fundamental, a constitutive quality of the ego as the agent of (resistant) negotiations between unconscious, imaginary and symbolic registers. For Lacan, moreover, the way in which the analyst positions their reaction to the resistances occurring in analysis can itself generate resistance, whether through the reductiveness that arises from overhasty explanation, or through the compromises caused by the desire to achieve assent or agreement with the analysand, or even because of the analyst's wish to overcome resistance itself. Lacan thus challenges the idea that the removal of resistances simply constitutes analytic progress. The analytic confrontation of resistance is as likely answered by the symptom as it is rewarded by advancement to the 'truth'. As such, analysis should be conducted not as an epic or heroic struggle between two egos, since merely opposing resistance can stifle the subject's desire and impede its role in therapeutic terms. When it opposes suggestion, resistance conveys the desire to maintain the subject's desire, and this important feature must somehow be included rather than dispensed with in the analytic process. For Lacan, moreover, the psychoanalytic conception of resistance is less tied to psychological processes as such, and acquires value principally in relation to the analytic work itself. Resistance is less to be considered from the point of view of the subject's psychic properties, but should be understood more specifically in relation to the work of interpretation, as a potentially creative element in what is effectively a creative process. The complexity of a resistance borne of analysis, pitched creatively in the contested domain it inhabits but also forms, resonates strongly throughout the pages of *Resistance and Psychoanalysis*.

This book pursues the question of psychoanalysis and resistance, then, through a number of readings and contexts (including those that recall the question of 'politics', whether more or less directly); readings and contexts which themselves make difficult any prospect of reducing these two terms, or their relationship, to a wholly single or fully stable set of meanings providing the grounds for a classically thetic presentation of the subject matter in question. Rather, my approach is one that hopes for a certain performative tracing of their conjunctural possibilities taking effect throughout the following pages, and in a number of different ways, echoing the formation of resistance in a psychoanalytic sense that I've been describing above.

The book's introduction sets the scene by recognising that more recent reinvestments in the 'political' facility and prospects of psychoanalysis, frequently routed through debates around Lacanianism, display a tendency to dismiss 'poststructuralism' (and, indeed, any vestige of a 'poststructuralist' Lacan), as they attempt sharp distinctions between, say, a materialism supposedly capable of addressing 'political' issues today versus unwanted traces of a longstanding idealism with which 'deconstruction' can now be historically aligned. Reviewing some of Derrida's writing on Lacan, the introduction moves on to assess the dismissal of 'poststructuralism' that one finds, for example, in Žižek's recently published doctoral thesis, originally from 1982. Since the 'political' implications of this dismissal are far from simply 'progressive', the introduction asks questions about the 'politics' of the performative in both Derrida's and Žižek's texts on Lacan, which in turn helps to explain why my own book is less dominated by, and often more critical of, recent critical trends in the field of contemporary continental thought, particularly in terms of its 'political' self-image.

The first part of the book is themed around the question of the possible relationships between violence, including 'political' violence, and resistance in its multiple senses. Taking its cue from a recent return to the work of Frantz Fanon, 'Impossible Divisions' concentrates on the section of *Black Skin, White Masks* entitled 'The Negro and Recognition', where the Hegelian theme of mutual recognition as the origin of man's self-consciousness and potential freedom is tested against the complex circumstances to which colonialism leads. Here, Fanon's idea that the 'Negro slave' is recognised by the 'White Master' in a situation that is *'without conflict'* suggests a possibly double, or self-resistant, meaning. More explicitly, it means that the colonial situation after slavery ushers in something like a phoney war. Perhaps more suggestively, it implies that colonialism's historical interpretation or provenance is not exhausted by the Hegelian master-slave logic. On the basis of this double reading or double possibility of the colonial, one may wonder whether, after Hegel, it is historical *interpretation* or the historical *process* itself that is broken or has gone awry. Such dynamic tensions exposed by Fanon's writing suggest, I argue, an imperfect or impossibly divided dialectics at work throughout his corpus. Indeed, the non–self-identical doubleness of colonial displacement and divided critique is perhaps what gives force and expression to Fanon's interventions in the world, not merely as a historical inspiration but as a multiply charged remainder, something that is still in the making. Lastly, I argue that the section of Fanon's 'The Negro and Recognition' devoted to a critique of Adler points to an earlier footnote in *Black Skin, White Masks* which offers a fairly lengthy engagement with Lacan, allowing us to reread the politics of racial difference into the scene of the Lacanian mirror-stage. Here, the resistant 'other' of psychoanalysis – specifically, the 'other' mirror-stage that Fanon is able to derive from his reading of Lacan in tandem with his psychiatric studies in Antilles – unlocks the possibility of another 'politics' capable of addressing, by better recognising, some of its most significant impasses.

The next chapter concentrates on the problem of violence and civility addressed in the work of Étienne Balibar, asking in particular whether his concept of 'antiviolence' is able to negotiate a lesser violence that preserves the possibility of civility, or whether it is fated only to redistribute the modalities of violence, including revolutionary 'counterviolence' and pacifist 'nonviolence', in a way that risks the greater violence of managed oppression and exploitation. Through references to the work of Hannah Arendt that connect their two 'texts', this chapter turns from Balibar's writings to the work of Jean-François Lyotard, in particular the short essay 'The Other's Rights', originally presented as part of the 1993 Oxford Amnesty International Lectures, in order to assess whether Lyotard's thought offers pathways beyond the seemingly irresolvable paradoxes of 'antiviolence'. Along the way, it contemplates the debts of both these thinkers to the psychoanalytic corpus. Lyotard's are perhaps better known. But Balibar revisits the Freudian legacy, for instance, in order to examine the idea of a 'cruelty or capacity for destruction' that goes beyond the Freudian death drive, so as to reimagine extreme types of violence which surpass the violent forms that we recognise as intrinsic to the nation-state's historic arc. This 'beyond' spills over into a violence arising from an *'idealization of hatred'*, as he puts it, that Balibar treats as an extra-national transformation of fascism. The touch-point for the theoretical possibility of such a mutation in the conceptual toolkit of Freudian psychoanalysis is, perhaps tellingly, Derrida's essay, 'Psychoanalysis Searches the States of its Soul: The Impossible Beyond of a Sovereign Cruelty'. If reconceptualising violence in its contemporary guises involves transformative re-engagement with psychoanalytic ideas and arguments, I suggest that Balibar's thought inherits and assumes a *resistance* of psycho-analysis that may also be a resistance *of* psychoanalysis.

'What is a Complex?', the next chapter in the book, evaluates the question of the 'complex' in a range of scientific, political and psychoanalytic contexts, asking not only where lines of connection and demarcation occur among specific distributions of meaning, value, theory and practice; but also probing the psychoanalytic corpus, notably Freud's writings on the notion of a 'complex', in order to reframe various implications of the idea that this term tends to resist its own utilisation as both an object and form of analysis. This section establishes connections between three sets of theoretical questions: the common practice of describing modernity and its wake in terms of a drive towards increasing complexity; the meaning and cultural legacy of phrases such as 'military–industrial complex' and sundry derivations in the political sphere; and the intricacies and ambiguities subtending the term 'complex' within psychoanalytic theory. As a concept that Freud both utilised and repudiated, the provocative power of the term 'complex' is linked to the way it thwarts various attempts at systemisation (providing nonetheless an apparatus of sorts through which contemporary science, Slavoj Žižek, Noam Chomsky, Freud, Eisenhower and post-war politics can be articulated to one another).

'Fleeced', meanwhile, returns to the problem of the relation of deconstruction to psychoanalysis, and within this reads the Genet column of *Glas* in terms of the deconstructibility of 'the deciding discourse of castration', as Derrida puts it. Questions of violence and sexual differentiation thus come to the fore in this chapter. The fleece that Genet imagines Harcamone wearing in *The Miracle of the Rose* takes centre stage, as much as Genet's flowers. The fleece is both garb and pelt, at once a talismanic scalp, a part that has been brutally cut away, and a covering used to shield or shelter what is vulnerable or exposed. It is both something stolen, and a protective barrier against loss. To get 'fleeced' already carries a double and ambiguous set of possible meanings, then, and Derrida puts it to work in the interests of a double-sexed deconstruction of castratability. If the erection cannot 'fall' without re-elevating the entire edifice or column of that phallogocentrism of which castration would paradoxically form an uncastratable part, Derrida's insertion of a deconstructive 'hole in erection' exposes to a powerfully deciphering and transformative reading just this tale of castration's uncastratability. Taking up Derrida's suggestion that the bi-columnar is in a certain sense uncastratable, the essay closes by reading into the Hegel column of *Glas* precisely this deconstructibility of a 'deciding discourse of castration', notably in terms of the Hegelian interpretation of Antigone's politics.

'The University and the Hysteric', the last chapter in this first section of the book, turns to Freud's writings on hysteria at the end of the nineteenth century, notably the case history of Elisabeth von R., where difficulties in walking, leg pains, uncertain balance and 'locomotor weakness' prompted Freud in his 'first full-length case study' of this particular illness to subscribe to a diagnose of hysteria. If this predicament sounds a little remote from more conventional questions of politics, it acquires relevance as a way to extend Derrida's discussion, in 'Mochlos', of the modern, post-Kantian university institution as constituted by a bodily division of its parts aimed at establishing proportion and balance but actually giving rise to certain difficulties that are somewhat akin to the 'locomotor weakness' that Freud associated with the hysteric. From this perspective, if it becomes possible to consider speaking of the university as itself hysterical or caught up in a case of hysteria, then this chapter considers the question of the institutional 'politics' that hysteria might allow or encourage. Despite her apparent inability to exert the leverage required to walk, what afflicts Fräulein von R. is a series of unresolved psychic transactions or transitions –

a psychic dynamic that remains in flux – for which the term leverage, as it is used in Derrida's 'Mochlos', might still be rather apt. To leverage against the other or receive leverage from the other, as seems to happen in the post-Kantian university, recalls the situation of desire in the case of the hysteric who appropriates the other's desire not least to gain just such an advantage where the other's arguably greater resources are concerned. (This, too, is a surely question of violence in some degree, or rather of certain *violences* pitted one against the other.) We might, then, cultivate our own institutional 'politics' in (and beyond) the university by weighing them in terms of the advantages and pitfalls of the hysteric's psychic strategies.

The second part of the book explores the questions of psychoanalysis, 'politics' and resistance from a 'phobic' perspective. For psychoanalysis, broadly speaking, phobias primarily result from a lapse in the paternal function or figure. The subject in question is thereby badly lacking in terms of paternalistic prohibition or authoritative limitation more generally in relation to objects of desire, so that drives themselves become sufficiently unmodulated or unregulated as to risk a terrible drift towards psychosis as a psychological state in which the subject-object relation itself begins to go awry. In this set of circumstances, phobic objects or situations stand in, simulating that which imposes separation between the two, in order to confront just such a possibility. To the extent that the diminution of any higher principle of authority combined with the intensifying production of unregulated desires might be taken to characterise key features of twenty-first-century existence as it seems to wheel out of all possible control (with Brexit and Trump being perhaps the most recent examples of this 'phobic' paradigm, Trump in particular emerging as a 'faux' substitute *par excellence*, a spectacular 'shock' replacement, in the phobic situation characterised by these combined forces), it would doubtless be feasible to describe modern life as always potentially phobic life. From this perspective, all of our objects would risk becoming phoney or partial objects substituting for a potentially devastating loss that threatens our psychic constitution as such. If the interpretation of, let's say, advanced global capitalism or recent neoliberalisms by way of categories derived from psychological analysis has become something of a trend, however, this part of the book does not settle for any such single pathway. Instead, it also asks whether phobia is as much the very medium of psychological interpretation in the wake of psychoanalysis as it is a potentially productive analytic tool for contemporary times. From this perspective, before we venture to apply the concepts and approaches associated with phobia to present-day social or cultural forms, we must first of all ask whether something like phobia (albeit a 'phobia' somewhat at odds with itself) pervades the very conditions of possibility of important swathes of psychological enquiry, turning itself back on the analytic resources it would seem to channel, as much as equipping us with the conceptual means to interpret the world around us. If we are phobic, in other words, this may well have something to do with our lived or imagined relationship with the world, but nevertheless such a 'psychological' description – if such a thing could be demarcated – needs to acknowledge that its very possibility may itself be inhabited by phobic conditions that can neither be reliably articulated nor satisfactorily comprehended, neither adequately controlled nor securely contained as such. What would remain, therefore, would be a highly complex and undoubtedly fraught series of shifts, projections and displacements in which the question of phobia was itself unstably pitched between the supposed 'object' of concern, whatever that may be, and its very own discourse.

The second part of the book is divided into four sections. The first traces Freud's interest in yet apparent aversion to phobia, from his earliest writings on the topic in the 1890s through to his reinterpretation of the Little Hans case study, originally from 1909, in the mid-1920s. Here, I argue, it is possible to detect something like a phobic reaction to phobia itself: what I call Freud's phobophobia. Furthermore, it may also be possible to find, in the subsequent literature on the case of Little Hans, traces of this phobic reaction contaminating sometimes sharply critical readings just as surely as they do Freud's own writings. Thus, for example, we might detect in Deleuze's markedly hostile attitude to this Freudian text an aversion to or recoil from what is in fact most 'phobic' about it. Through exploring the Lacanian idea that phobia prevents the onset of psychosis in the event of a certain lapse of the paternal metaphor (by presenting us with a faux or partial 'object' that may stand in for the mother as the focus of both paternal prohibition and subjective desire), I conjecture that phobia operates precisely through a certain resistance to itself, a doubleness that renders Freud's phobophobia not just a psychological curiosity but perhaps a feature of the very structure of phobia from the outset. In the latter stages of the chapter, I contrast psychoanalytic approaches to phobia with other possible ways to think about its subject matter. Since Freud's most famous early text on phobia takes the example of Pascal's fear of abysses, I turn to Blanchot's short essay on this topic, 'Pascal's Hand'. For Blanchot, the abyss is in this case less the phobic 'object' that saves the subject in want of an authoritative paternal metaphor, than it is the (non-)phenomenon which potentialises the conversion of the subject – whether

Pascal or his reader – into the wholly other-than-self. In this sense, for Blanchot what is abyssal in Pascal's text amounts to a 'detestable residue' that might prove just too much for psycho-phobic reading. If, nevertheless, the abyssal conjures something out of nothing, I develop this idea in connection with Lyotard's evocation of the 'mutic' quality of music. For Lyotard, it is the mutic – that which is not readily audible or sensible as such – that concerns the very matter or materiality of music, striking us bodily without conscious construction in some prior sense. Yet 'mutic' refers not simply to that which is mute, but to that which lacks defensive parts, such as claws or teeth, or to that which is blunt and lacks pointedness, or a point. Thus, Lyotard evokes music as mutic in a similar way that Blanchot writes of Pascal's text as a powerfully orchestrated and highly conscious exercise in demonstrative discourse that nevertheless finally gives way to an abyssal 'other' of itself. What is left behind (like the 'detestable residue' described by Blanchot) is, however, the very 'sound matter' of music itself. But that music seems to rely on a semi-repressed relation to its 'other' does not mean, for Lyotard, 'that music *would express* or *translate* a phobia among the living for whatever evokes their death', as he puts it. 'The terms of expression and translation are inappropriate', he writes.[2] Since mutic music it is not in search or in want of an object, whether desirable or prohibitory, it evades the objectival quandary – and thus the phobic 'game' – of psychoanalysis. Unlike the horse that inspires Little Hans's phobia, it is toothless, without bite or point. Taking as a cue the mutic allusion to toothlessness, the final section of this chapter examines Freud's treatment of dreams with a dental stimulus. In *The Interpretation of Dreams*,

---

2   Jean-François Lyotard, *Postmodern Fables*, trans. Georges Van den Abbeele (Minneapolis: University of Minnesota Press, 1999), pp. 226.

what we might term ondontophobic dreaming receives a double explanation. At one moment, it is linked with castration (teeth being pulled), while at another it is associated with masturbatory fantasy (the dream of pulling or knocking one out). While, as I argue, the first interpretation suggests a subject in (phobic) want of an object, the second offers the prospect of a subject capable of auto-erotically dispensing with the object altogether. Freud's very point in interpreting such dreams is therefore blunted by this double or self-resistant, and therefore perhaps phobic, interpretation. Dreams of tooth-pulling or of toothlessness thus complicate the phobic explanation which they nevertheless seem to performatively reinscribe.

The second section of this part of the book turns to the work of Quentin Meillassoux, the thinker perhaps most associated with the speculative-materialist turn in continental thought in recent years. Meillassoux argues that post-Kantian philosophy increasingly succumbs to a principle of correlation between thinking and being, wherein the one cannot be contemplated outside of the other. For Meillassoux, such thought limits itself to the correlationist circle in which the 'object' arises only on condition of subjective representation, with no opportunity consequently to access whatever may exist in an uncorrelated relation to my thought. (Meillassoux uses the phrase, the 'Great Outdoors'.) This chapter does not so much assess the degree of success Meillassoux has in seeking to break with this circle (if it can indeed be so generalised), although it does offer some analysis of the means by such an attempt is made, and their implications. Rather, it focuses on his argument about the necessity of contingency as something that is not to be confused with a probabilistic idea of chance, one that might condemn us to perpetual fearfulness. While the possibility of such trepidation – filed under the general rubric of 'Hume's problem' – is slighted and supposedly overcome by speculative thought of the Meillassouxian type, the fact that it is far from prevalent among or endorsed by even the strongest correlationists invites us to reconsider its perhaps ambivalent and divided resources, prompting us to ask whether they may indeed be reduced to an image of merely oppositional difference. This suggestion is further developed through the work of Melanie Klein. Moreover, the last part of the chapter observes that the 'unreason' (that which cannot be correlated as such) which accompanies the flight from so-called correlationism may not simply lead in the direction of science, as Meillassoux suggests. For with the demise of correlation, as Julie Kristeva pointed out long ago, we also risk a descent into psychosis. If the 'style' of the psychotic is characterised by unreflective certainty rather than fearful doubt, traces of such a style may be detected in the writings of Quentin Meillassoux to the extent that they may not simply represent some desire to overcome fear, but more precisely in the sense that they suggest the *want* of an object to be scared of. (The latter, of course, constitutes the means by which the phobic sufferer retains or regains subject-ness over and against the threat of a psychotic dissolution of subject-object relations.) It is therefore through recourse to the paradigm of psychological interpretation (not simply operative at some personal level but instead pertaining in 'structural' terms, if you will) that I seek to analyse what is at stake in Meillassouxian thought. Rather than assess speculative materialism's possible impact through drier forms of philosophical evaluation, in other words, I ask not just about its desires and fears more generally, but more specifically about its phobic and potentially psychotic dimensions.

The third section of Part II picks up on the theme of the 'outside', and the fears, desires, drives and indeed drift it seems to inspire, in order to raise the question of agoraphobia in a number of contexts. In particular, I argue that agoraphobia is not only about recoil or retreat from public spaces, but that surprisingly enough an abiding fear of the 'open' may in fact generate the conditions of possibility for a democratically oriented public sphere, however fragile and contradictory they may be (not least, where supposedly 'open' political assembly complexly interacts with ostensibly 'public' marketplaces). Agoraphobic fear of the space of the public square, whether crowded or comparatively empty, can produce inconsistent effects, provoking reactionary paranoia as well as inspiring political dissent. But if the appeal to the 'rational ground' of a public sphere is at least in part based upon agoraphobic, crowd-fearing impulses, its evocation of reason and duty is exceeded and resisted by a notion of Levinasian responsibility that has been described in terms of an 'ethical agoraphobia'. Furthermore, in 'The Outside', the last chapter of *Otherwise than Being*, Levinas critiques a philosophical tradition, finding its high-point with Kant, that ties essence to subjectivity in a way that regards being in terms of a certain inwardness to itself, producing effects beyond the merely philosophical that Levinas ties to European histories of conquest and defence. Such a tradition produces its relation to the 'other' principally in terms of what Levinas terms 'disclosure', by which is meant subjective access to entities, through modes of representation by which the spatial conditions of such entities transpire only inasmuch as they are given 'for' a subject. Levinas's critique of 'disclosure' therefore suggests certain affinities with Meillassoux's analysis of correlationism. Yet if the 'ethical agoraphobia' of Levinasian responsibility entails a step into the 'open' that cannot simply be faced fearlessly, then this surely prompts comparison with speculative materialism as in *want* of an object to be scared of.

In other words, Meillassouxian thought may do well to be more afraid than it is (or at any rate, more afraid than it is prepared to admit). This is especially true if we are right to conclude that any access to the 'outside' (complicated as it is bound to be) may depend upon it.

The last section of this part of the book returns to the question of phobia in so far as it may be not merely a psycho-analytic question (that is, one that might be addressed using psychoanalytic concepts or methods), but a question *for* psycho-analysis, indeed *of* psychoanalysis itself, a means to assess its highly complex and sometimes deeply problematic conditions of possibility. In 1929, Alfred Adler, noted one-time follower of Freud, produced a case study of 'Miss R.', the young daughter of a Viennese tailor, in which he offered a lengthy commentary on her lupus phobia. Lupus is an auto-immune disease linked to tuberculosis that reached its heights during the nineteenth century, before the bacillus causing tuberculosis was isolated and before light therapy treatments of the condition had been developed. (Since lupus was also linked to raw milk, the intro-duction of the pasteurisation process was seen as another factor in its long-term decline, and indeed Miss R.'s phobias include a love-hate relationship to milk.) Although it could affect several body systems, lupus was identified foremost with unsightly facial skin lesions that often developed into horrendous ulcers as the disease became chronic and progressive. Found at the crossroads between the sprawl of the city and the birth of the clinic, one might say that lupus's historic arc reflects the early history of psychoanalysis itself. Interestingly, Adler associates Miss R.'s phobias with a continual desire to avoid her own inferiorisation in the family setting, but also with a deep-rooted fear about life on the outside. The prospect of holding a safe and secure place within the family is thus always highly uncertain, and subject to competitive rivalries, but equally the world beyond the family is fraught with unimaginable dangers. The case study itself offers a clue to the relationship between analyst and analysand, who, so it seems, never actually met. Adler interprets most of the young girl's behaviour in terms of an egotistic desire to hold centre-stage, and not be overshadowed by others, on the part of a spoilt child; yet perhaps revealingly the case history itself is constructed out of extemporised remarks that Adler makes before a captive audience of zealous followers, presumably to show off his own analytic brilliance (in contrast to, say, Freud's, whom he takes every opportunity to disparage). As we begin to wonder whether Adler might be talking about himself as much as Miss R., then, the case study begins to offer some insights into the split with Freud in 1911. Not least, it is possible to trace connections between the auto-immune condition of lupus, the near auto-immunitary instability of the (paternalistic) family, and the self-destructive collapse of the Freud circle in Vienna in the early years of the twentieth century. That lupus receives its name through an etymological link to the wolf prompts recollection of the famous dictum used by Freud, *Homo homini lupus* (man is wolf to man): just as lupus eats away the face (a face glimpsed horrifyingly in the cracked mirror of this particular case study), so vulpine 'man' eats or devours himself. Here, lupus phobia is less the 'object' of psychological interests than it is their very medium. The resistances *of* psychoanalysis, then, are once more tied to the possibility of the *resistances* of psychoanalysis. This may be true, however such resistances might take shape, and in whichever 'political' form.

Introduction: The Love of Lacan
(Derrida, Žižek)

Loving Resistance

In a lecture from the early 1990s, Derrida is called upon to outline his attitude towards Lacanian psychoanalysis.[1] While still in the preliminary stages of his talk, Derrida exclaims that 'Lacan is so much more aware as a philosopher than Freud, so much more a philosopher than Freud!' (47). This is a striking assertion, and not only because most readers of Derrida would generally detect a certain preference for Freud over Lacan – or at any rate a more intricate, rigorous and sustained practice of reading of the Freudian text in tandem with the develop-ment of deconstructive thought and writing, in comparison to the somewhat less patient or admiring attitude towards Lacan in his previous writings. Derrida's contention is perhaps all the more unusual and conspicuous, since it seems to presume a philosophical standard – indeed a shared understanding of the 'philosophical' – which Lacan, more than Freud, fulfils. If Derrida's statement appears, in rather uncharacteristic fashion, to grant entry to the 'philosophical' on the basis of an entirely unquestioned or unstated set of conditions and attributes, then surely Derrida himself would probably be less philosophically 'aware' than those he is commenting on here (and, by his own implication, that might make him less of a philosopher than either of the psychoanalysts he is seeking to demarcate 'philosophically'). However, we shouldn't assume that granting Lacan the status of a 'philosopher' constitutes a straightforward compliment, albeit one that unintentionally backfires on its author. For Derrida promises that, as his text proceeds, he will attend to 'the paradoxical and perverse consequences that flow from the fact' of Lacan's comparatively more 'philosophical' leanings. If nothing else, this implies that to be a philosopher, to philosophise, or to exercise philosophical awareness, is not such a straightforward matter, not merely a given, consistent or self-identical practice. Indeed, the implication might be that philosophy – even, and perhaps especially, at the point it becomes self-consciously 'aware' – leads almost inevitably to perverse and paradoxical outcomes. Where this leaves the Derrida of this particular passage – the one who seems initially to lapse unawares into a philosophical slumber, but who is surely highly conscious of the 'textual' or 'rhetorical' effects that will surface from his bold exclamation – is an interesting question. Does it make him more or less of a philosopher, for instance? Or is the impact of this ploy that it stymies such calculations from the outset, deliberately pulling the rug from under the philosophical election of Lacan over Freud in the very same process?

Referring to the reading he undertook in *The Post Card* of Lacan's 'Seminar on "The Purloined Letter"', Derrida reiterates what he sees as the deconstructible facets of Lacan's discourse: the commitment to truth whether as unveiling or adequation; the priority given to speech in terms of its supposed relation to presence and plenitude (in contrast to the ostensibly mechanical, technical and auxiliary nature of the archive or the record); the

2

phonocentrism of the Lacanian text in its construal of language
(a feature of his discourse that Lacan sought to recast 'after-the-
fact', Derrida tells us); the transcendental positon of the phallus
and thus the phallogocentrism of Lacanian psychoanalysis; the
reappropriating return of the letter to the origin which precedes
the advent of a certain 'lack' (as Derrida suggests, it is this aspect
of Lacanian thought – concerning the inadequately treated
question of the divisibility of the letter – that most divides it
from deconstruction, since, for Derrida, the irreducible possibility of non-arrival is constitutive of the letter itself); the inability
to reckon with the fictional or literary dimension of narration;
and the extent to which the effects of the double in Poe's tale
are neglected in Lacan's reading. For Derrida, then, in all these
examples Lacanian thought remained too closely tied to the
most 'deconstructible motifs of philosophy', deploying them in
surprisingly 'strenuous' and 'dogmatic' ways at just the moment
they were being called fundamentally into question. 'I found
myself at the time faced with a powerful philosophical, philoso-
phizing reconstitution of psychoanalysis' (55), he writes:

> Lacan's discourse [was] too philosophical for me, too much at
> home with the philosophers – despite, of course, all sorts of
> disavowals on this subject – too much at home with all those
> with whom I was in the process, not of breaking, which makes
> no sense, as I've said countless times, but of reconsidering all the
> contracts; a Lacanian discourse, then, too much at home with
> a Sartrian neo-existentialism (which has not been sufficiently
> discussed or whose remainders have not been sufficiently
> pointed out in Lacan's discourse right up to *Écrits*, where the
> discourse of alienation, authenticity, and so forth prevails), too
> much at home with Hegel/Kojève the 'master' (and Hegel/
> Kojève is also Heidegger, for Kojève does not anthropologize
> only the phenomenology of spirit; he also Heideggerianizes it,

as you know, which was very interesting – and there would be much to say about this . . . (56)

From this perspective it is Lacan, rather than Derrida, who fails to question with sufficient rigour a philosophical tradition that includes not only Hegel and Sartre but also Heidegger and Husserl. On this point, Derrida's central criticism of Lacan, as we have already noted, concerns the question of the letter's 'divisibility', which, while it might appear philosophically 'minor' to some, leads to a dispute over the 'materiality of the signifier' as in fact an 'idealization' worthy of precisely the philosophical tradition that Derrida endeavours to 'deconstruct' (a dispute that would doubtless be reactivated in the context of resurgent materialisms today):

> Lacan says that it 'does not suffer partition': 'Cut a letter into small pieces,' he says, 'and it remains the letter it is.' Consequently, what Lacan then calls the 'materiality of the signifier,' which he deduces from an indivisibility that is nowhere to be found, always seemed and still seems to me to correspond to an 'idealization' of the letter, to an ideal identity of the letter, which was a problem I had been working on elsewhere along other lines for quite some time . . . I could read, then, this surreptitious idealization, not to say this idealism of Lacan's, only on the basis of a work that was already underway, in a deconstructive mode . . . to read him in a problematizing and nondogmatic fashion, it is also necessary to read, for example, Husserl and a few others, and to read them in a problematic or deconstructive way. (60)

Derrida's quarrel with Lacan therefore turns out to be Derrida's quarrel with philosophy in general – no wonder, then, that he had begun by elevating Lacan to the status of a philosopher! Nonetheless, as we already know, philosophy generally comes with certain perverse or paradoxical consequences. From a much earlier point in the text, Derrida is therefore happy to endorse René Major's allusion 'to an "underground" history in the trajectory of Lacan's discourse', through which it is not simply tethered 'to an identifiable circle', 'a geographic area', nor even to 'the advertised form of an academic and institutional program' that it indeed more explicitly flouts (44). For Major, this 'underground history' concerns the 'question of the question' (Derrida salutes psychoanalysis as a form of thinking that includes an irreducible resistance to dominant cultural programmes, institutions and media discourses bent on certain types of reductive and normalising representation); a 'question of the question' that is, as Major himself puts it, 'more vast and stems from procedures of translation and theoretico-practical issues that join up at the borders (of several disciplines) that they destabilize'.[2] The paradox of Lacanian psychoanalysis thus concerns the perverse relationship of this quasi-subterranean space of questioning to its more 'disciplined' philosophical complicities. And such a paradoxical configuration, for Derrida, makes possible another reading of Lacan, one he might be tempted – using a word that appears in this text – to label 'destinerrant':[3]

> There is here, if I may be permitted to say so, the outline of a new training, another curriculum for psychoanalyst readers of Lacan, at least if they want to read him otherwise than in an apelike, orthodox, and defensive manner. This parallels, in sum, the advice concerning a 'new training' that certain of us – the rare professional philosophers who read and published on Lacan in the philosophical university (I am thinking above all of Philippe Lacoue-Labarthe and Jean-Luc Nancy) – gave to philosophers when we told them to read Lacan, which advice was then, about twenty years ago, rather rare. (60)

Regardless of the 'philosophical' validity of Derrida's criticisms of Lacan's 'philosophy' (a matter that is itself complicated by Derrida's own remarks about the 'philosophical' as such, and indeed his evocation above of 'new' pathways in 'professional' or 'university' philosophy), 'For the Love of Lacan' throws up another series of questions. For in this text Derrida seems to profess his love for Lacan, a fellow Parisian whom he nevertheless met on just a couple of occasions, the most famous being outside of France,[4] though with whom he obviously corresponded on occasion. Or, rather, Derrida tests this proposition on his audience in a way that situates his own discourse somewhere between the undecidable possibilities of truth and fiction (in the process, perhaps, recalling the shortcomings of Lacan's practice of reading in his text on Poe):

> And if I were to say now: 'You see, I think that we loved each other very much, Lacan and I,' I am almost certain that many of you here would not stand for it. Many would not stand for it, which explains a lot of things. Many would not stand for it, and not because it surprised them, not at all; I even wonder if this idea is not strangely familiar to them. Not because of surprise, then, but because it is a thing that ought not to have happened and above all that cannot be said without presumptuousness, especially by a sole speaker who says 'we' all alone after the death of the other. Thus the Thing should not be said and especially not repeated; and yet, if I repeated 'we loved each other very much, Lacan and I, each as he will have pleased, each in his way or each in our way,' would that constitute a revelation, a confession, or a denunciation? Let everyone take this 'as it may please him.' (42)

If, by his own reckoning, Derrida's declaration of love for Lacan is less shocking for its surprise-value (given their past history) than for its post-mortem superciliousness, nevertheless

Derrida's readers might also want to test such an expression of deep affection against the rhetorical ploys of the text, of which this is clearly another example. What sort of love is this, where seeming praise so thinly masks damning condemnation? Yet to dispense with the destinerrant effects of those 'fictional' forms that put into question both Lacan's philosophical status and Derrida's personal appreciation of him would presumably lead to a form of love unable to resist those forms of domination or mastery for which Lacanian thought is subjected to criticism in the first place. Whereas a love that risks the ordeal of fiction's possibility, the chance of destinerrance, or the originary supplement of the divided letter may well constitute a love that many would not 'stand for' (such 'standing for' would doubtless strike Derrida as a motif closely allied to a phallogocentric metaphysics of presence), but which might nonetheless grant access to the 'underground' domains which transect Lacanianism's own disciplinary space and standing. The phrase 'for the love of Lacan' might then mean something rather different, just as the appreciation of him as a 'philosopher' turned out to do; not just a Janus-faced interjection belonging to a genre of impatience, outburst, dismissiveness ('for the love of God!), but instead a proposition that might be read otherwise, on the thither side of its always potentially fictional construction, opening new possibilities and horizons. For this reason, perhaps, Derrida finishes his paper in a particular vein:

> But if I had said that we loved each other very much, Lacan and I, and thus we promised each other very much, and that this was for me a good thing in this life, would I have been in the truth? Stephen Melville said that the promise always risked being also a threat. That's true. But I would always prefer to prefer the promise. (69)

The promise can always turn out to be a threat. 'Is that a threat?', TV characters are heard to say in a heightened moment of soap opera; 'No, it's a promise!' is the stock reply. But, still, what threatens – in the relationship of deconstruction to psychoanalysis, Derrida to Lacan, (every) friend to (every other) friend – also always 'promises', albeit promising otherwise.

The idea that deconstruction alone might save Lacanianism from itself would no doubt enrage Lacanians far more than the presumptuousness Derrida himself admits in one-sidedly re-articulating a relationship to the dear-departed friend. The notion that Derridean deconstruction is itself able to escape all the effects of power, control, dogmatism and discipleship attributed to Lacanian discourse and influence would doubtless strike them as a greater irony than any of those found amid the rhetorical ploys of Derrida's own text. Without aiming to resolve such disputes, if nothing else it is possible to say that Derrida's text does attune us not only to the problem of psychoanalysis's philosophical 'usage', but also to the idea that the philosophical 'politics' of psychoanalysis aren't easily separable from its own 'internal' politics – those of the master and the follower as well as the heretic or apostate, whoever they may or may not be. (Notably, and not entirely co-incidentally, via a reference to Heidegger, Derrida draws philosophy into the space of onto-theology.) Politics, philosophy and psychoanalysis are thus enjoined by relations which are as much *resistant* as they are convivial. For it is simultaneously always and never a matter of 'as it may please him' – a phrase that Derrida presents as a 'quotation from Lacan, from a quasi-private phrase between Lacan and myself' (thus in effect compounding the problematic with which we are dealing here).[5]

Fittingly, then, Derrida's lecture is included in the volume *Resistances of Psychoanalysis*, originally appearing in France in the mid-1990s.[6] Derrida prefaces this collection of three texts by noting an increasing resistance to psychoanalysis at the time, both at academic and institutional levels and more widely across the various spheres of society and culture. His aim, however, is to rethink this supposed opposition between psychoanalysis and its would-be adversaries, not only by suggesting that the various analyses resistant to psychoanalysis inevitably call up the psychoanalytic understanding of 'resistance-to-analysis', but also by affirming a resistance internal to psychoanalysis itself which complicates the very idea of a resistant 'outside' construed in terms of psychoanalysis's opponents. From this perspective, resistance to psychoanalysis cannot be thought 'outside' of the resistance *of* psychoanalysis – a resistance of itself to itself, or rather a resistance of the 'other' of itself to itself as the very form analysis takes – although equally this same resistance troubles any evocation of merely the 'internal' workings of psycho-analysis itself.

Resistance to 'Poststructuralism'

In a way that is perhaps symptomatic of a more general dissatisfaction with deconstruction that cuts across a number of approaches within the contemporary 'theoretical' field, Derrida's various commentaries on Lacan have been disputed by Slavoj Žižek as indicative of 'poststructuralism' at its worst. An example of this critique can be found in *The Most Sublime Hysteric: Hegel with Lacan*, published in English in 2014.[7] This particular title by Žižek is important in that it represents a reworked version of his 1982 doctoral thesis, completed under the direction of Jacques-Alain Miller at the University of Paris VIII. The event of its publication in revised form has been taken not just to present Hegel as a Lacanian *avant la lettre*[8] but to demonstrate that from his earliest writings Žižek pioneered an approach that would make possible the intersection of Lacanianism and Hegelianism to the benefit of forms of political thought capable of breaking through the 'poststructuralist' impasse.

One chapter, 'The Quilting Point of Ideology: Or Why Lacan is Not a "Poststructuralist"', is, unsurprisingly given its title, of particular interest in this regard. Here, the Lacanian notion of a 'quilting point' takes centre-stage as the 'fundamentally *contingent* operation through which the ideological-symbolic field retroactively receives its "reason," its *necessity*, or, to put it in Hegelian terms, through which it posits its own preconditions' (199). The stereotype of the 'Jew' in Nazi ideology serves as an exemplary figure of such a quilting point. Far from offering 'an inarguable refutation' that might 'cause the ideological edifice to collapse', the difference between the stereotype of the 'Jew' and the everyday experiences of Jewish people is '*already included in advance in the way anti-Semitism operates*': 'You have to be very careful with Jews, it isn't always easy to spot them because they can take on the appearance of ordinary people . . . in order to hide their true corrupt nature!' (196). Drawing on Ernesto Laclau's analysis of fascist ideology, Žižek therefore evokes the quilting point as that which operates as an exceptional element or 'master signifier' to unify a 'patchwork' of contingent elements into a single 'edifice' capable of 'totalizing the field and stabilizing its signification' (199). However, this exceptional element is not so much exempt from the differential play of relations that it otherwise unifies or stabilises such that it acquires the status of an 'abundant' signification or a 'fixed point of reference' (200); rather, it emerges on condition of a purely performative self-articulation that is sufficiently tautological or self-referential that the very idea of 'reference' is misleading, since the quilting point as ostensibly a point of reference is itself 'reference-less'. Thus, it is 'the mark of a lack, the empty space of signification' that nevertheless secures the field of signification. Put differently, the quilting point is always already the 'impossible' of itself. The quilting point actually does no more than to, in Žižek's terms, 'incarnate' and 'positivize' the impossible 'Real' whose impasses it seeks to overcome (201). Coming back to Nazi ideology, the 'Jew' would then be nothing other than *the way in which Nazism presentifies its own impossibility*', the exemplary or exceptional figure of 'the fundamental impossibility of the totalitarian project'. But Žižek's point here is not to herald the inevitable foundering of totalitarianism on the basis of this paradox, but to show how its contingent operation is always to include this knowledge in its own structural or systematic workings, as in the example of the 'sleight of hand' that sees all Jewish people reincorporated regardless into the stereotype of the 'Jew'. Totalitarianism is, in this sense, structured as a struggle not against the 'other' per se (Jewish people at large), but against its own conditions of (im)possibility configured as just this exceptional-impossible element we are calling the 'Jew'. And, for Žižek, that's precisely how fascism works.

As the chapter enters its final phase, Žižek's concern is to demonstrate how, despite appearances to the contrary, this form of analysis cannot be reabsorbed from a 'poststructuralist' perspective. Although it may seem that the quilting point might be reinterpreted as just another example of an always doomed attempt to arrest plurality or dispersion through the force of a totalisation that can never complete itself as such, leaving us in the position of a kind of 'bad infinity' where the irresolvable interplay of quilting and un-quilting constitutes itself as an interminable process, nevertheless Žižek wants to establish Lacanianism here in terms of a possible exit from just this 'poststructuralist' situation. He argues that Lacan's interest is not in affirming the inevitable subversion of totalisation, its unavoidable lapse into fragmentation or division; rather, his concern is to ask the question of the quilting point's very possibility, of what causes it to arise in the first place. For Žižek, this is a Hegelian question. And precisely the failure of the quilting point is, paradoxically enough, the very answer to this question of its origin:

> If totalization and the 'quilting point' fail, it is because they can only bring about their own existence through an element that incarnates this very impossibility itself . . . It is therefore superfluous to search for symptomal points, fissures that could cause the totality to collapse. It is superfluous to say that the quilting point tries to totalize the diffuse and diverse field but will always fail – *as if the quilting point itself was not the embodiment, the positivization of this fundamental failure, of this very impossibility as such*. (203–4)

The quilting point is 'evidence of its own impossibility' converted into contingent operations that make totalitarianism possible. This impossibility marks not so much the limit of totalitarianism, as 'poststructuralism' might have it (on Žižek's account), but instead accounts precisely for its emergence, indeed its constitutive power.

On the way to demarcating the 'poststructuralist' approach from that of Lacan, Žižek also wants to reverse the distinction that sees the former – 'poststructuralism' – resisting the forms of mastery it accuses the latter – Lacan – of stealthily reintroducing or readopting. Thus, *contra* Derrida, Lacan does not merely seek to arrest and master textual dissemination by re-anchoring lack in a positive sense, 'reducing or canceling lack by means of its very affirmation' (205) – if only because, through the exceptional example of the quilting point, the positivisation of an impossibility happens as precisely a contingent operation. Indeed, such a perspective on Lacan's thought is only made possible by means of a 'poststructuralist' perspective that, for Žižek, itself 'holds together' rather too well, holding to paradoxical formulations (there is no simple 'outside' of metaphysics; there is no self-contained 'inside' of metaphysics) which secure its position more or less 'unimpeachably', as he puts it (206). From here, we are treated to a torrent of criticisms about 'poststructuralist' or 'deconstructive' poeticisations which mimic the textual or disseminal effects of literature only to better conceal their 'firm', 'strict' theoreticism.

Be wary, then – 'poststructuralism' may not be what it seems. You have to be very careful with 'deconstructionism', it can take on the appearance of its opposite in order to hide its true nature. (Indeed, it risks the spread of its own infection to the extent that, in sly denial of its own character, it projects its own shortcomings on to others.) If I am deliberately re-invoking the language that Žižek uses to reflect the way that fascist totalitarianism constructs the figure of the 'Jew', then it is perhaps telling that Žižek resolves the question of the 'radical difference' between Lacan and 'poststructuralism' by insisting that it is precisely the performative 'utterances' of Lacan as an expression of 'impossible' mastery which 'prevent us from reverting back into the metalinguistic position' with which 'poststructuralism' itself might be associated (207). Here, it is not only that – on the strength of Žižek's own analysis – Lacanian performativity itself looks rather 'fascist' (for Žižek implies this is exactly how fascism works), but also that the language of 'reverting back' (and, later on, 'backsliding') recalls the Nazi discourse of 'Jewish' degeneracy projected onto a debauched 'poststructuralism'. One wonders, then, whether everything that Žižek has to say about the functioning of the word 'Jew' in Nazi ideology might not also apply to the way in which the terms 'poststructuralism' and 'deconstructionism' work in his own, 'Lacanian' discourse. A 'proper' understanding of the fascist discourse of the 'Jew' – non-poststructuralist, opposed to poststructuralism – also operates as the form through which Žižekian discourse positions 'poststructuralism' as effectively the 'Jew', more or less fascistically.

The point I'm making about this seeming paradox in Žižek's essay seems so obvious that it is hard to believe the effect isn't deliberate, a suspicion which is, in and of itself, further cause for concern. Regardless of whether his criticisms of deconstruction or 'poststructuralism' contain any truth or value whatsoever – a question I deliberately want to leave undeveloped here – my response is not merely a backsliding 'deconstruction' of his own discourse, operating outside of its own, pioneering terms and logic. On the contrary, I am only taking him at his word (something that deconstruction does rather well, in fact). But that, in itself, is a complicated matter, notably because, for Žižek, Lacan's statement in *Seminar XI* – 'That is precisely what I mean, and say – for what I mean, I say . . .' – is not a lapse that allows renewed allusion to the 'poststructuralist' straw man of 'mastery', but is instead an utterance of precisely the 'impossible' kind that one might be tempted to associate with the contingent operations of totalitarianism or fascism. Perhaps it is mostly in this sense, then, that Žižek is saying just what he means to say in 'Why Lacan is not a "Poststructuralist"'.

Žižek is of course not alone in advocating the combination of certain forms of psychoanalytic and political thought. There is currently a large industry devoted to the topic of relating Lacan to Marx, psychoanalysis to materialism, and 'theory' to 'politics' after 'poststructuralism'. We could survey any number of examples encapsulating this trend, but one in particular might suffice to bring out the concerns that emerge from the above analysis of Žižek's rebuttal of the 'poststructuralist' paradigm. Adrian Johnston's *Prolegomena to Any Future Materialism*[9] advocates a 'healthy dose of pig-headed, close-minded stupidity on behalf of materialism' (14), which is allied to his desire to purge the latter of all traces of religious thinking. Speaking of Lacan's attitude towards Marxism, Johnston thus writes of materialism's task in terms of the 'surprisingly incomplete and difficult struggle exhaustively to secularize materialism, to purge it of camouflaged residues of religiosity hiding within its ostensibly godless confines' (62). He proposes a Lacanian atheism that 'demands flushing out and liquidating' each and every 'stubborn investment' in 'the theological and religious', whether conscious or unconscious. Suspicion grows, however, that the enemy may be within, and that one must begin at home. Johnston writes that 'faithfulness to this Lacan dictates submitting to merciless criticism those Lacans who deviate from this uphill path' (72). The irony that such a purge is to be conducted with the theologico-political fervour of an inquisition is all too obvious, while growing recourse to the figure of the sly turncoat masquerading as a comrade-in-arms complicates the terms of engagement in only the most predictable of ways. Johnston proposes 'an enthusiastic call-to-arms that is simultaneously a warning of the danger of the return of old (un)holy ghosts' (77). Lacanianism must resist itself, then, in certain ways.

For Johnston, Lacanian psychoanalysis is better equipped than many post-Enlightenment rationalisms to deliver against materialism's aspirations. In particular, he argues that 'its placement of antagonisms and oppositions at the very heart of material being' (24) chimes with recent findings in biological science. The myth of biological immutability is countered in the contemporary life sciences through ideas of 'hyperdense complexity' (31) not reducible to any form of self-identical conceptuality or theoreticity. Johnston argues for a new materialism of the kind made possible by Catherine Malabou's thinking of plasticity, one that remains hospitable to scientific endeavour at its cutting edges, while at the same time speaking back to the ideological predilections of science and scientists, particularly where certain forms of determinism are concerned. Alongside the Lacanian Real and Badiouist mathematics, we also find the rather predictable evocation of Cantorian set theory as the gesture by which contemporary thought's resistance to totalisation is formalised. Yet Badiou's preference for the mathematisable is itself resisted in favour of a certain biological preference, one which permits the assertion of merely a 'weak nature' defined by 'heterogeneous ensembles of less-than-fully synthesized material beings, internally conflicted, hodgepodge jumbles of elements-in-tension'. Here, the 'material' in its non-reductive sense is depicted in terms of 'phenomena flourishing in the nooks and crannies of the strife-saturated, undetermined matrices of materiality, in the cracks, gaps, and splits of these discrepant strata' (37). At this point, the Lacan who seemed at certain moments to favour 'mathematical-type formalism' as an escape route from humanistic models of subjectivity (43) is comparatively downgraded in favour of a psychoanalysis able to rehabilitate aspects of Freud's biological scientism, as Johnston puts it, in the interests of a new pact between critical thought and the life sciences today. Unsurprisingly, Badiou's outsourcing of ontology from philosophy to mathematics is thereby contested as the basis of materialism proper. It is just too pure, it lacks the messiness demanded by an authentic dialectics and evinced by the findings of the natural sciences alike (messy bedfellows in themselves). It is as if, paradoxically enough, materialism must purge itself even of an untrustworthy purism: true materialism must up the ante on the 'ultra-rigour' of Badiouist 'purity'. Johnston therefore suggests that the assault on idealism by a purified materialism must of necessity also counter or resist itself in a certain sense. (Johnston's text is thereby much less a manifesto than a model, a performance rather than a policy statement, of resistance itself.) The messiness that transpires from this situation reflects the contemporary critical field as much as it does a 'nature' that is 'manifest in condensed form in the bodies and brains of human beings' taking inconsistent and heterogeneous shapes characterised by 'holes, gaps, and lags' (86). Badiou is presented, in the space of just a few pages, as at once averse to biology and as unclear on the borderline between idealism and material-ism as he is on that which separates biopolitics from biological science (88-90). If the 'good' rhetoric of a non-deterministic biology masks a highly determined political game played out across this particular landscape of 'materialist' theory in pursuit of (as well as resistant to) its own purification, one can't help but wonder if this is how the brain works, in so far as Johnston is concerned. Are its dynamics of self-organisation those of a perpetual self-cleansing? The messier story Johnston wants to tell is of the purifying gesture of mathematical formalisation being somewhat alien to neuroscientific understandings: thus, he questions what he deems the Badouist inclination to drive the life sciences towards quantum mechanics (95). But if the brain doesn't work on the basis of self-purification, why retain the motif for materialism, if that same materialism justifies itself on the strength of its affinity with science in its biological rather than mathematical form? Unless of course the plasticity of the brain 'as both flexible and resistant, as moving between the malleability of reformation and the fixity of formation' (102) establishes itself as the very medium and instrument of a politics that hygienises in increasingly intensifying ways. This seems a highly doubtful but nevertheless rather terrifying prospect.

Quentin Meillassoux, Son of the Badiouist Father, comes last in the Holy Trinity of thinkers tackled in Johnston's book. He is described as 'more of a realist than Badiou' (142) to the extent that the former, more so than the latter, encourages a certain passage from mathematical purity to a sense of extra-subjective or non-correlational 'matter'. Nonetheless, Meillassoux is deemed guilty of cherry-picking from the empirical realm when its suits, for instance in his arguments about the arche-fossil, while violently sealing off his brand of speculative materialism from the messy evidence of empirical science whenever the latter troubles the former's rationality (160–1). Here, Johnston's retreat from the comparative 'hygiene' of Meillassouxian thinking is, paradoxically, another expression of a logic of the purge, which comes ever closer to home in the sense that the nearest family member is always the most suspect: Meillassoux 'clings with one hand to what he struggles to cast away with the other' (60).

As his book nears its conclusion, Johnston argues that there is 'a big difference between arguing for materialism/realism versus actually pursuing the positive construction of materialist/realist projects dirtying their hands with real empirical data' (173). This critique is, fittingly, surely nothing but a self-condemnation, a case of chickens coming home to roost. By obsessing over the theoretical arguments, *Prolegomena to Any Future Materialism* makes no attempt at 'empirical' engagement. Hands get dirty in Johnston's book not in the sense that – going along for the ride on some life sciences field-trip – they enjoy digging in fertile ground. Instead, the logic of the purge and of purification that Johnston both resists and advocates in a curiously entangled gesture casts troubling light on such 'dirty hands'.

Performing Resistance

What we have seen is that debates between 'materialism' or a politics configured through new alignments between Hegel and Lacan, on the one hand, and the legacies and possible future of 'poststructuralism' or 'deconstruction', on the other, may rest – surprisingly enough – on a certain taste for their different, although not completely unrelated, performative conditions. (Not unrelated, in the sense that Žižek's attempt to expel or expunge 'poststructuralism' from the Lacanian 'text' puts his own discourse into a potentially deconstructible situation, the terms or basis of which cannot simply be projected on to an 'other'.) Does one prefer the *resistant* performativity of Derrida's double discourse of 'love' and 'philosophy' directed at Lacanianism or Lacan himself (and these are rather different propositions, perhaps)? Or does one identify instead with the performative conditions of a Lacanian utterance which, for Žižek, posits a certain lack of 'mastery' only in order to assume 'impossibility' of a kind that would seem to echo, or at least mimic, the contingent operations of totalitarianism or fascism? Which is the more or less 'political', and in what sense?

RESISTANCE AND PSYCHOANALYSIS

Notes

1 Jacques Derrida, 'For the Love of Lacan', in *Resistances of Psychoanalysis*, trans. Peggy Kamuf, Pascale-Anne Brault and Michael Naas (Stanford: Stanford University Press, 1998), pp. 39–69. Page references will be given in the body of the chapter.

2 René Major, 'Depuis Lacan', in *Lacan avec les philosophes* (Paris: Albin Michel, 1991), p. 387.

3 Derrida's thinking of *destinerrance* may be aligned to the logic of the 'postal' which dictates that the condition of possibility of every arrival is the chance that any letter may get lost in the post.

4 Derrida and Lacan first met, famously, at the 1966 Johns Hopkins conference in Baltimore, at which Derrida stole the show (and effectively began his Anglo-American reputation) with 'Structure, Sign, and Play in the Discourse of the Human Sciences'. Derrida tells us that Lacan, upon being introduced, commented drily on the fact that they had to travel to America to meet.

5 The comparable phrase in current English usage might be 'if you like!', which refuses as it grants, indeed doubly provokes as it seems to retreat or back down from the power it addresses.

6 Interestingly, Derrida proclaims his love of the word 'resistance', recalling as it does French resistance to the Nazi occupation, among other things.

7 Slavoj Žižek, *The Most Sublime Hysteric: Hegel with Lacan*, trans. Thomas Scott-Railton (Cambridge: Polity Press, 2014). Page references will be given in the body of the chapter.

8 See Jodie Matthews' review for the LSE on-line at http://blogs.lse.ac.uk/ lsereviewofbooks/2014/10/16/book-review-the-most-sublime-hysteric-hegel-with-lacan-by-slavoj-zizek.

9 Adrian Johnston, *Prolegomena to Any Future Materialism: The Outcome of Contemporary French Philosophy* (Evanston: Northwestern University Press, 2013). Page references will be given in the body of the chapter.

Part I Violence and Resistance

1

Impossible Divisions:
Fanon, Hegel and Psychoanalysis

In Frantz Fanon's 'The Negro and Recognition',[1] the penultimate chapter of *Black Skins, White Masks*, the Hegelian theme of mutual recognition as the origin of man's self-consciousness and potential freedom is tested against the complex circumstances to which colonialism leads, and, tellingly, Fanon's engagement with psychological thought and his clinical work constitute an important arena for this testing of the Hegelian inheritance. In this particular essay, as we will see, Fanon's idea that the 'Negro slave' is recognised by the 'White Master' in a situation that is *'without conflict'* suggests the possibility of a dual meaning, connoting not just a protracted phoney war in the aftermath of colonialism, but hinting also that colonialism's historical interpretation may not itself be exhausted by the Hegelian master-slave dialectic, or that its complications may not easily be reducible to the logic this implies. On the basis of such a dual reading of the colonial as it arises from Fanon's text, after Hegel we might well ask whether it is historical *interpretation* or the historical *process* itself that has somehow faltered. Unless resolved, the hesitation between these two possibilities would of course present considerable difficulties for any form of political thought remaining indebted to Hegel. Such dynamic tensions exposed by Fanon's writing may suggest, then, something like an imperfect or impossibly divided dialectics at work throughout his corpus. Indeed, the non-self-identical doubleness of colonial displacement and divided critique is, perhaps, precisely what gives force and expression to Fanon's interventions in the world, not merely as a historical inspiration but as a multiply charged remainder, something still in the making or yet to come. What we have termed the resistant 'other' of psychoanalysis has its part to play here, one not simply confined within the limits of psychoanalytic discourse alone.

'The Negro and Hegel'

Preceded by a chapter on 'The Negro and Psychopathology' in which Fanon cites and develops but also disputes Lacan, and engages with but also contests psychoanalysis, 'The Negro and Recognition' begins with a discussion of Adlerian psychology, but then finds its central point of reference in Hegelian discourse. For Hegel, the possibility of self-knowledge originates in the process of identifying an object of desire, in terms of which one can distinguish and thus experience oneself as such. But to ensure that the knowledge of the 'self' thereby attained is not merely transitory or superficial (as the fulfilment of desire can frequently be), I need to recognise myself by way of an 'other' that is independent and enduring rather than simply immediate or fleeting. This other must therefore be like me: another self-consciousness in which I recognise myself. This recognition founds the possibility of a community based on mutual self-recognition. However, since one's recognition as an independent self-consciousness relies upon a display of detachment or freedom which in turn ultimately entails staking one's very life, the possibility of community or mutuality comes at the price of an encounter with the other which is nothing less than a matter of life-and-death. During such a struggle, in which the possibility of recognition leads the protagonists to put their lives in fundamental danger, the risk is that both winner and loser lose: the latter, because failure means death; the former, because victory destroys the other who in fact establishes the very conditions of possibility for one's own self-recognition. Such mortal combat − as itself a spectacular dead-end − is thus recast by Hegel in terms of the living relations of master and slave. Here, so one might think, the conflict between the two is partly redeemed or resolved, in that it grants the master superiority, freedom and independence, while providing the slave with a reason or position by which to live, namely dependency upon or service of another. However, the recognition that the slave affords the master − in so far as it does not stem from another self-consciousness like me, but instead from one who has pulled back from staking his life − proves as unsatisfactory as that of a fatally vanquished opponent. Meanwhile, the pursuit of desires − which grants the possibility of knowledge or consciousness of 'self' in the first place − is dimmed by the presence of the slave, whose work on the master's behalf both interrupts the relation to the objective world that furnishes the possibility of desire's satisfaction, and places the master in a paradoxical situation of dependency. Ultimately, therefore, the slave affords the master neither true self-consciousness nor independence (in fact, it is the slave rather than the master who has experienced more directly the fearful prospect of death, and whose slavery entails a sort of detachment from nature in which the possibility of freedom would seem to arise). True recognition, then, must be fully mutual rather than one-sided and unequal. Achieving such 'recognition', or moving beyond its complex problematics, is however a far from uncomplicated matter (in any case, its understanding depends in no small part on the pathway taken through the various receptions and developments of Hegel's thought, not least in the twentieth century).

In 'The Negro and Recognition', the Hegelian theme of mutual recognition as the origin of man's self-consciousness and possible freedom is tested against the complex circumstances to which colonialism has led us. In the second subsection, entitled 'The Negro and Hegel', Fanon begins by stating that there is no 'open conflict between white and black'. Instead, the 'Negro slave' is 'recognized' by the 'White Master' in a situation that is *without conflict* (217). A few sentences later, returning to the theme of the master's recognition of the slave which he once more states occurs without 'struggle', Fanon suggests that, to the extent that the 'Negro' has been liberated from slavery without having to engage in mortal combat for his freedom, the grounds of the relationship between the two have not fulfilled their Hegelian destiny. The 'Negro' has neither properly cast off the shackles of slavery nor acquired anything more than a paltry semblance of mastery. In the process, the 'White Master' attains a certain personhood by recognising the other without entering into full conflict, but lacks genuine consciousness of the 'self' he truly is (219). Given these subsidiary comments, one may surmise that the lack of 'open conflict between white and black' to which Fanon refers is due principally to the historic evasion he attributes to slavery's ending.[2] Yet elsewhere in his writing Fanon also implies that the relations between 'black' and 'white' are not reducible to the master-slave dialectic; indeed, that the state of affairs we call colonialism arises in circumstances that are, in essence, not defined by original combat of the internecine kind that founds the possibility of the master-slave relation. Of course, for Hegel, such combat is never simply a 'natural' occurrence (depending as it does on a specific detachment of the 'self' from 'nature'), and thus it always acquires a historicality beyond some intrinsic necessity. Nonetheless, it is far from clear that Fanon uniformly or uncritically accepts its extension in the interests of a wholesale explanation of colonial history. From this perspective, the idea that the 'Negro slave' is 'recognized' by the 'White Master' in a situation that is *without conflict* may acquire a double meaning: more overtly, that the colonial situation 'post-slavery' ushers in something like a phoney war; but perhaps more suggestively, that colonialism's historical interpretation is in fact not drained dry by the Hegelian logic of master-slave. And, on the basis of this double reading or double possibility, one is left asking whether, in Hegel's aftermath, it is historical *interpretation* or the historical *process* itself that is broken or has gone awry, notably in terms of what we understand by the 'colonial'.[3]

Be that as it may, for Fanon the 'former slave' nevertheless seeks recognition of the Hegelian kind. Such recognition, he goes on to suggest, can only occur through a mutuality which must be humanly constructed since it relies on a certain disconnection of self-consciousness from 'nature', but one which at the same time has to transcend given human distinctions since it implies 'the universal consciousness of self'. Fanon writes: 'Each consciousness of self is in quest of absoluteness. It wants to be recognized as a primal value without reference to life, as a transformation of subjective certainty (*Gewissheit*) into objective truth (*Wahrheit*)' (217–18). Nonetheless, as desire meets resistance from the other (such resistance providing the essential ground for true self-consciousness to emerge), the pathway 'toward a supreme good that is the transformation of subjective certainty of my own worth into a universally valid objective truth' (218) seems bound to lead to conflict and violence. In order to achieve recognition (that is, to 'do battle' for a newly created 'human world' of 'reciprocal recognitions'), the black 'former slave' must, it seems, venture his life in a 'savage struggle' against the one who is reluctant to recognise him fully (218). And yet surely the Hegelian 'truth' of this situation – the radical possibility of overcoming the historic evasion Fanon associates with the end of slavery – is at the same time countermanded by the possibly *extrinsic* relation of the master–slave dialectic to the historical interplay between 'white' and 'black'? This ironic possibility affects not only the question of the status – both conceptual and strategic – of violence in Fanon's discourse, but once more raises the problem of what exactly obstructs decolonisation; whether the fault lies in the interpretative shortcomings of 'theoretical' forms and arguments that largely belong to a European tradition, or in contingent facts and constraints that might test their conceptual boundaries as much as call for their 'regulatory' operationalisation on the ground.

Such problems undoubtedly exist as the counterparts to Fanon's thought, or better still open up its frontiers rather than define its limits. They resonate with rather than negate the profound courage and still-disarming honesty of a text such as *Black Skin, White Masks*, the strength of which derives no doubt from its radical affirmation of a seemingly impossible task: namely, to imagine the chance of a decisive break from the conditions of guilt, self-loathing and psychological violence that Fanon – like every 'man of color' – perhaps inevitably inherits, when those very same conditions seem inescapably to embody and define the possibility of being in the world[4] – not merely the circumstances Fanon wants to analyse and transform, but also his capacity to think about them and respond to them. What remains striking to this day are the complex ways in which *Black Skin, White Masks* resists and subverts the anthropological genres with which it also plays, as time and again Fanon ventures, risks – or better, exposes, *ex-poses* – his own intricately inscribed participation in the condition he diagnoses. (What sort of combat does this constitute?) When set against the backdrop of a Judeo-Christian tradition to which he both does and does not belong, the idea of Fanon as a prophet of impossible invention, seeking to dismantle and overcome a vast legacy of guilt, self-reproach and tortured self-image (one which, in another sense, seems utterly intractable) no doubt helps to explain the discipleship and hagiography his work has attracted.[5] In similar vein, *The Wretched of the Earth* asks of us the near-impossible. How are we to reconcile, on the one hand, a call to arms in which colonial adversaries are imagined to be locked in Manichean relations of binary opposition at the structural level, and, on the other, a set of psychiatric studies and observations that not only put in doubt presumptions about the possibility of such clear-cut distinctions in the embodied experience of colonial subjects, but which leave largely unresolved the question of how one gets from the deeply ambivalent conditions exemplified by the pathological behaviour of Fanon's patients – all of whom endure the complex legacy of psychic violence that connects as much as separates 'coloniser' and 'colonised' – to the pure and absolute confrontation willed at the level of the revolutionary acts of de-colonisation, or, for that matter, to the single form of universal 'man' that he depicts as constitutive as much as ideal (in the sense that any post-colonial or post-Western, post-humanistic 'consciousness' would depend, in the terms outlined above, upon 'human' construction).[6] The problem of the relationship between 'theoretical' or conceptual analysis and contingent forms of interpretation, expression and understanding perhaps defines the complexity of Fanon's corpus. Something like a constitutive hesitation between the acknowledgement of flawed historical process and flawed historical interpretation might help to explain the distinctive differences between the near-confessional performance and performativity of *Black Skin, White Masks*, in which Fanon is figured much more as the participant in the discourse he produces,[7] and the cooler, methodical examination to be found in *The Wretched of the Earth*, where undimmed anger is perhaps matched by a certain ruthless detachment (although of course the final section of the latter, returning us to the world of mental disorders caused by colonial 'war', reproduces the potential schism it perhaps seeks to overcome).

Likewise, when seeking to relate Fanon's philosophical and professional training and practice to the grounds of his political thought, it would seem that it is no more helpful simply to assert than to downplay an underlying continuity or identity between the two. (Indeed, it is important to remember that while Fanon's political arguments derive from systematic theoretical analysis, they also seek to resist universalising theoreticism of the kind that, as he himself suggests, risks overly privileging a leftist-Marxist tradition of European origins and orientation.) If, as Richard Pithouse has put it, Fanon was – complexly enough – 'committed to some transcendent ethical axioms . . . which were in turn founded on a universal ontology', nonetheless to 'assume that his engagement with the dynamic particularities' of a specific political situation gives rise to 'a set of transcendent propositions for political praxis' may be to profoundly misconstrue 'the nature of Fanon's engagement'.[8] For it is not only that lived political struggle embodies a political theory that is prior to it, but also that political theory itself comes to embody and enact the struggle to which it addresses and commits itself. (Thus, if nothing else, the distribution of the 'particular' and the 'general' across the space of theoretical political discourse may be regulated to an important extent by the contingency of politics as a form of experience or engagement.) Nonetheless, it is probably over-hasty to describe the dynamic tensions in Fanon's writing – between flawed historical interpretation and flawed historical process, between philosophy, 'theory' and political thought, between participation, detachment and change, between the sense of arrested struggle and the sense of fabricated combat[9] implied by the double possibility of '*without conflict*' – in terms of dialectics, dialectics 'proper', dialectics *as such*. One might instead approach Fanon's corpus in terms of a possibly more productive notion of an 'imperfect' or impossibly divided dialectics at work throughout.

A re-reading of Fanon today may be occasioned by far-reaching concerns about contemporary international problems and crises, but its timeliness may also consist in the need – not always sufficiently acknowledged – to keep open the question of which critical resources might contribute to the potentially transformative analysis of such 'politics' on a general or worldwide scale. In this sense, it is worth observing that Homi Bhabha's description, over a quarter of a century ago, of Fanon's work as profoundly split 'between a Hegelian-Marxist dialectic, a phenomenological affirmation of Self and Other and the psychoanalytic ambivalence of the Unconscious' (x) continues to place him at the very crossroads of current theoretical debates. In particular, over the past decade, the return to various types of Marxist and communist thought, when set against the legacy

31

of another theoretical corpus more closely associated with deconstruction and poststructuralism more generally (one that is often considered to be in decline), risks a situation in which proponents of ostensibly different theoretical traditions lapse into mutually dismissive hostility and ultimately sterile opposition. Of course, psychoanalysis occupies a complex and contested place in this theoretical landscape (the claims upon it are at once multiple and somewhat ornately entangled), and therefore to some extent psychoanalysis provides access to the possibility of re-energising the debate outside of such dead-end conflicts. Fanon's work, meanwhile, suggests not only that such divergent positions may in fact be funded by intellectual or critical histories that remain far from mutually exclusive, but also that the complex interactions to which these histories give rise produce dynamic tensions which – for all their 'philosophical' inconsistencies – may nevertheless be extraordinarily instructive, highly significant, and, in the end, powerfully *constitutive*. Here, psychological thought is not merely a bridgehead, however precarious, between distinct forms of thinking; it is once more the resistant 'other' that supplements in order to mutate and re-orient them, or at any rate to *change the question* they may be capable of asking.

Despite longstanding arguments about Bhabha's 'theoreticism' (which I do not assume should simply be dismissed), let us therefore recall that his account of Fanon's 'jagged testimony of colonial dislocation' understands the latter as funded by formidably competing intellectual resources which its proponent at once powerfully embraces and deeply suspects. Bhabha thereby insists on the value of Fanonian discourse as precisely a refusal of 'total' theory. As Bhabha himself puts it, if 'Fanon opens up a margin of interrogation that causes a subversive slippage of identity and authority', 'nowhere is this slippage more visible than in his work itself where a range of texts and traditions . . . vie to utter that last word which remains unspoken' (xxiv). Perhaps more than anything, it is this absolutely constitutive 'refusal' of total theory that Fanon's text bequeaths to critical thought and practice today – a refusal not just of 'theoreticism' *per se*, but of the reductively 'theoreticist' type of stance that it would risk making possible (albeit as either an impossible pretence or a distracting straw man). The non-self-identical 'doubleness' of colonial displacement and divided critique is, perhaps, precisely what gives force and expression to Fanon's interventions in the world, not merely as an historical inspiration but more importantly as a multiply-charged and far from indivisible remainder, something still in the making or yet to come.

'The Negro and Adler'

But what of the opening section of 'The Negro and Recognition' devoted to the topic of 'The Negro and Adler'? Fanon begins with a quotation from *The Neurotic Constitution* which suggests that psychogenic conditions, despite their seemingly complex and chaotic features, should be understood in terms of simple causal finality, whereby once the ultimate goal of the condition is revealed, the patient may be read like a book. Fanon wastes no time in declaring this conclusion totally wrong-headed, arguing that such theoretical positions form the basis for 'the most stupendous frauds of our period' (211). Applying Adler's individual psychology to the Antilleans, Fanon argues that since their identity is entirely 'contingent', saturated by continual exposure to 'The Other' that defines them, their case marks the limit of possibility of the Adlerian approach. Nevertheless, the Antillean 'is characterized by his desire to dominate the other' (211–12), to instrumentalise, brutalise or otherwise objectify only in order to securitise the 'self', not least to emerge as unrivalled centre of attention, a model of superiority. Such absolute narcissism amounts to 'Me, nothing but me', and yet because it is 'The Other who corroborates him in his search for self-validation', for Fanon the always insecure Antillean is locked into a dynamic set of relations that for him remain inconsistent with an Adlerian idea of human communication and action (212–13). Adler's psychology of the individual doesn't square with the collective neurosis of Antilleans in general. They are caught in a struggle between inferiority and superiority, one that can only be 'individualised' at the cost of an enormous misrecognition of what is at stake in this situation. While the 'Adlerian comparison' is binary – ego and other – the Antillean comparison is 'surmounted by a third term' in that the relation to the other is always mediated by the 'social fiction', as Fanon puts it, of racial difference (215). Moreover, Fanon suggests that Adlerian psychology would be utterly incapable of mobilising change, instead endorsing the project of aping the 'superiority' of the white man only to then diagnose 'an indisputable complex of dependence' (216), thus effectively advocating resignation about one's place in the world as a more viable psychological option.

It is easy to see how this introductory section of 'The Negro and Recognition' establishes the trajectory of the ensuing commentary on Hegel in all of its difficulty. But these pages also point backwards, perhaps, to a lengthy footnote on Lacan in the preceding chapter, concerning in particular the Lacanian idea of the mirror-stage. Here, Fanon wonders what would transpire if the black man were introduced into the mirror-stage of the

white European, insisting in fact that this would actually constitute the mechanism by which white identity is acquired (161).
If this is a critique as much as a development of Lacan, perhaps
here Fanon downplays the element of splitting, heterogeneity
and difference that enters into the formation of the 'I' during
the mirror-stage. Be that as it may, Fanon also implies that there
is no straightforward mirror-stage for the black man, or at any
rate that it somewhat mutates the paradoxical conditions of
the mirror-stage itself: namely, those of deriving a sense of self
by repressing difference in relation to the 'other' from whom
identity is in fact derived. 'I contend that for the Antillean the
mirror hallucination is always neutral', he writes. 'When Antilleans tell me that they have experienced it, I always ask the same
question: "What color were you?" Invariably they reply: "I had
no color"' (162). Here, the repression of difference inherent in
the mirror-stage results in the neutralisation of colour which
presumably, for Fanon, profoundly controls and constrains as
much as it enhances or liberates the Antillean 'self'. This phenomenon he links to the fantasies of Antillean children to run
rosy-cheeked, like little Parisians, through open fields. Colour
neutrality turns out to license fantasies of whiteness: what is
repressed in the mirror-stage of the Antillean, in other words,
is not the otherness of the white Other but blackness itself.
Just as it does in Fanon's commentary on individual psychology, rereading the politics of racial difference into the scene of
the Lacanian mirror-stage once more introduces a critical 'third
term' into the field of psychological discourse, in the process
producing an analysis that might have been explicitly directed
towards the Hegelian problematic and its limits for which the
second half of 'The Negro and Recognition' is a kind of pretext.
What is crucial, here, though, is that it is the resistant 'other' of

psychoanalysis – specifically, the 'other' mirror-stage that Fanon is able to derive from his reading of Lacan in tandem with his psychiatric studies in Antilles – which may unlock another 'politics' capable of addressing, by better recognising, some of its impasses.

Notes

1   Frantz Fanon, *Black Skin, White Masks*, trans. Charles Lam Markmann (London: Pluto Press, 1993). Page references will be given in the body of the chapter.

2   For Homi Bhabha, writing of *Black Skin, White Masks* in his 'Foreword' to the English edition, 'recognition' in its Hegelian sense 'fails to ignite in the colonial relation where there is only narcissistic indifference' (xxi); in other words, where the desire of the colonised for recognition-through-struggle is met with an historic evasion of this very desire.

3   This recognition (along with my broader suggestion concerning an 'imperfect dialectics' at work in Fanon's writings) may resonate productively with Bhabha's assertion that Fanon 'may yearn for the total transformation of Man and Society, but he speaks most effectively from the uncertain interstices of historical change . . . To read Fanon is to experience the sense of division that prefigures – and fissures – the emergence of a truly radical thought that never dawns without casting an uncertain dark' (ix).

4   As is well known, Fanon supplements Merleau-Ponty's phenomenological account of embodiment in the world by developing an epidermal historico-racial analysis as a critical rejoinder to what may be seen as Merleau-Ponty's overly inclusive corporeal schema.

5   One wonders about the possibility of reading Fanon's psychiatry in terms of – indeed, against – Foucault's notion of a 'discourse of the exercise' which, for the latter, defines Descartes' 'rational' approach to madness in the *Meditations* (in fact Foucault's rejoinder to Derrida's critique of his work on madness turns on this point: see Michel Foucault, 'My Body, This Paper, This Fire', in *Essential Works Volume 2, 1954–1984: Aesthetics, Method, and Epistemology*, ed. James Faubion (London: Penguin Books, 1998)). For Foucault, contra Derrida, such a 'discourse of the exercise' intervenes at a highly specific, highly determined moment in Descartes'

text, such that the 'test of madness' and the 'test of dreaming' (412), far from functioning as near-identical operations, remain quite distinct in their purpose. Foucault insists that the *Meditations* 'require this double reading' whereby we are confronted with 'a set of propositions forming a *system*, which each reader must follow through if he wishes to feel their truth, and a set of modifications forming an *exercise*, which each reader must effect, by which each reader must be affected, if he in turn wants to be the subject enunciating this truth on his own behalf' (406). The reference to madness in the first Meditation is, Foucault argues, part of a distinct process linked to the 'discourse of the exercise' which therefore relates more to the second than the first aspect of this 'reading': 'the meditating subject had to exclude madness by qualifying himself as not mad' (412). 'Once this qualification of the subject has finally been achieved', says Foucault, 'systematic discursivity' is once more allowed to 'take the upper hand' (410) – a process which, indeed, also allows a certain exclusion of madness from philosophical discourse. One wonders if, in the colonial setting described and indeed inhabited by Fanon, this process isn't just as much impeded as that of Hegelian 'recognition'.

6   Time and space permitting, I would have liked to develop this point as a response to Bhabha's pejorative claim that Fanon experiences an overcompensatory hunger for 'humanism' (xx).

7   A performative discourse which, as Bhabha observes, stakes itself precisely upon a refusal to objectify and thereby narrate the colonial experience according to the classical forms of sociology, anthropology, historicism or empiricism which are funded by the 'text' of the West (xiii).

8   Richard Pithouse, 'The Open Door of Every Consciousness', *South Atlantic Quarterly* 112:1 (2013), 91–8.

9   Of course, the fabricated or humanly constructed nature of combat is inherent to the Hegelian account of the master-slave dialectic, although its possibility is not exhausted by Hegelianism, as Fanon's own writing on colonialism perhaps demonstrates.

2

Civility and its Discontents:
Balibar, Arendt, Lyotard

In 2015, almost a decade and a half after their original delivery, Étienne Balibar's Wellek lectures appeared in English, under the title *Violence and Civility: On the Limits of Political Philosophy*. This chapter will evaluate the book's contribution to the critical thinking of citizenship, civility and violence today. First of all, however, a word about the role played by psychoanalysis throughout these lectures, one that if anything seems to have intensified rather than diminished during that long editorial period between their original presentation and final publication. While it would be wrong to say that the entire thesis is explicitly framed and developed through continual recourse to psychoanalytic concepts, arguments and ideas, nonetheless I would argue that in crucial ways the 'psychoanalytic' is resorted to, albeit through a deliberately transformative gesture, as a vital resource for the *form* of thinking that Balibar deems necessary in relation to his subject matter. In particular, it seems to me that the 'limits' of political philosophy alluded to in the book's subtitle are traced out through a distinctively *resistant* relationship to psychoanalysis which amounts neither to a rejection nor a critique, but which instead exploits the resistances *of* psychoanalysis in the interests of the most relevant questioning concerning the 'political' today.

Obviously the question of violence is a key motif for this project. At a number of points in the published text, as he re-engages the legacy of Freud, Balibar considers the idea of a 'cruelty or capacity for destruction' that is located beyond the Freudian death drive itself, in order that he might re-think extreme types of violence which exceed the forms of authoritarianism, domination and oppression that are familiar within the historic arc of the nation-state. This 'beyond' tips over instead into a violence that stems from an *'idealization of hatred'* (perhaps more and more recognisable today), which Balibar considers in terms of an extension or transformation of fascism beyond its 'ordinary' or state form.[1] The reference point for the theoretical possibility of such a mutation in the conceptual toolkit of Freudian psychoanalysis is, interestingly, Derrida's essay, 'Psychoanalysis Searches the States of its Soul: The Impossible Beyond of a Sovereign Cruelty', which was presented as an address to the States General of Psychoanalysis held at the Sorbonne in 2000 (four years after the Wellek lectures were originally delivered, hence my remark above concerning Balibar's revision of the text over time, and the apparent intensification of an interest in psychoanalysis). Thus the thinking of violence in its contemporary guises comes to entail, for Balibar, critical re-engagement with psychoanalytic concepts, categories and forms of thought in the broader sense. In particular, through the reference to Derrida, it is clear that an understanding of sovereignty in its current manifestations (operating as a shifting ground as much as a stable phenomenon) benefits from this critical interaction or alignment. Importantly, however, the grounds of psychoanalysis are themselves transformed in the process. Picking up once more on Derrida's evocation of 'the beyond of the death drive', for Balibar the latter entails 'the dissociation of the tension or "unity of opposites'" between life and death, resulting in drives which we must recognise in terms of the modern principle or contemporary problematic of sovereignty itself. Balibar writes:

> This no longer has anything to do with the psychological analogy of ill-will or human 'evil'; the hypothesis is, rather, that the constitutive association of death with life is turned back against life itself, inverting the function of defense of the 'ego' or of individuality and turning it into a process of unlimited appropriation (including – perhaps most importantly – *self-appropriation*). (143)

The 'beyond of the death drive' exposes psychoanalysis to the 'other' of itself, then; a resistant other which in fact threatens to unseat the 'psychological analogy' from which new understandings of sovereign or political forms might otherwise seem to derive. That said, on closer inspection this mutation in the 'psychological analogy' may not in fact obliterate its relevance so much as restore and re-emphasise the paradoxical or perverse consequences of Freudian thought itself:

> I say that we are beyond psychologism here, but we naturally find ourselves on a very uncomfortable tightrope, as in Freud himself, between psychology and metaphysics, or between two ways, empirical or speculative, of invoking the idea of human nature. The idea of the 'death drive' and its beyond or limit can be reduced neither to Hobbes' 'war of all against all' nor to Darwin's 'natural selection' and all its applications in the political realm. (143)

Here, the death drive – never simply reducible to 'nature' (so that the 'uncomfortable tightrope' is not happened upon 'naturally'!) – itself tends to denature, distort or otherwise deconstruct all the borderlines between psychology and metaphysics, the empirical and the speculative, the 'original' and the 'historical', between natural and non-natural 'war' or 'selection', good and evil, and so on. In this sense, the death drive as much as its 'beyond' or limit already pertains to a situation in which the 'psychological analogy' that would permit 'applications in the political realm' is subjected to an altogether different logic. The normative form − that of analogy or application − which an orthodox psychologism grants is not so much dispensed with in favour of a move 'beyond' psychoanalysis itself, as it is reconstituted in a manner that is more faithful to the 'origin', if one may put it that way. To go *beyond* psychoanalysis or the death drive is in fact also to go *back* to them in the most vigilant and rigorous fashion. From this perspective, in its thinking of the modalities of violence in both their historical and contemporary cast, Balibar's book should to a certain extent be read and evaluated according to a rather complicated procedure whereby the conditions and characteristics of psychoanalytic discourse are transformed and renewed at just those moments that 'psychology' might seem to be left behind. For sure, psychoanalysis surfaces explicitly in many places throughout Balibar's lectures, but the frame of reference it makes possible is operative not only when he discusses anxiety, the Möbius strip, the mirror-stage, *objet petit a* or the Real in Lacan (through which access to relevant forms of political thought is sought), but also − and perhaps precisely − where the book deals more generally with questions of sovereignty, 'life', violence and civility. This is another way of saying that psycho-analytic thought once more seems to become most powerful at the point of a certain *resistance* to itself; a resistance one might be tempted to call 'internal' since it is far from merely extrinsic, but a resistance that is nonetheless also a radically 'other' force operating within that of which it is still an essential part.

41

Civility and Violence

One point of departure for these texts, then, is the enduring question of citizenship (dealt with in a range of writings by Balibar, including those found in *Equaliberty* and *We, the People of Europe?*). Citizenship was of course a hugely important problem at that time, in terms of the allied question of Europe in all its senses, as much as in terms of the not unrelated (though not simply identical) issue of world populations in flux, the relationship between the 'local' and the 'global', and so on. These are questions that have of course been powerfully renewed in more recent times, under different yet connected conditions and circumstances, making the English publication of Balibar's Wellek lectures far more timely than belated. The appearance of this book, in other words, reopens the question: Whither citizenship? Given the rising instance and intense complications of statelessness and forced migration worldwide, given the finance politics that, in Balibar's own terms, make Europe an 'apartheid' of sorts,[2] given the increasing privatisation of public and welfare provision as an example of the erosion of what citizenship means in its practical as well as ideological sense, given the ongoing transformation of the various relationships of nation-states to the private interests of multinational companies (and, for that matter, the transnational social and economic effects of certain nation's or groups of nations' fiscal policy on the world's stage), given the far-reaching effects globally of debt capitalism, given the intensifying lack of separation between the political and economic spheres that would seem to mark the transition from liberal democracy to neoliberalism,[3] given the impact of certain nationalisms and fundamentalisms of various types over the past decades, given the politics of security and 'counter-terrorism' that affects rights of all kinds – given all of this, what is to be made of citizenship today?

Though we should be highly wary of any elision or hasty slippage from one key word to another in a certain family of terms, for Balibar the problem of citizenship raises related questions of the 'civic' and the 'civil' (although, for him, these do not go straightforwardly in the direction of any received sense of 'community', especially when construed in terms of settled communal or consensual belonging,[4] not least since Balibar is fond of describing the 'intrinsically antinomic'[5] relationship of citizenship to democracy and the state). These are questions, then, that he groups under the general problem of 'civility' in an attempt to conceive of the possibility of a more progressive or even emancipatory politics. This is a 'politics' that Balibar analyses primarily in terms of the problem of 'violence', not just in the sense that the world seems to be becoming progressively more violent – regardless of whether such violence is predominantly state-sponsored, whether it is inspired by certain fundamentalisms or nationalisms somewhat beyond (though not simply outside) the current reach of the state form, or whether it is, as it were, more purely market-led (as if one could ever totally separate these different types of 'violence'). The question of violence is central to that of politics, for Balibar, not just to the extent that violence is growing (almost beyond the reach of 'politics' itself), but more properly because to conceive of the question of politics with any rigour, even and perhaps especially when one chooses to concentrate on motifs of, let's say, the public realm and the common good, citizenry and indeed civilisation itself, is inevitably to raise the spectre of the question of violence, whether one likes it or not.[6]

For Balibar, then, the possibility of a progressive or emancipatory politics must negotiate carefully with the question of violence that it frequently tends to resist, to recoil from, or to otherwise resolve somewhat too readily. It is not enough simply to denounce or repudiate violence *per se*, or, alternatively – if one accepts its usage as at times unavoidable – to justify its appropriation or 'conversion' as sometimes indispensable to radical political programmes, even if their ultimate aim is the abolition of violence as such. Instead, such a 'politics' must first consider more deeply its complexly constituted and at times highly entangled relationship to violence. In broad terms, such a relationship may take three possible forms, Balibar tells us; albeit forms which, far from being simply mutually exclusive, have proven historically interdependent or at least inter-implicated in a number of ways. Balibar names this triumvirate according to the threefold designation, 'nonviolence', 'counterviolence' and 'antiviolence'.

Balibar's aim here is to seek an alternate pathway for politics that succumbs neither to the naive idea of a total 'abstraction from violence' (what he terms 'nonviolence'), nor to a political strategy based on the co-opting of violence in the interests of a revolutionary transformation of the conditions of power, or in other words the 'conversion' of violence in its repressive form into a source of emancipatory possibility (which he designates by the term 'counterviolence'). Instead, Balibar seeks to develop a conception of 'antiviolence', tied to a renewed idea of 'civility' that is not merely received intact from certain political traditions, but which instead, if it is to have the chance of a future in terms of the current needs of political thought and action, must be transformed in significant ways.

Balibar rightly spends time, therefore, outlining what 'civility' is not, or must not be. Civility is not to be reduced, through its etymological history and connections, to concepts of politeness, proper behaviour or good manners in the public or political realm. It is not simply equivalent to ideas of moral or ethical uprightness or decency, regardless of the extent to which such notions are conceived culturally or politically in terms of either the requisite facets of individual 'character', or alternately as the apt expression of the social bond, or both. Instead, 'civility' is that which answers 'contemporary extreme violence', as Balibar puts it, neither from an imagined 'outside' (the position of 'nonviolence'), nor from an 'inside' turned upon its head in the interests of the revolutionary 'conversion' of violence (the position of 'counterviolence'), but which instead re-marks otherwise the deconstructible limits and possibilities of violence as we understand it.

Identity of Violence

Civility refuses both the idea that violence can decisively be brought to an end and the notion that it is simply without end or limit, in precisely the sense that both of these positions tend to objectify or homogenise violence as such. The first position grants violence an historical coherence or consistency in terms of conditions that are fully determined or inscribed in a sufficiently secure way that their 'beyond' can be imagined in terms of a more-or-less simple 'outside' capable of decisive non-participation in the *identity* that violence thereby acquires. ('Violence is *this*, and *this* can be stopped.') The second position, frequently identified with post-Hobbesianism, seems to assert violence as the originary and thus inescapable condition of all human existence. Yet the imperious generality of such a claim is marked by a certain contradiction, in the sense that violence in Hobbes turns out to be less a state of nature than the originary condition of 'politics' *per se* ('violence' *means* 'politics'). Hence, violence *as always 'political' violence* cannot therefore be naturalised as such. (Incidentally, this conception of politics in terms of *instituted* violence is of course by no means simply opposed to the classical construction of the political realm in terms of the 'polis', public space, citizenship, social 'virtue', etc.) In Hegel, meanwhile, this notion of the discontinuity of violence and nature arises with his idea that history may be construed in terms of the 'violent conversion of violence conceived as a process of incessant denaturation' (47). For Balibar, such 'counterviolent' conversion of violence does not merely confirm violence's essential ubiquity, to the extent that violence is thereby marked by a radical unnaturality that is difficult to reconcile with essentialist claims. As such, the 'negative' movement of Spirit, whereby the seeming 'demonstration of the inevitability of violence' in fact leads through the dialectical process to 'a sublime elimination of violence' (48), leads not only to debates about the predestined nature of violence (whether it is destined to exist or, contrariwise, destined to end). Instead, the Hegelian 'conversion' of violence raises the prospect of violence as itself denatured or denaturing, and therefore as groundlessly artificial, baselessly errant, or, one might say, radically perverse.

Civility, then, is not just the matter of reintroducing good manners, proper behaviour, politeness, courtesy or decency into a 'politics' always bent on violence, or devoted to the violent end of violence; instead, it is the name Balibar wants to give to certain 'political' strategies founded on the recognition of the always double and deconstructible limits of what is 'violent' (i.e., 'politics' itself). In other words, civility is what Derrida might call the *supplement* of violence, which means neither that civility is that which *finesses* violence in order to make it palatable (thus, in effect, to augment and extend it); nor that civility aims principally at violence's lessening or amelioration (in order to guard against its worst extremes, thus in a sense to preserve its possibility); nor even that civility marks that pure and noble line in the sand from which violence must retreat (an expulsion of sorts which, if one turns to historical instances of this kind of standpoint, hardly guarantees violence's diminution). At its best, civility does not merely settle its accounts with violence in any of these ways, all of which would leave what might otherwise be termed its 'good conscience' open to further scrutiny. Instead, to follow Balibar's thinking, civility is an impurity – a negotiation if not a compromise – that seeks at each turn to capitalise on the always impure economy of violence in the interests of an 'antiviolence' that neither immunises nor converts.

In the first instance, as Balibar himself recognises, civility may correspond to little more than just this 'question' of the excess of violence over its own conceptual determination in various, though hardly opposed, forms (65). If the revolution must be 'civilised',[7] then, this is not merely in the sense – to which we might all too hastily resort – that proper behaviour and good sense must regulate violent excess. Otherwise, critics of Balibar might be right to point out that such strategies in fact tend to permit or even encourage the most extreme and violent forms of inequality by other means. (That is, they risk a certain managing-down, subtle-ising or taking-one's-foot-off-the-pedal of violence which, perhaps more than sheer violence or unbridled force, ensures that inequality is safely maintained.) From this perspective, then, to 'civilise' the revolution is to seek an alternative to the impasse of either 'nonviolent' or 'counterviolent' attitudes which not only mistakenly reduce the contradictory or even aporetic problematics of violence, but in the process risk succumbing to the force of an *identity* (or the identity of a 'force') that is in fact at once impossible and impossibly violent. To lay claim to such 'civility' is therefore to inscribe the resistance of violence within the aporias of violence, rather than within a *conditioned* (or 'civilised') violence – aporias that, if they create in themselves the impression of a certain violence, nonetheless cannot merely be collapsed back into the conceptual fields that govern our sense of what violence is, remaining instead non-objectifiable in terms of, and thus irreducible to, 'violence' as such. In other words, 'civility' is that which somehow partakes of the 'unpolitical' supplement that is the wellspring of the very possibility of politics (whether that politics is more or less 'violent' or more or less 'civilised' – and indeed who could ever take the measure of any such combination?) *as much as it is also precisely the limit of such possibility.* 'Antiviolence' thereby re-marks the aporia or the 'unpolitical' of politics that both makes and un-makes it.[8] Such thinking on Balibar's part may thus be characterised in terms of reformism or revisionism only through a desperate misunderstanding of its intellectual ambit.

In theoretical terms, this is dizzying stuff, not to mention pathbreaking in a certain way. But surely we need to take further steps to clarify if not concretise 'civility' – a 'concept' that, it must be granted, would necessarily lose some if not much of its force were it to be referred or restricted too hastily to the available discourses of 'violence' or 'politics' that it seeks to deconstruct – before we can assess its capacity for political transformation. Here, certain questions arise, and should be broached before further headway can be made on this topic.

Violence Management

If to '"civilize" a revolutionary movement from within', as Balibar puts it – and to thereby 'introduce the antiviolence I call civility into the very heart of the violence of a social transformation' – is not simply a matter of ending violence or converting it into the violent 'other' of itself, it is surely still less to be understood as the attempt to regulate or *manage* violence. (The term regulation, in its possible relationship to that of management, may prove interesting here: are the Kantian regulative principles and ideas evidence of a less 'managed' scenario where the orientation of the understanding is concerned, or on the contrary are they indicative of an ingenious 'management solution'?) For surely, as history teaches us, such regulation or management of violence is inherently paradoxical, risking amplifying and intensifying the effects of violence and inequality at the very point of ostensibly lessening them. This is true, even and perhaps especially up to the extreme point of a complete termination of violence. Balibar himself reminds us of Derrida's point about the utter violence – the irresistible domination – that would likely accompany the complete cessation of violence in all its forms. To figure progressive nonviolence proceeding to its optimal point as the ultimate aim and aspiration of 'civility' or 'antiviolence' might therefore be to yoke civility itself to the same nightmarish course followed by 'violence', 'counterviolence' and 'nonviolence' alike.

What, then, *is* civility? If it is, quite rightly, to be denuded of all the hypocritical trappings of high-minded morality, or denied the stylised *accoutrements* of good manners and politeness, or for that matter stripped of the more shop-soiled garments of worldly pragmatism to which, for instance, neoliberal governments so frequently resort, what remains of civility beyond the sheer *management* of violence that inscribes its task within an extremely thorny paradox? What would it mean to introduce antiviolence into 'the very heart of the violence of a social transformation', and to thereby 'civilise' revolution itself, if, by evoking civility, we must be extremely wary of resorting to the idea of a certain managerialism (or administration or governmentality, as Foucault might put it) — even one that may be deprived, however improbably, of the historical sense of morals, manners, or even current forms of pragmatism — *precisely because every form of management that we might imagine risks serving the interests of violence by other means*, even if 'violence' sometimes violently resists just such violent management? How might civility escape this terrifying, vertiginous problematic in which all opposition to repression or tyranny seems ultimately to remain trapped, whereby to reduce violence may only be to increase it, whether inadvertently or not; where to minimise violence risks maximising it?

What, then, *is* civility? The very form that this question takes ('What *is*?') entails obvious 'philosophical' or 'theoretical' shortcomings, yet it cannot easily be sacrificed without risking some doubtless unwanted consequences. We might rightly balk at getting caught up afresh in an identity-based formulation of just the kind that traps the 'thinking' of violence in the dead-end circularity of 'nonviolence'/'counterviolence' ('violence is *something* that can go away/violence is *something* that won't go away'), one that circles back to the impossible identity of violence 'itself'. Yet to forgo the question entirely is obviously to clear the ground for certain predictable complaints against this particular form of political thought as ultimately just too 'theoretical', abstract, abstruse, impractical, and so on.

In order to take forward the question of civility, then, Balibar evokes Rosa Luxemburg's call for revolution to find its 'representative moment' (104). To offset the strong chance of revolution 'being overwhelmed by the very barbarity that it was trying to expunge' (104), Balibar foresees the possibility of a certain detachment from violence through collective empowerment. In other words, for Balibar, representativity might offer the opportunity for mutual, critical self-reflection. The 'representative moment' of emancipation might foster, and indeed license, diverse responses to violence that were not merely reactive or conformist. Here, it is the *critique* of violence as much as its 'management' that is at stake. As Balibar puts it, it is a question 'of introducing *another dialectic* (that of violence and antiviolence) into the practice of transformation itself on the basis that political violence can never be completely controlled' (105). Such critique seems destined neither to reproduce violence through counterviolent repetition, nor to succumb to the orthodoxy of nonviolence as a dominating ethical imperative.

Here, one might say that the dialectical relation of 'antiviolence' to violence is somewhat distinctive in relation to that of both counterviolence and nonviolence, in that what violence and antiviolence share is precisely a *resistance* to management. Violence resists management, because it is the always excessive supplement of politics, being at once the condition of possibility of the political yet also its radical limit or challenge. 'Antiviolence', meanwhile, resists management in the sense that it earns its name only when it proves itself capable of effectively mobilising that part of the critique of violence that fully appreciates the paradoxical plight of every strategy of *managing* violence.

Pluralism and Civility

But what would this dialectical interaction between 'violence' and 'antiviolence' actually look like? Might it leave antiviolence in too weak a position to counteract sheer violence unfettered by regulative controls? Is there not still a risk that its own critique of the paradoxical elements of every strategy of resistance to violence risks putting the discourse of 'antiviolence' out of business before it ever had a chance to get going? Balibar's call for '*different strategies of civility*' bases itself on what he deems 'the *intrinsic pluralism* of the notion of civility' (106) – a 'pluralism' that would seem the necessary corollary of antiviolence's retreat from the absolute control, sovereignty or mastery over violence which itself risks a symmetrical repetition of violence. And yet the risk of a discourse of 'pluralism' is inevitably that it fuels complaints about the overhasty dilution of emancipatory will, or that it threatens to place counter-revolutionary obstacles in the pathway of concerted radicalism of, say, a vanguardist type. With good reason, Balibar might well be uninterested in answering back such criticisms at any great length, allowing instead the critique of (historical) counterviolence to speak for itself. On the other hand, however, without a robustly articulated response to these objections one may risk depriving civility of a fully stocked critical armoury of the kind that might be needed to effectuate it as a 'strategy'.

Accordingly, Balibar delineates three specific strategies of civility. The first, a 'hegemonic strategy' derived from Balibar's reading of Hegel, involves 'a regulated, controlled construction of "pluralism" as a politically structured relationship between state and society', whereby a diverse variety of 'communitarian affiliations' take hold, but also where members are brought into

relationship with one another not merely on the basis of identification with a greater whole, but also on the strength of a
certain distance taken within such identification to in fact make
it possible at another level of universality. In other words, here,
the 'dialectic of the particular and the universal' is shaped by a
certain distantiation internal to identificatory possibility, which
allows the individual some degree of separation in order to find
self-recognition in a form of citizenship that guarantees partial
yet critical detachment from each and every communal identity
within the larger social bond. Historically, the hegemonic strategy
works to progressively denaturalise ties of a more primary kind
(family, clan, etc.) in the interests of the reconstruction of one's
sense of belonging that is mediated by the institutions of civil
society, ultimately in the interests of the state. As Balibar points
out, Hegel hardly foresaw the terrible risk of political abuse
embedded in this model, for instance by fascist states of the
twentieth century. Nevertheless, what qualifies the 'hegemonic
strategy' for consideration as a type of civility is that the intricate
interplay of belonging and non-belonging, of particularity and
universality, that organises the hierarchical construction of social
identity at the various levels of family, community and state
introduces a degree of self-difference within identification that
borders on a paradox, if not a contradiction. Henceforth divided
by this paradox, the state cannot be 'total' or absolute. The
hegemonic strategy thus becomes interesting to Balibar since it
is in this way that 'pluralism' may be thought to constitute itself
more concretely in terms of a specific social dynamic that has
built-in resistance, as it were, to the violence of an absolutist
type. Nonetheless, Balibar is the first to point out that, historically, the tensions that exist within this 'hegemonic' model
when combined with its commitment to certain hierarchical

transitions lead to violence in other ways. The antinomies that structure such hegemonic systems not only protect the whole edifice from absolutist retrenchment, but they also mean that the requisite forms of transit from the particular to the universal on which the hegemonic model of the social bond essentially depends must on occasion be brought about by more or less forceful means (whether the violence is 'physical' or 'symbolic'). In particular, such a 'Hegelian politics of civility', writes Balibar, 'includes a restrictive or even repressive condition, normality' (113). The processes of normalisation upon which the hierarchical interactions of the hegemonic model rely tend to purge so-called pluralism of any perverse elements. It is perhaps no surprise that, as Balibar points out, such a model insists first of all on *sexual* normality; not least, perhaps, to restrict the meaning of perversion to a manageable 'sexual' form, i.e., one that might be used to affirm types of normalcy that ground the operativity of the entire hegemonic system. At such a point, where perversity is not just stigmatised or illegitimised but reduced to an identificatory 'prop', so-called pluralism lapses back into the more or less violent management of what is perceived as 'violent', and the hegemonic model risks becoming drained of its potential to escape the paradoxes of every 'strategy' that pits itself against tyranny or repression.

That said, Balibar is reluctant to totally dismiss the hegemonic strategy. Its internal self-differences make possible a powerfully deconstructive reading of the Hegelian text, specifically in terms of Hegel's interpretation of Sophocles' *Antigone*. Of course, we find this reading rigorously pursued in Derrida's *Glas*, which must have been in Balibar's mind when writing this section of the text, although he does not make explicit reference to it. In *Glas*, the spiritual and ethical purity of the sister-brother relation seems guaranteed both by the lack of conjugal desire and by the absence of epic conflict between parent and child, so that in transcending internecine struggle this very same relation provides grounds for the 'free' dissolution of family into felicitous civil life. Thus, the brother–sister bond at once provides an exemplary image of filiation in its full plenitude or synthetic possibility, uninterrupted either by longing or resentment; and yet it also places Antigone outside the possibility of dialectical incorporation according to the dominant logic of filiation (that of the 'masculine' in the conventional fatherly or state form, which Antigone powerfully resists in defying Creon as the embodiment of a state–substitute for the father). In other words, Antigone represents at once the possibility and impossibility of the synthesising universality of Spirit, and thus of the Hegelian system itself. Violence, here, cannot fully overcome a certain plurality, one that is perverse in a deeper sense than the merely 'sexual'. However, even though this scenario short-circuits the system, resisting it through neither exactly a mere repetition nor a straightforward rejection of its violence, for some it might be difficult to see how a text such as this makes possible a better world, ending as it does in self-destructive tragedy rather than with the affirmation of liberatory hope. To be sure, the inherent instability of such a 'plural' text would permit rewritings 'otherwise', not fully dominated or exhausted by the tragic mode. Doubtless, though, more work would need to be done before an 'antiviolent' civility with potentially progressive social and political effects might be founded on a certain interaction with such 'pluralism'.

The second strategy of civility that Balibar identifies is of the majoritarian type. This he locates principally within the traditions of Marxism, including certain debates internal to Marxism

(107), which endow the majority or the 'mass' with the greatest political efficacy and potential. The third, minoritarian in nature, takes inspiration from the work of Deleuze and Guattari. What these strategies have in common, yet what also distinguishes them, 'involves the way one takes a distance from the state and the imperatives of its constitution', as Balibar puts it (116). In the majoritarian strategy, what is highlighted by Balibar is the possibility of a 'bottom-up' invention of emancipatory politics not shackled to the counterviolent strategies frequently adopted by, say, a revolutionary vanguard. This 'bottom-up' approach entrusts itself with responsibility, rather than yielding to some slavish reaction to mastery of the kind that tends to repeat the cycle of violence. Here, pluralism is to be reconstructed not as a 'state function' bent on normalising 'social conflicts in hierarchical fashion' (117), but develops instead in terms of the negotiation between genuinely diverse emancipatory movements free from exhaustive statist determination.[9] For Balibar, if this vision of majoritarian civil emancipation is as improbable as it is inspiring, such strategies and movements nonetheless remain important in opening up potential new spaces of political freedom, although he does not exclude Deleuze and Guattari's criticism of all majoritarianism as intrinsically at risk of mass violence and subjection. Nonetheless, Balibar is also able to show that, in Deleuze and Guattari, 'the terminology of becoming-minoritarian' frequently tends to

> invert, term for term, the scheme of the emancipation of humanity through emancipation of a 'universal class.' Like every inversion, however, this one, too, preserves an element of its point of departure. The idea is still that of a process that simultaneously affects both poles of an asymmetrical relation of domination. (121)

Thus, for Balibar, the minoritarian strategy risks becoming merely the obverse of counterviolence as the negative expression of dialectical history, albeit that minoritarian 'becoming' is imagined in terms of non-teleological fluidities. As he sees it, then, minoritarianism – not least since it rests on a binary term – remains dialectisable despite Deleuze and Guattari's intentions. In this way, rather than simply standing outside of other 'strategies of civility', it partakes of similar problematics, and is vulnerable to the same criticisms it levels at other positions, concerning both its own effectiveness in combating violence and indeed the 'latent tendency to reproduce extreme violence' (123). If, from the perspective of a 'micropolitics of desire', majoritarianism always drifts towards a 'hegemonic project', nevertheless from a broadly Marxist viewpoint the politics of deterritorialisation are always at risk of serving the interests of power, not least in its most recent global forms. It is as if, for Balibar, these two strategies are locked in a confrontation whereby the faults they detect in the other position are also the risks they must negotiate in their own. The encounter, if one may say so, threatens to become self-destructively counterviolent, even as it indicates a certain self-difference that, as we have already seen, may be taken in more than one direction.

Inconclusive Civility

Such insights bring us to the close of Balibar's 1996 Wellek lectures, although the English edition of *Violence and Civility* concludes with an essay from 2003 on the question of the 'un-political'. (The book is also introduced by the text that Balibar gave at Cerisy-la-Salle in 1992 on the work of Jacques Derrida, itself devoted to the topic of violence.) In the preface to this edition, Balibar suggests that the significant time lag between the delivery and publication of the lectures was in part to do with his own dissatisfaction that they lacked 'a clear conclusion' (viii), a possible shortcoming that the intervening years had not yet fully rectified. For him, it was then a matter of finding ways 'to relativize the formal thesis' of these lectures, namely that civility or antiviolence 'forms as such a "politics of politics" (or a meta-politics in charge of "creating" the conditions for the institution of the political, including this very special form of institution which is a revolution)' (ix).[10] Such a 'politics of politics', then, is not to be considered reducible to a single 'modality', but is to be located instead at the shifting intersections of violence and civility, that is between counterviolent, nonviolent and antiviolent problematics, hegemonic, majoritarian and minoritarian politics, and so forth. Balibar concludes that this mixed and plural set of 'modalities' and problematics, falling short of a comprehensive system (while still demanding systematic analysis of sorts), provided something of a solution to the problem of his lectures' inconclusive ending, indeed making a solution out of the very problem itself. Why, then, add another essay to bring the collection to a close?

In '*Après-Coup*' – the text in question – the demand for civility arises on the strength of a particular equation: the answer for which it calls equals the inability of politics to do away with 'liberating insurgency (which may itself require violence)' plus its incapacity to fully resist 'the nihilism of violence' (128). This extremely elegant formulation nicely captures what Balibar describes as the problem or question of civility, without requiring its author to restrict the plural possibilities of civility to some exemplary case or instance. As the essay proceeds, once more civility seems to be optimised where the distantiation internal to the forms of identification upon which civil models of politics rest might be productively accentuated. It intensifies where such distantiation fosters an inventive renewal of politics neither restricted to the 'counterviolence' of reactive servility nor to the absolutist idealism of nonviolence, but committed instead to creative kinds of remaking whose grounds are neither foundationally 'given' nor teleologically determined. This is a 'politics of politics' that would try as far as possible to be responsible for itself. It would be measured by standards of its own making that were indeed always 'in the making'. And yet the promise of such a politics is always tempered by the fact that 'the debate with "violence"'. . . is essentially interminable' (149). If violence cannot be entirely ignored or negated, civility must interact with it in ways that ensure 'antiviolence', unlike nonviolence or counterviolence, is not ultimately dominated by violence. Yet for this to happen, 'civility' must remain constantly vigilant to the risk of simply economising with violence, which means, above all, understanding the risks implicit in the temptation to manage violence, whether in the form of regulation, amelioration, or the making palatable of violence. To economise with violence, as we have seen, may be to risk maximising it in the very attempt (whether genuine or not) to minimise it. This is true, even if, as Balibar rightly asserts elsewhere, '"civility" does not necessarily involve the idea of the suppression of "conflicts" and "antagonisms" in society, as if they were always the harbingers of violence and not the opposite. Much, if not most, of the extreme violence we are led to discuss in fact results from a blind preference for "consensus" and "peace".'[11] At times, no doubt, the task of 'civility' is to accentuate – to maximise – and not to inhibit – or minimise – conflict and dissent, albeit to lessen once more the greater violence that is frequently waged in the name of 'consensus' or 'peace'. Thus, the challenge remains to imagine forms of civility that could forgo violence-management without in the process changing the 'civil' equation, such that the liberating insurgency at the (aporetic) heart of the political[12] when combined with the ineradicable nihilism of violence might lead us in terrifyingly precarious directions. How, then, can civility rid itself of the demand to manage violence? This is civility's dilemma: to forgo violence-management to the maximal degree might be to remain vulnerable the worse violence; yet to embrace violence-management to even a minimal degree may be to risk the worse violence. Since it is forced, however unfeasibly, to negotiate between these two 'alternatives' – and I use the word 'forced' deliberately – civility *must* therefore economise with that which it must not economise, *and impossibly so*, in conditions where to minimise may be to maximise, and vice versa. What, in these circumstances, prevents 'antiviolence' from succumbing to the same fate as 'nonviolence' or 'counterviolence', i.e., simply getting recycled back into violence, licensing violence whichever way it turns? 'Antiviolence', from this point of view, seems only to redistribute all of the modalities of violence (including 'counterviolence' and 'nonviolence') between the risk of an unavoidably violent destiny, on the one hand, and – given Balibar's recursive insistence on the limits of prior determination – the chance that any of these modalities may enjoy the contingent possibility of a more progressive relationship to violence, on the other. In which case, surely 'antiviolence' ceases to stand out as a special instance, offering a distinctive pathway out of the dead-end paradoxes of the other two 'strategies' waged against tyranny and repression?

To put matters in yet another way: as much as it forms a 'politics of politics', given its paradoxical predicament 'civility' would also appear to be a supplement in need of some sort of supplement. *Après-coup*, one may seek to remake Sophocles' tragedy from the plural materials at its disposal, but unless such acts of invention can be concretely specified so as to address the contingencies of today and tomorrow (as well as, perhaps, yesterday), civility might end up being the name for something we could turn to if only violence was not what it was. If nothing else, Balibar's book convincingly demonstrates that such a scenario, however likely and depressing it may seem, is neither necessary nor fated, *precisely because violence is not what it is*, because it is not reducible to the names and forms by which we recognise it, and through which it seems increasingly to surround and entrap us. If it is an equation we are after, then, a genuinely transformative civility depends on the transformation of violence (one that envisages neither its decisive ending, nor its sheer acceptance, nor even such resistance as takes its 'object' for granted). This transformation includes the question of civility on the successive levels of its theoretical meaning or intention, its agency or efficacy, and its outcomes. In what ways is civility's 'antiviolence' violent, if not in intention or design, then at the level of its exercise, or in its effects? Is 'violence' of whatever degree distributed differently at each of these levels, or is the manifestation of any such violence to be considered constant throughout the various stages or phases of 'antiviolence', from beginning to end? Would such distribution, if uneven, change in different circumstances, and if so what would be the key factors at work? I raise such issues in order to ask what seems a critical question. How, if at all, does violence change as it passes through 'antiviolence', and how, if it all, is 'antiviolence' changed by it? Such problems seem highly apt given Balibar's own emphasis on plurality, contingency and the dynamism of social interactions not reducible to given determination.

Civility and Rights

One way to conceive of civility with a greater degree of clarity
or concreteness may be to pursue its linkage to the question of
rights. (Of course the question of rights raises a further question:
rights in what sense? My purpose here, however, is less to debate
versions of rights – Arendtian, Balibarian, or otherwise – than it
is simply to register the question of rights as a civil 'supplement'
having the capacity to enjoin the question of politics in potentially concrete ways.) In a number of places in Balibar's writing,
then, this connection between civility and rights crops up. For
instance, in the essay, 'The Antinomy of Citizenship', included
in *Equaliberty*, he notes that citizenship is necessarily constituted
within the horizon of a social and political community defined
by the 'reciprocity of rights and duties', one that places certain
limits on forms of rulership, therefore constituting citizenship
in a dynamic and potentially unstable relationship to power and
authority. Yet precisely because of and not despite this situation,
citizenship is 'permanently traversed by crises and tensions . . .
it is a fragile institution'.[13] Citizenship is thus always susceptible to remaking or transformation, not least in terms of the
inconcludable negotiation between freedom and equality, insurgency and constitution, that defines the so-called democratic
situation. In other words, the antinomic conditions of possibility
of citizenship provoke continual re-invention as much as serene
conservation, and this instability begs the question of 'rights' as
much as it reinforces a need for them.

The question of the precise relationship between 'civil' and
'human' rights is taken up in another essay included in *Equaliberty*. In 'Hannah Arendt, the Right to Have Rights, and
Civil Disobedience',[14] Balibar shows how Arendt negotiates the

apparent tension between, on the one hand, an insistence on a politics of 'right' as the basis of a democratic surplus, and, on the other, critical dissatisfaction with the notion of fundamental human rights more generally. For Arendt, rights are to be constructed not asserted, made not given, claimed not bestowed; or, as Balibar puts it, 'the rights of man cannot be conceived as an *origin* to be rediscovered or restored (as was postulated in their name by the revolutions of the Enlightenment), but only as an *invention* (one of the meanings of *auctoritas*) or a continuous *beginning* (*archè*)' (167). Rights are thus always 'in the making', forged in the context of living conflicts and contradictions that make them as radically precarious as they are radically apt.

We might think of 'civic' or 'civil' rights as largely the derivative outcrop of a notion of fundamental human rights. However, Balibar asserts that since history often teaches us that personal and human rights may typically be swept away precisely when civil rights are abolished or diminished, the 'civic' is the effective context and practical condition for human rights, and not the other way around (170–1).[15]

Following Arendt, Balibar argues that the 'civil' construction of rights (as opposed to their human 'givenness') implies that the principal or 'first' right may be thought of in terms of 'the right to have rights', the *political* demand for rights, or 'the right to petition' in a classical sense. Here, emphasis is placed less on the statutory nature of rights than on the claiming of rights as integral to rights themselves. The right to have rights is therefore at once 'absolute *and* contingent' (172). From this perspective, rights are not 'relativized', far from it; instead, they reclaim their absolute demand in the very context of the active 'construction of the human' through the 'historical invention of political institutions' (173). (Thus, the absolute is maintained only in the context of contingency.) Henceforth, humans do not simply 'have' their rights – they *are* their rights. Once more, however, this represents a precarious state of affairs since the very institutions through which rights are gained also tend to threaten the rights they make possible. From this point of view, as Balibar later puts it, 'the construction of the political, and thus the definition of the citizen, can thus only be antinomic' (175). This antinomy is plural, divided between the positive and negative roles of institution(s), between constitution and insurrection as twin poles of the democratic, between the good and evil that may occur on the strength of the political risk always inherent in active citizenship and the 'claiming' of rights, and so on. As Balibar writes:

> It is striking that here Arendt . . . cites Tocqueville's notion of 'dangerous liberty' and refers to the 'perils of equality' that are inseparable from democracy. These ideas are at the center of the political dilemma inherent in movements of dissidence and civil disobedience, caught between the authoritarianism and conservatism of the state and the possibility of an essentially totalitarian internal degeneration. (176)

In fact, Balibar closes his essay by noting that 'the collective exercise of judgment, which is rooted in freedom of speech and tests itself to the point of risking disobedience', forms not simply an 'ideal foundation of legislative power, but the everyday reality of its exercise and control by the community of citizens'; and yet it 'would no doubt be illusory to imagine that a state or a society in which civic disobedience figures among the fundamental rights would in itself be immunized against totalitarian degeneration'. That said, this problem or dilemma is the very one that, on Balibar's reading of Arendt, 'should orient our understanding of the political' (186). That Balibar characterises this orientation in terms of a 'regulative idea' (presumably attributed to Arendt's Kantian interests) may threaten to reduce the complex interplay between insurrection and constitution – the very trace of *equaliberty* – to a question of violence-management, at any rate in part. One wonders whether the mediation 'by a community of citizens' of the violent antinomies of state politics and civil disobedience via the exercise of 'judgment' might itself produce unwanted outcomes, not least in the interests of repression and inequality, especially given that all claims are not statutorily given but are instead forcefully made. But does the problematic opened up by the reading of Arendt's work so readily succumb to such a disheartening conclusion?

Lyotard, Civility and Rights

Reference to Arendt's work on the question of rights informs a short talk by Jean-François Lyotard, 'The Other's Rights', originally presented as part of the 1993 Oxford Amnesty International Lectures.[16] While the latter may be considered a relatively minor text in relation to Lyotard's corpus overall, one context for its continuing significance is the repeated allusion made to this text by Jacques Rancière in support of his critique not only of Lyotard but more generally of an 'ethics of the other' position that is blamed for the curtailment of emancipatory possibility in the political field. Such a position, Rancière argues, is tied regressively to an ethical consensuality dictated by the unrepresentable horror of the Holocaust. It is therefore presented as at once constrained by traumatic repetition and driven by a sense of redemptive entitlement that hardly squares with egalitarian activism. However, predicating such a critique on the 'The Other's Rights' couldn't be more misplaced. Far from presenting 'rights' in terms of an ethical consensus that impedes political transformation, when read carefully Lyotard's lecture in fact evokes a radical civility that might effectively confront forms of domination and power without succumbing to the paradoxical predicament of 'antiviolence'.

Lyotard's point of departure in this text is the 'other than human' that for him founds the possibility of human rights. Such rights, he argues, accrue only at the point at which 'the human is other than *a* human being', that is to say more than just basic or bare human life. As its primary historical instance, this 'other' or excess of the human is embodied in the notion of the citizen. (Here, then, the relation between 'human' and 'civic' rights is once again not straightforwardly derivative.) Lyotard affirms that it is only on condition of being other-than-human that such a being may become 'an *other* human being' within the social realm. 'Then "the others" can treat him as their fellow human being' (136). As Lyotard points out in a footnote which follows up on Arendt's evocation of fellow feeling in *The Origins of Totalitarianism*, in French 'fellow man' is *semblable*, which implies likeness. If what makes human beings alike is, therefore, 'the fact that every human being carries within him the figure of the other' (136), this 'other' emerges as the other-than-human in the other human that I also am. If this situation constitutes the inaugurating possibility of citizenry in general, nevertheless its concept is formulated outside of notions of the absolute identity of the social bond.[17] One would never attain 'full' citizenship pure and simple, citizenship without remainder, since the figure of the citizen is also that of the '*other than*', meaning that human lives can never be unproblematically reduced to the citizen-form as an identity to which they nevertheless tend.

In answer to the question 'what is this figure of the other in me?', Lyotard's response, following Arendt, is 'nothing but a man', or, even more minimally, 'nothing other than an individual of the species Homo sapiens' (136). For him, the specificity of such a 'species' is tied to the communicability which underpins human interlocution, albeit one characterised by a certain heterogeneity to the extent that human language entails forms of address which are necessarily dissymmetrical (I speak, you listen; and, alternately, vice versa). While animals can instinctively and sensorily 'merge into a community based on signals', argues Lyotard, the very circumstances of interlocution mean that human beings cannot (138). While in retrospect Lyotard may be guilty of a too hasty contrast between the instinctual and sensory communication of the 'animal' and the non-instinctual operations of human language, his thinking of the conditions of speech is what is most important for our purposes here. For such speech marks a double and deconstructible condition. What in one sense founds human community (the other-than-human in me which makes me an-other-human) also establishes the frontiers of communal identity, or in other words the limit of the community's integrity or coherence as such. It does so precisely to the extent that what founds civil life is the heterogeneity and dissymmetry which grounds the operations of language or speech construed as a form of address to another.

For Lyotard, nevertheless, 'the citizen is the human individual whose right to address others is recognized by those others' (138). The formulation of the human being as other-than-human/an-other-human, routed through the dissymmetry or heterogeneity of interlocution, is explicitly linked to the specific historical forms that civil society will have taken, entering in as a decisive yet non-integratable element (that is, non-assimilable and yet indispensable to both the language and the time of civility). The principle of the right to address the other, and of the other's recognition of this right, founds the historical possibility of human society in its modern sense, whether it be 'the Greek *politeia* or the modern *republic*' (138). Nevertheless, amid the available models for social forms, it is for Lyotard the 'republican principle' in particular which introduces 'civic interlocution' into the community, and which therefore maintains the principle of heterogeneity or alterity in the realm of human communication. Without it, he suggests, the 'demos' or 'demotic' in its pure form risks a fall into absolute consensuality.

Within this model of interlocutory civility, silence is paradoxically the condition of possibility of address. It is only through recognising the value of his own silence before the teacher's address that the pupil in his turn earns the right to speak. (In a phrase that the Rancière of *The Ignorant Schoolmaster*[18] must have blanched at, Lyotard argues that 'the exultation of interactivity as a pedagogic principle is pure demagogy' (142).) The pupil's silence, in other words, teaches the value of the right to speak. Yet what the master or teacher has to say is not easily reducible to 'interlocutory expectation' (142). The discourse offered by the teacher conveys things that the pupil does not already know and may not, indeed may never, understand. Thus, this form of speech more radically *estranges* – although, of course, it does not simply threaten to destroy the community, far from it, since what is estranging about pedagogic language also profoundly confirms the alterity or heterogeneity at the core of the civil contract (i.e., the right of the other's address), so that the teacher from this perspective becomes as much the cornerstone of civil life as the stranger or foreigner in 'our' midst (although such a teacher is, equally, far from just the conservative guardian of 'what is'). As Lyotard puts it, if nothing is 'announced', if there is no innovation in the content or for that matter no inventiveness at the level of form, we are doomed to 'repetition and to the conservation of existing meanings' (143). The right to speak is just this duty to announce, which in fact offers itself as a prime source of resistance to the consensus that deadens, silences or excludes. As Lyotard puts it, through the repetition and conservation of existing meanings human community even as it 'spreads' will 'remain the same, prostrated in the euphoria it feels at being on such very good terms with itself' (143). Indeed, such estranging communication beyond 'interlocutory expectation' is also a matter of 'speaking otherwise than is my wont and saying something other than what I know how to say' (142). It thus estranges the teacher as much as the pupil from himself, as the radical condition of possibility of the interlocutory situation of civil life, and of the right to speech posed against 'the interlocutory consent of the community' inscribed within the always fragile and unstable historical formation of the civil contract.

The interlocutionary situation of dissymmetric address, not to be confused with any form of securable hierarchy or hegemony, is thus founded on a type of violence (or, as Lyotard puts it, 'distress') which nevertheless paradoxically offers significant resistance – not least through its constitution in terms of 'rights' – to various structures of hegemonic normalisation, hierarchical control or excessive power. If only because this discourse of rights entitles the citizen to 'address' in a situation that must be understood as constantly reinventable (one closely related, perhaps, to what Arendt presents as the right to claim one's rights), Lyotard's re-elaboration of 'civil' life establishes the horizon for a politics that is permanently in tension with anchorable forms of domination, a politics which affirms a radical pluralism that would seem incapable of normalising as such. Violence of the kind inherent in the claiming of such 'other-human' rights means that Lyotardian 'civility' resists both the violent desire to abolish violence (for a certain violence in fact inaugurates the other's rights) and the reactive wish to convert it into new forms of repression (since the 'civil' dynamics of inter-locution and address insist upon something like the permanence of an insurgent or revolutionary possibility that is inexhaust-ible by any form of tyranny). The 'other-than-human' Lyotard detects at the origin of so-called human rights thus generates the conditions of possibility for a transformative politics that, while far from immune to the fragile nature of 'civil' felicity, remains comparatively well-resourced to delegitimise domina-tion without succumbing to the paradoxical fate of that violent relation to violence we have so far given a variety of names (violence-management, violence-reduction, violence-abolition or violence-conversion). In other words, it neither curbs the potential of insurgency nor licenses dominance. In this way, Lyotardian civility may be comparatively well-equipped to avoid the paradoxical predicament of a regulative form of 'civility' without at the same time risking an ultimately ineffectual relationship to extreme violence. It changes, perhaps, the very question of violence-management.

Notes

1 Étienne Balibar, *Violence and Civility: On the Limits of Political Philosophy* (New York: Columbia University Press, 2015), pp. 59–60. Page references will be given in the body of the chapter.
2 See, for instance, 'Outline of a Topography of Cruelty: Citizenship and Civility in the Era of Global Violence', included in Balibar's *We, the People*

of Europe? Reflections on Transnational Citizenship (Princeton: Princeton University Press, 2003), pp. 115–32, esp. pp. 121ff.

3 Drawing on Wendy Brown's 'Neoliberalism and the End of Liberal Democracy' (in *Edgework: Critical Essays on Knowledge and Politics* (Princeton: Princeton University Press, 2005), pp. 37–59), Balibar offers some commentary on this topic in his own essay, 'Antinomies of Citizenship', *Journal of Romance Studies* 10:2 (2010), 1–20; this material also forms the introduction to Balibar's *Equaliberty: Political Essays* (Durham, NC: Duke University Press, 2014), pp. 1–32, under the title 'The Antinomy of Citizenship'.

4 On the question of imagining forms of citizenship without strong ties to existing conceptions of community, see especially 'Citizenship Without Community?', in Balibar's *We, the People of Europe?*, pp. 51–77. Here, Balibar argues that the problem is not so much about deciding '*which community* should be instituted as a priority and form the overall horizon of citizenship' but concerns instead the issue of '*knowing what the speculative concept of community means* and how we should understand it in an age of crisis of nation-states' (65).

5 See Balibar's essay, 'The Antinomy of Citizenship', p. 2.

6 In 'Outline of a Topography of Cruelty' Balibar asks whether 'extreme violence has generally replaced politics' or, instead, if it is the case that 'politics and violence' are 'no longer separated' (125).

7 In 'Outline of a Topography of Cruelty', Balibar uses just this formulation: 'It is not only the *state* or the *economy* that needs to be "civilized" or to become "civil," but also *revolution itself*' (131). This insistence is made in the context of another reflection upon the risks of revolution 'falling back into the very *symmetry* of political methods' that, as the history of the twentieth century shows, ironically reconnect emancipatory projects to the forms of power and tyranny they ostensibly oppose. As I suggest throughout this chapter, it is extremely difficult to rid 'antiviolence' – Balibar's answer to this seemingly unbreakable predicament – of the task of violence-management that echoes in part some of the most effective strategies of regimes of power and domination.

8 On this topic of the 'unpolitical' see the fourth chapter in Balibar's *Equaliberty*, 'What is Political Philosophy? Notes for a Topography', pp. 135–44.

9 In connection with this, we might note that in 'The Antinomy of Citizenship', Balibar offers some further reflection on the possible contexts that create the contemporary conditions for such groupings to arise, although here, tellingly, he draws our attention to 'outsider' factions that gravitate

not so much to diverse forms of emancipation, but that are driven instead by the 'compensatory' drives of 'negative or impossible communities', including those we might recognise in terms of organised crime or religious fanaticism (15).

10 In 'Outline of a Topography of Cruelty', Balibar describes this 'politics of politics' as 'politics in the second degree, which aims at creating, recreating and conserving the set of conditions within which politics as a collective participation in public affairs is possible' (76). As I suggest elsewhere in this chapter, perhaps more needs to be said concerning this difficult interplay between creating, on the one hand, and conserving, on the other, notably in terms of the question of violence, which may not remain stable or self-same in the transition or interaction between the two. Thus Balibar is quick to admit that, at this point in the analysis, 'civility' remains an ambiguous notion (certainly throughout his writings he makes a convincing case for the partial necessity of this very same ambiguity).

11 See 'Outline of a Topography of Cruelty', p. 116.

12 In his essay, 'Citizenship Without Community', Balibar describes further the 'insurrectional' power at the heart of the project of democratic emancipation that always vies uneasily — if sometimes productively — with the institution(s) of the 'democratic' state (67). Here, Balibar is keen to present an image of the 'democratic' interplay between citizenship, 'community' and state as always a matter of ongoing negotiation without 'ultimately definable solution' (77) — a kind of work in progress, or something forever 'in the making', for good or ill. In 'Outline of a Topography of Cruelty', meanwhile, Balibar turns to the writings of Hannah Arendt to reflect further on the 'insurrectional element constitutive of democratic citizenship' and its potentially dialectical relationship with a politics of civility. Here, again, the upshot is at best an 'intrinsically *fragile* or *precarious*' democratic political order 'continuously recreated in a politics of civility' in the interests of avoiding, effectively, a 'state of war' (120). At the kernel of such formulations, we still have the problem of 'antiviolence' as unable to escape some degree of violence-management or reduction as central to its task, which troublingly echoes some of the most familiar strategies waged by power against a politics of civility or emancipation, i.e., seemingly 'managing-down' violence in order to preserve and even maximise it all the more. The opposition between genuine and disingenuous strategies in this regard does not offer a robust distinction by means of which 'power' and 'civility' could be distinguished from one another: violence-management on the part of any dominating power or authority is of course not always

merely conspiratorial, and might at times even be, to put matters rather glibly, 'well meaning'.

13 'The Antinomy of Citizenship', p. 5.

14 *Equaliberty*, pp. 165–86. Page references will be given in the body of the chapter.

15 In 'Outline of a Topography of Cruelty', included in *We, the People of Europe?*, Balibar alludes to a similar idea when he suggests that 'the recognition and institution of citizens' rights . . . practically command the development of human rights' (132).

16 Jean-François Lyotard, 'The Other's Rights', in *On Human Rights*, ed. Stephen Shute and Susan Hurley (New York: Basic Books, 1993), pp. 135–47. Page references will be given in the body of the chapter.

17 Lyotard therefore continues: 'The likeness that they have in common follows from the difference of each from each' (136).

18 Jacques Rancière, *The Ignorant Schoolmaster: Five Lessons in Intellectual Emancipation*, trans. Kristin Ross (Stanford: Stanford University Press, 1991). The premise of this book is that the scene of teaching is characterised by an equal intelligence shared by teacher and student alike and thus that the beginnings of education are to be found in such 'equality'.

3

What is a Complex? Freudian Resistances

Complex Complexity

From the mid to late twentieth century onwards, the notion of complexity gathered momentum as a new way of doing science. The modelling of complex systems intersected with new developments in information theory, chaos theory and network theory (as well as innovations in other areas) in such a way as to define and address non-linear and non-mechanical systems problems across a number of disciplinary fields. Mathematicians, physicists, computer scientists, engineers, neuroscientists, molecular biologists, meteorologists, economists and social scientists have all benefited from the new approaches made possible by complexity, developing powerful analytic and computational tools used in a wide range of academic and non-academic settings.[1] While the origins of complexity theory can be traced back to forms of thought from earlier periods that arguably made its emergence possible, and while it is undoubtedly composed of a variety of theoretical approaches for which the prospect of unification or integration is still some way off, nonetheless the traction that complexity has attained seems a singularly modern phenomenon. During the past century, however, this terminology has gained ground against a backdrop of various uses of the word in a number of discursive fields, which at first glance seem distinct, even though one might readily trace connections between its 'scientific' production and developments in certain technologico-political, governmental and socio-cultural fields, as a rich critical literature testifies.[2] The term was imported into the political sphere most famously through the introduction of the phrase 'military-industrial complex', popularised after Eisenhower's farewell presidential address of 1961, which seemed to align with the comparative dominance of structural perspectives in the post-war period, and which provided a means of critical interpretation and indeed a basis for activist resistance centred not just on forms of government power but on an entire system of social, political and economic control. (Perhaps ironically, this is reflected in the fact that it was an outgoing US president that alerted his people to the existence of just such a 'complex'.) In the realm of human psychology, meanwhile, the notion of a 'complex', deriving largely from psychological and psychoanalytic forms of thought, acquired increasing explanatory power or at any rate widespread discursive usage where the problem of personality disorders was concerned. But both these examples of use made possible big claims about human life, individually and collectively; about what organised, determined, motivated or afflicted it.

As we will see, despite the comparative specificity of each of these utilisations of the word, their discursive exercise often entailed interesting elements of overlap (for instance, Eisenhower's references to the 'military-industrial complex' seem increasingly to psychologise the phenomena to which he alludes). Nevertheless, it would doubtless be possible to argue the relative specificity of these three major forms of terminology we have identified – all based on the same or similar words – by locating them in terms of the specific distribution of structural or systemic thinking that applies in each case, the particular formation of which enables or institutes each, but which also forms a resistant limit to the self-definition of each. (How systematic or non-systematic, structured or non-structured, holistic or non-holistic, predictive or non-predictive could or should each approach be?) If the terms 'complexity' and 'complex' have established a fairly major foothold in the way we think and talk about ourselves and our world (scientifically, politically, psychologically, etc.), the fact that they have been used in different ways across the domains of human knowledge, enquiry and practice probably says as much about the conceptual tensions as about the possible connections or configurations to which they give rise. That said, what potentially separates or divides them – how to handle the question of systems – is surely also what also links or aligns them, or at any rate what polices their borders, and manages passage across, as much as marks their boundaries.

Political Complexes

One of the earliest and most memorable recorded uses of the phrase 'military-industrial complex' can be found in President Dwight Eisenhower's 1961 farewell speech to the American people.[3] Looking back over a half-century of distinguished public service that also saw the world embroiled in a series of horrific conflicts, Eisenhower is swift to set his remarks squarely in the post-war context. He recognises the growing strength, over the course of his political career, of the US as an international super-power. Its military prowess, industrial productivity, economic wealth and political might are acknowledged as important co-requisites of its moral leadership in the world. But at the same time they are seen as a potential threat to precisely those values that, for Eisenhower, make America great: 'free government', 'liberty, dignity, and integrity', 'human betterment', and so forth. Showing a prescient sense of the near-permanent crisis that would come to define global history after the Second World War, Eisenhower worries that America might profit from, perhaps even exploit, such crises in the interests of even greater power, but that in the process it may alter its personality forever. Ever-increasing spending on national defences coupled with spiralling investment in national research programmes intended to maintain the competitive advantage of the US over its international enemies and rivals risks unbalancing the very character of the United States. The post-war 'military-industrial complex' that arises from and fuels this situation jeopardises the balance of private and public interests on which the nation is founded. Balance, indeed, becomes a crucial and thus frequently repeated term in the address: balance between the interests of the individual and the nation, between current preoccupations and a lasting concern for the future, between desire and duty, and so on. 'Good judgement' is required to keep this balance; without it, the nation will indeed become 'unbalanced', in more senses than one. If the language of the 'military-industrial complex' registers the growing importance of structural perspectives within post-war political thought and discourse (albeit those that may potentialise critical points of view, even from the Presidential office), then at the same time this 'military-industrial complex' is described in terms that undoubtedly seem increasingly 'psychological' in nature. For such a 'military-industrial complex' will have potentially 'grave consequences' if 'an alert and knowledgeable citizenry' *that it precisely puts at risk* is not consciously and deliberately maintained. The moral and mental health of the nation – its very sanity – is as much in danger, we are made to feel, as its organisational or structural 'balance'. And when this 'balance' is registered in terms of a battle for the heart and soul of America, the struggle of an 'alert and knowledgeable citizenry' against occult forces that are more or less subterranean, and more or less irresistible, plays itself out on a terrain that is undeniably presented as a 'psychic' one, as much as it is political or social or cultural.

Eisenhower almost tangibly shudders at the sudden and un-precedented development of a 'permanent armaments industry of vast proportions'. He is awestruck by the massive post-war outlay on 'military security'. It is as if the President himself – the figurehead of the nation and custodian of its values – is thrown off-balance by those terrifying forces that he himself, as representative of the national psyche, has been unable to control or even foresee. The interests of the 'military-industrial complex' increasingly conflict with those of 'free govern-ment', and threaten to overpower democratic processes and liberties through the 'acquisition of unwarranted influence', in much the same way that Jekyll turns into Hyde. We stand on the brink of a nightmare in which America's 'unconscious' might overwhelm national consciousness itself. In the realm of science, the clear-minded personality of the inventor as American pioneer has been usurped and superseded by an inhuman 'task force' of highly funded research-workers devoted to the instrumental value of technological development. The university, once a haven of 'free ideas', is beset by nationally sponsored research programmes that are increasingly 'formal-ized' and 'complex' (thus, without moral direction or compass).

The spirit of 'discovery' and the value of 'intellectual curiosity' are violently displaced by machinic laboratories and computerised operations. And the irony remains that the much-needed 'balance' which might serve as a corrective to this state of affairs is precisely what is eroded by this state of affairs. If it is the task of the statesman 'to mold, to balance, and to integrate these and other forces' – a task in which Eisenhower, by his own admission, has singularly failed – then the 1961 address reads not only as the farewell speech of an elder statesman, but as the swansong of statesmanship itself. Our future, the future of our children, is increasingly mortgaged away. The prospect of an 'insolvent phantom of tomorrow' looms as we desperately over-exploit our resources in the present. As much as its vital importance is urgently asserted, 'balance' already seems lost, a thing of the past. Hopes for its guardianship of the future look merely nostalgic. It is hard to know how 'the proud confederation of mutual trust and respect' that for Eisenhower seems to characterise the American tradition can withstand the onset of a 'community of dreadful fear and hate'. Peace is far from won, all that can be said is that war has been temporarily avoided. In the meantime, Eisenhower withdraws proudly – and with an obvious sense of relief – into his newfound private citizenship, finding there the personal values (faith, charity, goodness) that once supposedly founded a nation, but which are now elevated only in retreat. (And, to take Eisenhower's text at its word, such flight promises descent into madness as much as sane refuge.) The 'military-industrial complex', it seems, is not just a structural formation – an elaborate system of complexly interrelated parts – but also the figure of a certain psychological condition, a mental state. It is not just an operative organisational arrangement, but the agent or mechanism of collapse.

Despite its prescience in some regards, one may still wonder why we should revisit this scene from long ago, especially when the term 'military-industrial complex' has historically flourished – and more recently faded – in its capacity as mainly a term of general descriptiveness or even sweeping polemical value, rather than as a category of sound analytic or academic worth. (The fortunes of this phrase were perhaps predictable enough, given the direction and tone of Eisenhower's remarks.) And yet the question of whether the term encourages or resists explanatory possibility, whether it facilitates or undermines political consciousness, whether it provokes or restricts rational thought (or more complexly, both) is rather in the nature of the problem of the 'complex' itself – a problem that continues to be ongoing. It registers itself, for instance, in more recent engagements with the term. For instance, more than forty years after Eisenhower's address, Noam Chomsky argued that 'military-industrial complex' is a misnomer in the sense that militarisation or the 'military-industrial' is just one form that industrial society has taken as a pretext for its economic objectives.[4] (One might argue that 'industrial' society is equally a pretext for capitalism, rather than its formative 'core'.) Chomsky, then, offers a repudiation of the term in favour of a more penetrating and perspicacious analysis, one which restores analytic sanity against the backdrop of what is seen as a rather imprecise and ambiguous concept. As much an idea as a fact, the 'military-industrial complex' is to be rejected as an overly sprawling configuration that needs critical policing in the interests of properly lucid political thought. (Although, as I've just suggested, Chomsky's own retention of the 'industrial' risks a certain ironic repetition of the problem he seeks to clarify.) Here, like the post-war American citizenry evoked so optimistically by Eisenhower, it is surely in his capacity as an 'alert' and 'knowledgeable' subject that Chomsky finds himself able to resist the 'creep' or spread of the complex's insidious logic. At the other end of the spectrum, meanwhile, Slavoj Žižek ventures an extension or rather modification of the term amid a deepening of its psychological resonances.[5] Writing about the arrest of Radovan Karadžić in the aftermath of the conflicts that saw the break-up of the former Yugoslavia, Žižek speaks of a 'military-poetic complex' in which the amateurish verse of Karadžić – a would-be poet – sheds light on the psychology as much as the politics of ethnic cleansing. Karadžić is described as a 'ruthless political and military leader', but was also – as Žižek reminds us – 'a psychiatrist by profession'. The 'complex' which helps to explain the phenomenon for which Karadžić might stand as a representative figure – one which connects poetry, psychology and political and military power – is understood very much in terms of Žižek's own take on psychoanalysis. Karadžić's poetry thus represents:

the obscene call of the superego: all prohibitions should be suspended so that the subject might enjoy a destructive orgy without end. The superego is the 'godhead' which forbids the people nothing. Such a suspension of moral prohibitions is a crucial feature of 'postmodern' nationalism. It turns on its head the cliché according to which passionate ethnic identification restores a firm set of values and beliefs amid the insecurity of global secular society, and serves instead as the facilitator of a barely concealed 'You may!' It is today's apparently hedonistic and permissive society that is, paradoxically, more and more saturated by rules and regulations (restrictions on smoking and drinking, rules against sexual harassment, etc.), so that the notion of a passionate ethnic identification, far from demanding further restraint, functions instead as a liberating call: 'You may!

Whether or not one has any sympathy with Žižek's insights and approach, it is worth noting that at the point where the 'complex' extends rather than contracts itself, we are once more in the midst of not only an operative organisational arrangement, as I put it earlier, but also of a psychological understanding of relationships of power. (Although, even where it contracts itself, as in Chomsky's example, the competing forces of rational egoity and ironic repression may still be detected.) So it's not that I want to 'psychologise' the term, *per se*; more that it remains difficult if not impossible to sustain its usage without some degree of psychological 'drift', as it were (whether or not it is purged or augmented in these terms).

Psychoanalytic Complexes

There is a third contribution made by the Swiss School, probably to be ascribed entirely to Jung, which I do not value so highly as others do whose concern with these matters is more remote. I refer to the theory of 'complexes' . . . It has neither itself produced a psychological theory, nor has it proved capable of easy incorporation into the context of psycho-analytic theory. The word 'complex', on the other hand, had become naturalized, so to speak, in psycho-analytic language; it is a convenient and often indispensable term for summing up a psychological state descriptively. None of the other terms coined by psycho-analysis for its own needs has achieved such widespread popularity or been so misapplied to the detriment of the construction of clearer concepts. Analysts began to speak among themselves of a 'return of a complex' where they meant a 'return of the repressed', or fell into the habit of saying 'I have a complex against him', where the only correct expression would have been 'a resistance against him'.

Sigmund Freud, 'On the History of the
Psycho-Analytic Movement' (1914)[6]

Looking back on psychoanalysis's early history near the beginning of the first Great War in Europe, Freud takes time to formulate some critical remarks about the idea of a complex, which at this point he attributes almost entirely to Jung, thus effectively distancing himself from responsibility for its entry into the psychoanalytic lexicon. Not for the first time, Freud is rather dismissive of the term, at any rate downplaying the contribution it has made to genuine psychoanalytic categories and forms of thought. For Freud, the word 'complex' has unfortunately succumbed to the inaccuracies and simplifications for which the popularisation of an interest in psychology is largely responsible (although, here, the casual misuse by analysts themselves is the object of even sharper reproach). Freud feels that this word in its habitual usage somewhat dilutes and distorts more rigorous psychoanalytic terms, in particular 'repression' and 'resistance', which for him have much greater theoretical and explanatory force. (Jung is targeted for equivocating over this essential connection of the 'complex' to unconscious processes and materials.) And yet the term is not entirely abandoned. Instead, it retains an at times 'indispensable' value in precisely its descriptive capacity, which one might take to mean its ability to evoke precisely the complexities of a given psychological state in more or less summary form. In a certain sense, what damns the idea or discourse of the 'complex' − its seductive generality or catch-all quality − is thus also what saves it, partially at least (and Freud is far from guiltless when it comes to using the term 'descriptively' in several places in his writing). Here, then, we find an interesting ambivalence displayed towards the very concept or quasi-concept of the 'complex' which surely invites further investigation, not least since by *resisting* psychoanalytic theory in its proper form, the word 'complex' actually performs that for which it is purportedly an unfortunate misnomer: resistance itself. If the term is of little psychological value other than as an inexact yet eye-catching byword, how are we to explain Freud's hesitation in dismissing it completely, especially when the grounds for its retention are precisely those which would seem to demand it be banished from psychoanalytic parlance altogether? Why keep it, when the rather slight reason to do so is probably also a fairly compelling reason to discard it? And why, in reference to this term, does Freud's dissatisfaction with the popularisation of psychological thinking outside of psychoanalysis 'proper' so quickly revert to criticism of analysts themselves? As we will see, Freud, no less than other figures associated with the movement, was fond of identifying and naming complexes: might it be that psychoanalysis – Freud, even – has a 'complex' that remains as tenacious as it is problematic, as hard to resolve or pin down as it is to denounce or displace elsewhere?

Several years previously, Freud had written a paper on the potential value (and limits) of psychoanalytic procedures in the field of legal evidence, one which includes a much earlier record of his attitude to Jung, to the Zurich School and to the theory of complexes.[7] Writing in 1906, Freud seems more approving of the term 'complex' derived from this particular origin, although his admiration is perhaps tempered by a background of implied criticism. Freud entertains the idea that once knowledge of a specific complex is developed, one might use associative or stimulus-words in a legal setting to establish whether the person under examination is a sufferer or not. Freud relates this technique to that of the magistrate, who might use his own knowledge in leading ways to establish guilt or otherwise. This somewhat tentative connection between the fields of psychoanalysis and law is further pursued. (Tentative, because Freud later acknowledges – albeit not without the possibility of irony – a key difference between the psychoanalyst and the legal practitioner, whereby the latter may not as a rule take the subject by surprise). Indeed, it is sustained as Freud itemises the rather involved processes through which the subject might commit 'psychical self-betrayal' (107). The basic ground of comparison, having to do with the exposure of what has previously been kept secret, nonetheless remains susceptible to a critically differentiating factor. While the criminal deliberately hides the truth from the court, the patient – the hysteric, say – has no more prior knowledge of what he conceals than does the analyst (and sometimes less). Nevertheless, Freud stays with the idea that psychoanalysis is just another kind of detective work, and argues that when the spontaneity of the associative technique begins to run aground, this provides evidence that repression is at work, and that the analyst may be on to something. Each hesitation or obfuscation is an expression, and thus evidence, of resistance. Here, then, delay in reaction-time is as critical for psychoanalysis as it is for the courtroom in the suspicion of 'guilt', while odd or ambiguous answers also betray the guilty subject. Equally, when the answer to a question asked for a second or third time is altered, the nature of that alteration and that inconsistency provides vital clues which may aid the legal investigation as much as the analytic process. It is only a pity, suggests Freud, that the tempo of courtroom proceedings is that much faster than the laborious work of analysis, since this deprives the law of some of the benefits enjoyed by the latter.

If the connection between legal questioning and psychoanalysis starts out on a rather tentative footing, however, Freud persists in his keenness to demonstrate appreciation of their different spheres and activities. The criminal deliberately conceals his guilt, while the patient's secretiveness is not intentional; the criminal consciously adopts an adversarial relationship to the law, whereas the patient seeks to cooperate with the analyst. However, these distinctions – aimed at qualifying the very connection that Freud began by pursuing, and thereby establishing some limits to the value of psychoanalytic techniques in the field of law – remain highly questionable. For who is to say that the patient is never deliberately resistant to the forays of analysis? Is it so easy to draw the line between resistances that are merely altogether unconscious and those in which the subject consciously participates? Equally, who is to say that criminals do not sometimes wish to betray themselves? Freud of all people should be capable of disputing such simplistic distinctions. This is important because Freud goes on to write:

> The aim of psycho-analysis is absolutely uniform in every case: complexes have to be uncovered which have been repressed because of feelings of unpleasure and which produce signs of resistance if an attempt is made to bring them into consciousness. The resistance is as it were localized; it arises at the frontier between unconscious and conscious. In your cases [i.e., legal cases] what is concerned is a resistance which comes entirely from consciousness. (112)

The dissimilarity between the practice of law and of psychoanalysis therefore comes down to a particular conception of repression – for Freud, the very origin of the complex – that provides the latter (psychoanalysis) with both its raison d'être and modus operandi, while placing the former (law) decisively outside of the analytic scene. But if the differences that Freud seeks to establish between the criminal and the patient are arguably untenable, then this distinction begins to collapse and, in the process, the conception of repression 'proper' to psychoanalysis is open to question. And if this is the case, then Freud's attempt to retain usage of the term 'complex' beyond or outside of its Jungian sense, by insisting on the critical specificity of repression as he himself understands it, surely becomes less convincing all of a sudden. Once more, the idea of a 'complex', much less than being clarified through various psychoanalytic treatments, begins to impose its own problematics – one might say, its own 'complex' – on psychoanalysis itself.

Freud, of course, is not so slow to sense such difficulties. Within just a few lines, he is to be found reminding the legal profession of a further complication that they must face, namely that the accused may behave in ways that seem to imply guilt but which might in fact arise from psychic abnormalities, for instance neuroses. Here, then, Freud partly abandons his previous distinction – upon which the specificity or propriety of both psychoanalysis and repression was constructed – between the accused and the patient: the subject in the dock may be either guilty or unwell, or both at once. But Freud relinquishes the difference only in part, since he fails to acknowledge the obvious corollary, namely that the analysand may also be 'guilty' in the sense that Freud had previously assigned purely to the criminal, and that as a consequence his own idea both of psychoanalysis and repression might need a second look. The 'frontier' between deliberate or conscious acts and the 'unconscious' is acknowledged as simultaneously a complicated point of connection, yet this insight is not fully grasped, far from it. Once its supposed qualifications begin to crumble, what starts out as a tentative relation between psychoanalysis and law is transformed into a much more telling interaction, not just because we appreciate that despite the rulebook legal practitioners may in fact cruelly bait highly vulnerable people of uncertain responsibility (i.e., that law may break its own rules), but because we also become aware that the scene of analysis – and the drama of the 'complex' – may not be all that Freud imagines (i.e., that psychoanalysis's own rules, laws and boundaries are not themselves inviolable).[8]

How, then, to get to the bottom of this problem of the 'complex' (assuming that such a thing was ever possible)? Let's begin by reviewing some of the earliest associations of the term found in the psychological writing we'd identify with Freud, beginning with *Studies on Hysteria* (1895), parts of which were of course contributed by Breuer. In fact, on the subject of complexes Breuer seems keener on the word than Freud, and more liable to use it as a proper noun rather than merely a descriptive term. But across the texts found in *Studies on Hysteria*, a 'complex' emerges as that which may arise on the basis of an assemblage of associated ideas, ideas that might not be – indeed, are highly unlikely to be – consistent with one another, or, for that matter, intelligible in relation to one another. While some features of the complex may well be registered at a conscious level (a somewhat Jungian idea that Freud will later have cause to dispute more explicitly), by definition the general structure is itself therefore formed of elements that are not consciously appreciated by the subject, and that cannot be faced all at once, if they can be faced at all. A complex thus seems to be made up of interconnected yet frequently contradictory or irreconcilable materials, and it takes shape on the basis of interactions between its constituent parts that, while they are almost impossible to control or stop, nonetheless remain consistently and inevitably liable to repression and resistance of just the kind that Freud will increasingly insist upon. For analysis, what is at stake in the appreciation or treatment of a complex is thus a move beyond the more tangible or visible components of the complex, those that alert us to the possibility of a certain psychic condition, towards a retrieval of its highly complicated structure or form. This is easier said than done, however, if we recall that by its very nature a complex arises on the strength of powerful tensions, forceful repressions and highly charged resistances that are incredibly difficult to appreciate, let alone overcome.

In some of his first remarks on the notion of a complex, slender and embryonic though they may be, Freud seems to associate complexes – or at any rate a 'complex' situation – with difficult or problematic emotional states such as anxiety and grief, and with painful and unresolved memories. Breuer, meanwhile, notes the intrusive quality of unconscious materials, and an unhealthy yet unchecked compulsiveness where the associative tendency is concerned. He remarks that the complex is characterised by involved trains of thought or chains of associations in which key elements nevertheless *resist* associative contact. While complexes are described here as 'ideational' (i.e., as formations of ideas) it is nevertheless hard for the reader to decide whether distinct and discrete ideas – ideas *as such* – are brought into contact with one another to form a complex; or whether the complex is itself the precondition and setting for the 'ideas' in their specific (and typically non-self-identical) form. Two questions arise from this state of affairs: not only 'what is an idea?', but also 'what is a complex?' if the latter may be constituted by that which it constitutes as such?

However, despite these conceptual difficulties in the determination of a 'complex', within the space of just a few years one may detect in Freud's texts a perhaps surprising willingness to *name* certain complexes, even a rather florid enthusiasm for such activity. One may think of *The Interpretation of Dreams* (1900), among other writings. For example, Freud feels able to speak of an 'eating complex', a 'prostitute complex', and later on, here and in other places, a 'hunger complex', a 'masturbation complex', an 'excretory complex' or 'constipation complex' or '*lumf* complex', a 'horse complex', an 'infantile complex', a 'death complex', a 'love-hate complex', the 'sexual complex', and so on. But perhaps most interestingly, the Freud of this period alludes to the 'parental complex', closely allied to his famous ideas about the castration complex and the Oedipus complex. This naming tendency may seem odd, given the original conception of a complex as an intricately woven and perhaps impossibly nebulous matrix composed of disparate and indeed irreconcilable elements through which associative chains run in ways that seem resistant to a unified perspective, or to a dominant term or a single idea as such. And yet to 'master' a complex, as Freud sometimes puts it, entails for him reconstituting something of its *structural* composition. To retain its coherence *as such*, a structure – as Derrida and others have taught us – must be determined and controlled by a key element that is not contingent upon the vicissitudes of structural relations, even though structures are in essence defined by relationality. In other words, the structurality of a structure depends on an element that is, as it were, non- or a-structural, an element that is by definition at once central to the structure's possibility and yet exempt from (or outside) its contingent structural interactions. (The difficulty of the complex's 'structure' is compounded by the question of the *resistance* to association offered by some of the unconscious elements, since they would seem both to curtail the non-finite or compulsive associativity that might otherwise threaten the structural formation or structurality of the 'complex' while nevertheless acting as precisely its enabling condition.) In these terms, it is especially interesting that the 'parental complex' and its derivative or developed forms – in other words, its family members – begin to take centre-stage where the whole idea of a 'Freudian' complex is concerned, since the very notion of the 'parental complex' as it takes shape within psychoanalysis is at the same time precisely the problem of the complex *itself*: namely, that of a seemingly interminable, ungovernable series of relations in want of a proper or family name, a base or basis, a master or head(ing), as an impossible yet necessary injunction. Put differently, this suggests that the name given to a 'complex' may not resolve the question of its interpretation so much as add but a further layer or wrinkle to the complicated problem with which it confronts us.

As we have already seen, despite his frequent enthusiasm for *naming* complexes Freud nevertheless suggests in subsequent texts that we should be somewhat wary of the word, since it is at risk of substituting itself as an *improper* name for the sharper and more robust categories of resistance and repression. (Thus, it is also at risk of becoming part of an over-simplified psychological terminology that is susceptible to crude popularising uses.) One might venture to say, however, that the term resists or even represses that which it improperly names: resistance or repression itself. Through the very act of misnaming it enacts what it misnames. It performs what it also represses or resists (resisting resistance, repressing repression). The relationship of the complex to the name – a relationship that one might hope to clarify in order to resolve the question 'what is a complex?', or at any rate to identify a possible answer – thus once more partakes of the problem it seems to name. It seems that the very *idea* of a complex – if such a thing were even possible – makes us crave an organising term or a 'name' which it perhaps inevitably eludes even as its interaction with this term or name helps to clarify precisely the problem of the complex's elusiveness. Throughout his references to the notion of a 'complex', Freud is fond of alluding to the 'nuclear' aspect or 'nucleus' of the complex, but for the reasons we are describing this term itself surely achieves only a highly ambivalent standing in relation to the concept it seeks to supplement.

Equally, Freud's own allusions to his 'professional' or 'personal' complexes may do little more than seek to confer upon a psychoanalytic discourse of the 'complex' both the authority and glamour of the name of its father-figure, in a way that surely has an ironic connection to the idea of a 'father complex' that remains a family member among related terms such as 'castration' and 'Oedipus', which in turn give us Freud's most protracted engagements with the very notion of a 'complex'. At the beginning of the twentieth century, in 'The Psychopathology of Everyday Life' (1901), one can therefore trace the incidence of the term 'complex' through a series of uses on Freud's part that lead from the 'personal' to the 'professional' to the 'family complex'. Here, patterns of identification, association, dispersal and deferral – so characteristic of the problem of the 'complex' – themselves pull the text, and its author, in more than one direction. In this game of identity and difference, such twists and turns are of course additionally complicated in Freud's oeuvre by the attribution of the term to Jung, as we've already seen. Freud's allusion to a 'personal' complex, and indeed its motivation, is therefore highly questionable (even if his attribution of the term 'elsewhere' seems to carry highly personal motivations). For how could a complex be 'personal' any more than an 'idea' might be single?

On a similar front, while on certain occasions Freud distinguishes the psychologically 'normal' from deviant forms of psychic life, at other times he alludes to complexes suffered as much by the healthy as by the sick, once more unsettling the project of delineating the 'complex' in any proper sense. The effect here is, unsurprisingly, not dissimilar to the upshot of Freud's highly questionable demarcation of the criminal and the patient in his 1906 text on psychoanalysis and the law. Equally, the idea of a 'stimulus-word' that might unlock a complex, an idea pioneered by the Zurich School but entertained by Freud at least partially in the 1906 lecture, surely only reactivates the aporia of the complex's 'structure' just as much as the effect of naming. Where complexes are concerned, as we have seen, the family of terms which might otherwise scaffold a certain coherence around a principal figure is itself aberrant or errant to the extent that the 'complex' also somewhat depropriates the head(ing), the cap or the capital letter, the correct term or the proper or 'master' name. But if it seems to castrate, the complex also sutures, stitches (i.e., it *associates*, although by cutting as much as joining, as Breuer himself insightfully observed). Yet what is re-connected is not simply sewn back together, which would presume an original unity to be restored, but is instead worked into potentially new forms that prevent masterful 'unlocking' of the kind offered by a standard key. This idea of 'unlocking' is one that Freud himself is often resistant to, dismissing it as an unfortunate effect of the vulgar popularisations of psychological discourse, just as he had done concerning the devalued usage of the idea of a complex. Thus, the notion of a stimulus-word as the proposed point of entry to the entire 'complex' falters on the basis of the characteristics of a 'complex' that it precisely seeks to overcome. In other words, such a notion may be less an effective solution or approach to complexes themselves than a questionable response to the problem of the complex more generally, an unconvincing if rather predictable effect of their complexity.

These comments of mine on the notion of the 'complex' arise in part from engaging with those writings of Freud that precede texts published during and after the first decade of the twentieth century; texts where the notions of the 'castration complex' and the 'Oedipus complex' really come to the fore and are consciously developed in terms of their (capital) importance. Such investigation on my part establishes, then, the rather uncertain – maybe even unconscious – background against which the usage of the term may be evaluated. In 'The Dissolution of the Oedipus Complex' (1924), meanwhile, we find the perhaps inevitable corollary of the complex's inner problematics, played out less at the beginning of complexes than at their end. Here, Freud looks at two possibilities. On the one hand, he considers the idea that complexes are eventually destroyed through their lack of success, psychologically speaking. In other words, they founder on the basis of their own internal impossibility, which is in the end sufficiently shocking or striking in psychic terms to bring about just such a dramatic and decisive decline.[9] The other view Freud entertains, however, is that the complex's collapse occurs when the time has come for it simply to disintegrate. If these alternatives sound similar in a certain way, their difference is also somewhat obvious. For in one scenario, it is as though the complex facilitates a progressive psychological state, and as such enjoys a more or less functional status, not really resisting that which supersedes it; while in the alternative perspective, the complex combusts rather suddenly and brutally in such a way as to make possible – albeit fortuitously – another situation that presumably the complex itself would otherwise resist, had it the resources to do so. However, Freud's consideration of these two possibilities (in the end, he dismisses both) perhaps captures perfectly both the complexity of psychoanalysis's relationship to the term in question (is it a productive or on the contrary a resistant category, indeed might it be both?), but also the somewhat double and ambiguous relationship of complexes themselves to the resistance that for Freud establishes their defining possibility and conceptual integrity. Even at the point it seems to pass out of existence, whether melting away or violently imploding, the complex therefore puts psychoanalysis, at the beginning of its own thought, in a situation where it remains confronted by its own 'complex', as it were.

The 'Complex' Complex

When we talk about complexity theory, Freudian complexes or the 'military-industrial' (or some other, semi-equivalent) complex, obviously we are not talking about quite the same things, despite the fact that certain connections are obvious and well documented. As I noted earlier, the terminological cluster around the word 'complex' not only constitutes an important feature of the self-identity we inherit from the previous century, but invites critical analysis of the linkages between developments in the realms of techno-scientific knowledge and the 'political' field itself. I've done little more than to point out certain internal and distributive tensions in the way 'complexity' has taken hold, but also moments of curious – or perhaps not so curious – drift, for instance when a phrase owing its import to a 'structural' perspective gets 'psychologised'. What I would say, though, is that while complexity theory and discourse (which overspills the hard sciences into inquiries in the social sciences and humanities) may imagine itself capable of leaving other usages behind as simply archaic, irrelevant, or non-scientific, it might still be valuable to assess the trouble the word has caused this past hundred years or so. For Freud, in particular, this has to do with the extent to which the term resists its own utilisation as an object or form of analysis, at once gaining and losing its specificity on precisely this basis. If the problem of the complex, or of what is complex, comes down to the formation of a complex, if the two amount to the same thing (i.e., to if to talk about complexes invariably means having one), then what emerges is a certain quasi-'triangulated'[10] dimension – whether we call it heuristic, phenomenological, psychological, or by some other name – at once complexifying what is 'complex', and yet also undermining its capacity for 'complexity' in a certain way. This quasi-'triangulated' dimension, in other words, forms the resistant limit of complexity itself (a limit that is far from merely a constraint), enabling or rather extending what it also renders impossible or unattainable.

Notes

1 While complex problems have been studied since long before the advent of the twentieth century, they do seem to have a 'modern' quality. Statistical physics, information theory and non-linear dynamics derive those equations that support the modelling of complex systems, but such systems are used to model processes in a range of disciplines and multi-disciplinary fields including computer science, cybernetics and AI, economics, meteorology and climate studies, biology, chemistry and physics. Complexity theory, in its various forms, is itself complexly connected to systems theory, network theory, chaos theory, and research on adaptive systems that gained ground in the post-war period. Perhaps most famously, during the 1980s the Santa Fe Institute (SFI) was established to study the fundamental principles of complex adaptive systems, including physical, computational, biological

and social systems. (See also my note below.) More broadly, there is a large literature devoted to the use of complexity theory in understanding organisational change, and in management studies. One could readily trace connections throughout the latter half of the twentieth century in particular between these fields of study and the knowledges they produce, and certain developments in the technologico-industrial-economic-administrative-political field (one could extend or modify this series, no doubt), most notably in North America.

2 There is, of course, evidence of quite diverse usages of the term 'complexity' that can be found in relation to the defence and security (not merely 'military') 'complexes' of North Atlantic societies since the dissolution of the Cold War. On the 'edutainment military industrial complex', see the work of James Der Derian, especially his book *Virtuous War: Mapping the Military-Industrial-Media-Entertainment Complex* (London: Routledge, 2nd edn, 2009); see also the extensive discussion concerning the promotion and application of the move from cybernetics to complexity in Michael Dillon and Julian Reid's book, *The Liberal Way of War: Killing to Make Life Live* (London: Routledge, 2009). See also Stephen Stockell and Adam Muir, 'The Military-Entertainment Complex: A New Facet of Information Warfare', *The Fibreculture Journal* 1 (2003), http://one.fibreculturejournal. org/fcj-004-the-military-entertainment-complex-a-new-facet-of-information-warfare; and Tim Lenoir and Henry Lowood, *Theaters of War: The Military-Entertainment Complex* (Stanford: Stanford University Press, 2002). Reference might also be made to Dillon's other work including 'Poststructuralism, Complexity and Poetics', *Theory Culture and Society* 17:5 (2000), 1–26, and *Biopolitics of Security: A Political Analytic of Finitude* (London: Routledge, 2015). Complexity discourse also has widespread usage in the literature on complex emergencies that has developed in the last twenty years. See for example Louise Amoore, *The Politics of Possibility: Risk and Security Beyond Probability* (Durham, NC: Duke University Press, 2013). Such work is useful in balancing the psychological with the techno-scientific and wider policy-related popularity of complexity discourse, and it links also to the complexity-inflected literature connected to the Santa Fe Institute, Military Universities and Defence and Security research agencies like DARPA over the last twenty years or so. More generally, one might refer here as a primary context to the wider securitisation of western societies following 9/11, the advent of the so-called war on terror and the widespread preoccupation with complex emergencies and related strategies of resilience.

3 Dwight Eisenhower, 'Farewell Address to the Nation, January 17, 1961', http://mcadams.posc.mu.edu/ike.htm.

4 Noam Chomsky, interview with David Barsamian, 'War Crimes and Imperial Fantasies', *International Socialist Review* 37 (September–October 2004), https://chomsky.info/200408.

5 Slavoj Žižek, 'The Military-Poetic Complex', *London Review of Books*, 14 August 2008, p. 17, http://www.lrb.co.uk/v30/n16/slavoj-Žižek/the-military-poetic-complex.

6 Sigmund Freud, 'On the History of the Psycho-Analytic Movement' (1914), in *The Standard Edition of the Complete Psychological Works of Sigmund Freud*, Vol. XIV, ed. and trans. James Strachey (London: The Hogarth Press and the Institute of Psycho-Analysis, 1957), pp. 7–66. For this particular passage, see pp. 29–30.

7 Sigmund Freud, 'Psycho-Analysis and the Establishment of the Facts in Legal Proceedings' (1906), *The Standard Edition of the Complete Psychological Works of Sigmund Freud*, Vol. IX, ed. and trans. James Strachey (London: The Hogarth Press and the Institute of Psycho-Analysis, 1959), pp. 103–14. Page references will be given in the body of the chapter.

8 Freud concludes his lecture by advocating that legal investigation, in order to benefit from the insights offered by psychoanalysis, would need to test the psychological approach outside of actual criminal trials where the analytic situation could not be properly reproduced. Such experiments, in other words, could not yet provide the basis for the 'practical administration of justice' (114), but should instead be conducted through dummy exercises based on real cases, with the findings withheld from courts and prevented from influencing their decisions. (Only through a painstaking comparison between legal and psychoanalytic findings after many years could the value of such experiments be determined, Freud suggests.) This weirdly hybrid situation imposed upon the law, as if to recognise a certain grey area between psychology and justice, seems nevertheless to exempt psychoanalysis in all its propriety and purity from the bizarrely mixed scenario it demands. And yet one wonders whether – as the concluding testament of this lecture and final answer to the question of psychoanalysis and law – it sounds sufficiently odd to raise questions in the mind of any lawyer, as if Freud might be hiding something.

9 By way of comparison, in 'Some Psychical Consequences of the Anatomical Distinction Between the Sexes' (*The Standard Edition of the Complete Psychological Works of Sigmund Freud*, Vol. XIX, ed. and trans. James Strachey (London: The Hogarth Press and the Institute of Psycho-Analysis, 1961),

pp. 248–58), Freud writes: 'The Oedipus complex, however, is such an important thing that the manner in which one enters and leaves it cannot be without its effects. In boys . . . the complex is not simply repressed, it is literally smashed to pieces by the shock of threatened castration. Its libidinal cathexes are abandoned, desexualized and in part sublimated; its objects are incorporated into the ego, where they form the nucleus of the super-ego and give that new structure its characteristic qualities' (257).

10 I put this term in inverted commas as if to provoke disbelief that the 'phenomenon' I am seeking to describe might either be reduced to the numerical consistency or self-identity of the 'three', or that it might be explained simply from a 'perspectival' point of view; whereas in fact the problematic I am trying to develop in fact engulfs such stabilising props or supplements.

4

Fleeced: Derrida and 'the Deciding Discourse of Castration'

Derrida's interest in psychoanalysis spans, of course, a large number of texts. For the relationship of the psychoanalytic archive to the psychoanalytic thinking of the psyche *as* archive, or psychoanalysis's relation to its own technical conditions of possibility, one would consult *Archive Fever*. For psychoanalysis as a possible source of resistance to the forms of sovereignty which give us the death penalty, one might look to *Without Alibi*. Of course, much could also be said about psychoanalytic traces and resistances where Derrida seeks to think mourning, memory, life, death, alongside an array of other themes. Psycho-analysis may be borne in mind everywhere that Derrida treats sexual difference.

Certain affinities between deconstruction and psycho-analysis were often suggested to Derrida, and in some prefatory comments to 'Freud and the Scene of Writing', found in *Writing and Difference*, he acknowledges some connections between the two. The interminable repression of writing, *différance*, trace, supplement or non-present remainder which deconstruction gives us to think is recalled in the psychoanalytic conception of a 'repressed' that returns in the form of a symptom. The idea of an identity divided – yet constituted, too – by its own re-marking or repeatability not only calls up certain psychoanalytic themes but, indeed, reminds us of some of psychoanalysis's analytical models, or, perhaps better still, some of the *problems* of analysis with which it is confronted. Moreover, for the Derrida of 'Freud and the Scene of Writing', Freud's understanding of the psychic apparatus as a writing 'machine' suggests psychoanalysis's resistance to the phonocentric tradition inherited by phenomenology and linguistics, and perhaps draws close to Derrida's conception of a 'general writing' which cannot be dominated by speech, presence, and so forth. However, in the same early essay on psychoanalysis, Derrida's prefatory remarks differentiate his own work from psychoanalysis on the basis that the latter still remains too in thrall of metaphysics. Consequently, in a later text, 'Le Facteur de la *vérité*', included in *The Post Card*, Derrida argues that Lacan's seminar on Poe's 'The Purloined Letter' continues to be funded by the metaphysical construal of truth as revelation, a revelation which it is the task or destiny of psychoanalysis to deliver – in the form, here, of restoring the letter's 'lack' to its proper place: the truth of the phallus as the signified. As we've already seen, this theme is taken up once more in 'For the Love of Lacan', a still later text found in *Resistances to Psychoanalysis*. In *The Post Card*, then, we find a postal principle at work which is that of a disseminating *différance* that cannot be surely 'posted' to an ultimate addressee or destination, but which is marked instead by the irreducible and constitutive possibility of non-arrival. Relatedly, in 'To Speculate – on "Freud"' Derrida puts in question the very idea of 'Freud' as the ultimate addressee of psychoanalysis, the proper name to which psychoanalysis must restitute itself.

In *Resistances of Psychoanalysis*, the resistance to psychoanalysis offered by deconstruction (or, for that matter, any other discourse) is to be thought only alongside psychoanalysis's own conception of 'resistance-to-analysis', which implies a resistance *internal* to psychoanalysis itself. Analysis and resistance are, in other words, intensely knotted together in the very movement or production of psychoanalysis, since each depend on and supplement the other. The title of Derrida's book is therefore marked by a double genitive: resistances *of* psychoanalysis implies at once the resistance offered to psychoanalysis both by its opponents and analysands, and the resistance which it gives itself as perhaps the very condition of its possibility (the fraught institutional history of psychoanalysis – its internal conflicts, feuds and factionalisms – in some sense embodies this constitutive self-resistance). Deconstruction's complex relation to psychoanalysis – neither simply oppositional nor identificatory – must be thought in terms of such resistance, a resistance which both challenges and constitutes, questions and affirms.

Derrida's *Glas* is a less frequent point of reference when considering the relationship between psychoanalysis and deconstruction. The Hegel pages of this bicolumnar text are usually approached through the question of the family of terms which in Hegel's thought connect marriage, education, property and civil society, and the effect that Hegel's reading of *Antigone* has upon this series. The Genet column is thus frequently read in terms of its transgressive resistance to Hegelian logic (one not free from its own internal resistances, as Derrida points out), notably where questions of sex and sexual difference are concerned. The political dimensions of the Genet column have been extended to reflect wider questions of Genet's 'politics', for instance his relationship to the Palestinians and the Black Panthers. But, without at all opposing or contesting these approaches, it is also possible to pursue a sustained reading of the Genet column of

Glas – to one side of psychoanalysis, as it were – in terms of the problem of the deconstructibility of 'the deciding discourse of castration', as Derrida puts it. Here, the fleece that Genet imagines Harcamone wearing in *The Miracle of the Rose* takes centre stage just as much as Genet's flowers, more commonly thematised in *Glas* commentaries. The fleece – indeed, to get 'fleeced' – carries a multiple, ambiguous and unstable set of possible meanings (to cover and to strip, to protect and to expose, to sheathe and unsheathe), and Derrida puts this 'motif' to work in the interests of a double-sexed deconstruction of castratability (via Genet, a sort of theft beyond the possibility of theft). If the erection cannot 'fall' without re-elevating the entire edifice or column of that phallogocentrism of which castration would paradoxically form an uncastratable part, Derrida's insertion of a deconstructive 'hole in erection' exposes to a powerfully deciphering and transformative reading just this tale of castration's uncastratability. This, I argue, is how *Glas* fleeces us. Taking up Derrida's suggestion that the bi-columnar is in a certain sense uncastratable, this chapter closes by reading into the Hegel column of *Glas* precisely this deconstructibility of a 'deciding discourse of castration', notably in terms of the Hegelian interpretation of Antigone's 'politics'.

Of Flowers and Fleeces

What does it mean to get fleeced? What does it mean, for instance, to get fleeced by *Glas*,[1] described by Derrida himself as a 'fleecing text'? The fleece is both garb and pelt; it is at once a talismanic 'scalp', a part that has been brutally cut away, and a covering used to shield or shelter what is vulnerable or exposed (sometimes, working like a highly prized charm). It is both something stolen, and a protective barrier against loss. To get 'fleeced' already carries a double and ambiguous set of possible meanings, therefore – as if we may get 'fleeced' in the very process of subjecting the fleece to, let's say, hermeneutical inquiry. As if the warm embrace of (one) meaning always comes at the expense of another; and indeed not just at another's expense, but potentially one's own, since the very possibility of the 'fleece' is founded on sudden and violent (re-)appropriation. If 'fleecing' has no stable, single meaning, then, what is it to be 'fleeced' in or by *Glas*, this spellbinding concoction that is *Glas*? What, if anything, does it expose us to? And what, if anything, does it defend us from?

Perhaps in a similar vein – that of the seeming colloquialism – one may ask not only how the reader might approach a text so extraordinary as *Glas*, but how one might *wear* it: that is, how one might stand or bear it; how one might put up with it, or live with it, swallow it or suck it up? These phrases are not just fortuitous ones, in the sense that the entire fabric of the Genet column of *Glas* seems to be woven around images of garb (as well as of spittle, sputum, the mouth, etc., to which we'll return): depictions of types of costumery, jewellery and other clothing accessories, described by Genet and Derrida alike with a degree of stylisation that often seems to match their highly contrived and ornamented appearance. As if the style of such garb, of Genet's writing and of *Glas* itself are themselves intricately woven together. We are told, for instance, that *The Thief's Journal* and 'the costume of the prisoners' are in fact 'cut from the same material, the same flowery fabric' (129b). The qualities of this material in turn fashion the particular sensibilities of the reader. Meanwhile, a little later on, it is again 'the outfit of the convicts' that spurs desire, compels writing, and fosters the very language of both the text and its reader (137b). 'A column and a textile', a 'style', too, attain semblance of one another, through an intricately woven play of detachment and substitution that intimately ties the philosophical or critical concerns of the Genet column to its textual operations, construed each time as a 'made' or stylised fabric (137b). The details of a pair of denim slacks, of a criminal's gait, of a false limb (the 'wooden peg . . . fastened to a stump cut off below the knee by a system of straps and buckles' (139b)), of a plastic bunch of grapes pinned inside the trouser fly as if it were the cock's head-dress, of a military uniform or a fine tapestry, of an arrangement of cut flowers: pose, posture, postiche, prosthesis – all combine to manifest a 'simulacrum', a 'parade', a 'parry' or 'masquerade' (of erection, among other things, but also castration: the 'peg' for example is likened to a 'stony colossus' (139b)) that seems ornately and inseparably plaited, stitched into the work at hand. As if the 'style in question' were itself a 'fetish' of sorts (223b). The relation between style, fetish, erection and castration will therefore be one of our problems.

If it regales itself, *Glas* regales itself in flowers. The text is indeed composed 'in liana and ivy' (18b) – that which weaves, braids, entwines, binds, grafts, overlaps and sews together with some decorative aplomb the parts of the text that would otherwise appear to stand starkly apart, banded erect. The flower, so *Glas* tells us, is as much what gathers – '"the poetic object par excellence"' or the very 'figure of figures' (14b) – as it is that which is gathered or cut. What we might gather on the strength of the flower-gathering is that *Glas* is itself gathered by the flower that styles the text, whether in literary or rhetorical terms. The cut or gathered part nonetheless allots the whole of which it is a part. How, then, is one to comprehend or gather (cut) the flower, if it in fact determines the entire field within which – and of which – it becomes the principal figure? The part is larger than the whole of which it is a part, while still being a potentially detachable part of the whole whose intrinsic integrity it supposedly assures, and therefore it cannot with any simplicity support what supports it. (Later, as we will see, this will recall the deconstructive problem of the column and colossus, perhaps of erection itself.) And, performing this very problem perhaps, Genet 'has made himself into a flower. While tolling the *glas* (knell), he has put into the ground, with very great pomp, but also as a flower, his proper name, the names and nouns of common law, language, truth, sense, literature, rhetoric, and, if possible, the remain(s)' (12b). If the style of *Glas* has to do with 'the erectile stem – the style – of the flower', nonetheless when the flower blossoms at the stem's summit, 'the petals part' (21–2b) and the flower head (the proper) divides or decapitates itself. The bloom thus becomes, as Derrida puts it, '(de)part(ed)' (*partie*). No longer just a part of a larger whole (that it never simply was), but the very part that (however impossibly) partitions or demarcates it as such, the flower holds or harbours in itself 'the force of a transcendental excrescence' (15b). This suggests an odd outgrowth or projection, a distended body or architecture, an impossibly elastic supplementarity that both enlarges a figure, making it larger than the whole (of itself), larger than the rhetoric or poetics it comes to distinguish or define, but which also distorts, ruptures and interrupts the entire economy and very idea of the 'whole', of which it somehow remains an (excrescent) part. The flower – as the part that is and is not gathered – is '(de)part(ed)', then, by force of this 'transcendental excrescence' that somewhat sets it apart from the 'series of bodies or objects of which it forms a part'. Like the 'appearance' or 'apparition' of a 'hole in erection', the spectral remains of the '(de)part(ed)' part are therefore always already 'at work in the structure of the flower' (the stem, column, erection) as a 'practical deconstruction of the transcendental effect' (15b):

> In little continuous jerks, the sequences are enjoined, induced, glide in silence . . . They are always only sections of flowers, from paragraph to paragraph, so much so that anthological excerpts inflict only the violence necessary to attach importance [*faire cas*] to the remain(s). Take into account the overlap-effects [*effets de recoupe*], and you will see that the tissue ceaselessly re-forms itself around the incision [*entaille*]. (25b)

But what of the fleece, among these other regalia and insignia of the text? What of the especially talismanic golden fleece, fleece of the winged ram? As perhaps a byword for *genêt*, the gold-blossomed bush, so Derrida will say? The fleece 'surrounds the neck'. In the French the 'toison d'or' also refers to the necklace of the 'Order of the Golden Fleece' that Genet imagines Harcamone wearing, so it *is* a necklace as well as a fleece that is 'worn like a necklace'. Worn this way, the fleece festoons the person like the proper name in all its fragile grandeur (67b). As such the fleece marks the spot or line of the cut, the place where the head is at once prioritised, one might say fetishised through both severance and suspension, and at the same time degraded or demeaned, at once raised up and cast down, rendered proper and improper at a stroke (the head, therefore, as a double and no doubt duplicitous part of the 'whole' it at once participates in and allots). The fleece thus summons the problem or question – the spectre – of castration (though, as we shall see, transforming it, too). It therefore comes to be associated with 'the apparition or the appearance of a hole in erection', and furthermore with both erection itself, as it seemingly fulfils itself through the penetrative act (which entails the opening of a hole), and a certain lapse or failure of erection – a gap or hole in erection – so that we end up with the extraordinary image of a fleece-lined volcano, a vertiginous, erupting black hole, a shadowy pit, a lair for thieves and murderers armed with the sharpest of blades, that is also a 'spitting gulf', 'an inexhaustible eructation of letters in fusion': 'the text is a golden fleece' (67b). What we have, then, is a double-sexed image of the fleece: with the fleece, we find that which opens or gapes, and that which erupts, ejaculates; that which screens the exposable (detachable?) part, dissembling the promise of revelation, folding in and over on itself as it thrusts and spills forth. The text as golden fleece is a precious 'scalp', a cuttable part no doubt, the trophy-effect of a violent incision in language (something like a cut phallus or flower); but it is also a woven or braided mesh, a textual veil, an ornate fabulation, a near-spectral trace that spaces what it membranously nets together, an extended dissimulation covering both the whole of the hole, and the hole of the whole – in other words, the entirety of the void that it at once dissimulates and dissembles. In part, then, by casting holes over holes. So that in multiple ways the whole-hole lacks itself. The fleece-like text fleeces, then, in a double sense – if it steals away, what it takes from us is perhaps the thievable or detachable object itself, leaving hanging, suspended, in its place the fetish that it fabulates, as we'll see. As such, the seminal act to be associated with this woven 'scalp' is not simply that of theft, but theft of theft, theft of a certain possibility of theft. Where theft is to be committed, in other words, we find a certain abyss, as if another thief has come before the thief himself, but leaving only the trace of a certain abyss that no longer conforms to what is thievable or castratable in any simple sense. It is as if, through this textual fleecing, castration is put into double-sexed deconstruction, suspended above or below itself (like the fetish?), subjected to repetitive scenes of concocted re-enactment and re-embellishment, for good or ill.

Such a fleece is therefore not simply wrapped around a 'spitting gulf' conceived of decisively as either an ejaculating erection or the raw wound of castration; instead, it is refigured as a near-transparent sheath of spittle, fragile perhaps in the sense of being somewhat ethereal, but mucoid and gluey nonetheless. Mobile, elastic, strangely 'intact' (67b) (its increasing viscosity perhaps a gesture of hospitality towards the small tube of Vaseline that Genet so famously introduces into his text). This spittle smears, spreads like a thin, watery milk; worked in the mouth as a form of technique, it mats, pastes together hairs (pubic hairs, for instance). The white spit over the lips enframes as much as it sheathes the opening, coats rather than covers the genital parts to which it sticks, decorating as much as hiding them. A delicate silken veil rolled in the head's orifice folds over and in on itself, an oddly fascinating secretion that perhaps secretes nothing but itself – or that perhaps secretes secretion itself. What is discharged here, then, is not pure seminal fluid nor, for that matter, menstrual blood, but an enveloping drool that may mix and intermingle with others to form a strange, hybrid solution, a woven garment of liquids, juices, the flow and ebb of tides, a fine regalia befitting the watery pomp of a 'fleet of screens with purple sails . . . a fleet guarding itself at the prow and the poop, gold spurs for the parade' (67b). Elsewhere in the text, we find highly ornamented descriptions that culminate in Derrida's evocation of 'the agglomerate web-veil-spittle'. Here, amid a complex interaction between the 'membranous partition' of the soft palate, the jagged pillars of the tongue's edges, and the saliva that produces 'gluing contiguity', the 'text is spit out' (140–2b). It is even 'spat out into my mouth' perhaps: 'an almost unconscious movement of deglutination made me swallow' (147b) – providing another answer to the question of how one might 'wear' the text, how one might *swallow* it or suck it up. With this watery image of a purple-sailed, golden-spurred fleet parading itself before us, however, it is as if the fleece as modesty panel, as layered covering ('fleet of screens'), now comes to disport itself almost brazenly. Promising to sail or slide across vast expanses of hidden depths, it nonetheless seems to cover or conceal nothing at all. But, for all that, it is a parade that never seems to get going, never quite getting itself out of port: 'The parade always stays behind.' This 'behind' or *Derrière* calls to mind the tomb of the (late) father (tomb of the proper name marked by the 'capital letter', the 'D' of Derrida), but such that the logic of castration woven into the family romance can never quite be separated, severed, isolated or extracted from this watery solution, this spat-out secretion that mixes blood and sperm with itself. If the text is a 'fleecing text' in the sense that it reminds and thus robs us anew of the dead father (the figure behind the veil), nevertheless the 'phallic' cut that may be 'fervently celebrated in private, behind the curtain' is still a sort of cultic adornment, the occasion and pretext for another fleece-like weaving – another fleecing – another floral display of flowers and phalluses that are as much ornately braided as they are violently cut. What follows is a festival of preening, a hybrid arrangement of stems and stalks, hairs and feathers mixing together all plant, animal and human life in a wild orgy of miscegenation. Borders make way for braided flowers, the fleece-like text '*tricks out* its writing' such that the 'gulf' or abyss over which it seems to glide is at once divested of all border-lines of the 'self-same' – those which might grant identity or delineate being, for instance – and endures instead a weaving-dissimulation in which 'the erection is produced only in *abyme*', in the abyss (or the abeyance, the suspension) of the abyss. As Derrida writes:

> The tangled tracing of its filial filaments assures *at once* (imposs-ible castration decision) sewing and overlap cutting again . . . : of the mass of flowers as a phallic upsurging *and* a vaginal concavity (small *glas* grown, summarized in between, at the back of the glottis), intact virginity *and* bleeding castration, *taille* (clipping and size) of a rose, of 'the red rose of monstrous size and beauty' that will soon open up into a 'shadowy pit'. (68b)

As it joins and separates at once, this '*and*' – 'a phallic upsurging *and* a vaginal concavity', 'intact virginity *and* bleeding castration' – represents and yet transforms the 'impossible castration decision' that in its very impossibility allows weaving, braiding, concoct-ing, textual fleecing – 'the tangled tracing of filial filaments' – to happen. Elsewhere, Derrida speaks of the 'economy of the fetish' (antagonistically inseparable mix of separation and attach-ment) that overpowers the 'deciding discourse of castration': at bottom, 'the fetish is not opposable'; like the '*and*', one 'cannot cut though to a decision' concerning its always double function, 'any more than between the sexes', he writes (227b; 229b). (Meant to overcome castration anxiety, the fetish nonetheless suspends or substitutes every decision about castration in an ongoing way.) Such 'grafting', like that of the flower, is however precisely a matter of the text's 'style', one that cannot be secondarised in relation to its supposed 'substance' or 'matter', since the latter is everywhere spat, discharged, woven, worn, formed, stylised, seeming to pass between and across. The over-powering force or 'style' of the fetish in relation to the 'deciding discourse of castration' – like this double-sexed discourse of the '*and*' – connects, moreover, to Derrida's suggestion that the bi-columnar is in a certain sense uncastratable. Instead, the '*and*' fleeces, intricately and impossibly knotting what is separate and joined at one and the same time, undecidably giving and taking, exposing and covering. With this, the membranous, agglutinating, clumping '*and*' steals away from under our very noses the 'castration decision' – a decision that would indeed maintain the distinction between property and theft, presence and absence, 'monstrous size and beauty'/'shadowy pit', and so forth – a decision that it nevertheless cannot help but suspend, letting it hang, undecided, in a certain way. (A 'clump' is not exactly an erection but neither is it simply a non-erection.) This is perhaps the whole tale (hole-tale) of the 'taille' – of 'clipping and size' – that the 'fleecing text' weaves. From this 'maddening, atopical place' we get 'more or less (*than the*) truth, more or less (*than the*) veil' (69b), not simply causing the whole erection to *fall* (recall the winged ram, at once brought down and raised up), but putting such erection into deconstruction – fleecing it, if you will (where of course 'fleecing' retains its multiple sense).

Genet may well write for money – yes, and why not? (217–19b) – but, still, he fleeces us by means of a double and duplicitous economy in which – through theft of theft – what is taken from us (or given in return, who is to say?) is more and less than money, property, profit and loss.

For the erection to 'fall', to fall purely and simply or to be thought vulgarly in terms of mere 'falling', one would still have to maintain – to hold up – the entire edifice or column of that phallogocentrism of which castration would form an (uncastratable) part; whereas to deconstruct the phallus in its erection would be to expose to a powerfully deciphering and transformative reading just this tale – *taille*, since such a tale is also a cut and a tailoring – of (uncastratable) castration. Immeasurably taking its measure.

The Colossus

How, then, is one to take the size of the column, or bi-columnar text? How can it possibly measure against the erection, the stone stump, all-supplementing prosthesis, colossal perhaps beyond (its own) measure – 'the sublime, immeasurable, sizeless super-elevation' (260b) that is as much (and undecidably so) a portent of death as it is a sign of pure potency? Appearing as the supplementing part of 'Parergon', buried deep in *The Truth in Painting*,[2] we find Derrida's reading of Kant's Analytic of the Sublime, under the name or title of 'The Colossus'. The colossus, erect, upright, sublimely overhangs, looms above us, almost too high, 'almost too large'. Outsized, it seems at first beyond size, albeit according to a certain disproportionality which nonetheless implies the 'vast', the 'gigantic', the 'massive', the 'enormous'. Size (*taille*), Derrida tells us here, referred more originally to 'the line of a cut', to the incision which not only comes to 'broach a surface' (to circumcise, let's say), but also to 'delimit a contour', to distinguish but also to pattern, perhaps (120). In order to retain the latter sense of the French word *taille* – cutting, incision – in its uncertain relation to its other meaning – scale – Derrida's translator chooses to deploy the term 'cise', an obsolete spelling of the English word 'size'. 'Cise' therefore appears repeatedly throughout the text in order to preserve and indeed cultivate this ambiguity or complexity. 'Size', then, opens a track or pathway that goes from the question of magnitude or scale, to a certain opening or breaching, to the delineating mark of the *parergon* – as impossible mark, given the very problematic that the parergon itself implies (what intervenes to establish or limit the limit, and how might we delimit whatever this may be?). Thus leading to the complex relation, if it could be called that, between the 'size' of the outsized and the impossible logic of the cut (problem of the phallus).

Henceforth, a certain double antagonises (itself), a double-effect occurs, deconstructibly, between the over- or outsized and the tracing or drawing or marking of a line: 'between the Greek *kolossus* and the *columna* or *columen* of the Romans, a sort of semantic and formal unity exerts an irresistible attraction', Derrida writes (120). A sublime attraction, perhaps – we should wonder a good while longer how to describe it, though doubtless in a form which turns such 'unity' (indeed such a desire for unity) nearly inside out. For the column is not, in the end, the colossus; or, rather, the column is not purely and simply colossal. The column that supports an edifice as its prop, as a *parergon* – 'supplement to the operation, neither work nor outside the work' (121) – constitutes itself as a supporting structure, and is therefore necessarily of moderate and measurable size. As Derrida remarks, 'a measure of its erection can be taken' (122). Although, of course, deconstructibly so, since by constituting itself as an indispensable part of the object it delineates, the *parergon* serves, not simply as the outer limit or boundary of 'form', but more fundamentally as its enabling condition and hence most 'interior' property. Which begs the question, if the parergon is an intrinsic facet of the 'work' as much as its extrinsic border or edge, what then serves as the parergon of parergon, the limit of the limit, that which limits the limit itself? Thus, according to an impossible measure (that of the 'erection'), the parergonal-deconstructible limit of the column vies strangely with the colossal sublimity or sublime colossus that attracts it, or raises it up, elevates it, only to 'out-size' it.

How does one take the measure, or get the size, of this situation? As if to maintain a distinction between the two (however unstable this may be), Kant in the Analytic of the Sublime highlights 'quantity', in contrast to the analytic of the beautiful where, as Derrida notes, he had begun with 'quality'. Kant distinguishes the mathematical sublime, where the imagination is overwhelmed by spatial or temporal magnitude, from the dynamical sublime, in which a sense of overbearing power (for instance, an irresistible force of nature) may cause sheer terror, impeding cognition, immobilising the will. Kant commences with the mathematical sublime, then, taking 'quantity' as his cue. In these terms, he describes the sublime − irreducible to the simple measure of 'form' − as that which is *absolutely large*. Nevertheless, the absolutely large, as Derrida points out, 'is not a dimension, in the quantitative sense' (135). The 'absolutely large' acquires a magnitude that is beyond measure, that is wholly disproportionate, asymmetrical, incalculable, incomparable, and thus unequal, unscaled, to anything save itself. And yet, all the same, the 'absolutely large' allows itself to be 'represented under the category of quantity' (136) which it unavoidably evokes as much as decisively eschews. Moreover, while ostensibly it may not be compared with anything, the absolutely large as a 'figure' of the sublime is, Derrida tells us, nonetheless *preferred* by Kant to the absolutely small. Indeed, since 'the more and hence largeness are inscribed in the movement and in the very concept of preference' (136), it is not just that the (non-rational)

115

elevation of the large over the small on Kant's part raises the question of a particular preference, but instead that the *very question of preference itself* is at issue here. 'If no mathematics can as such justify a preference', writes Derrida, 'it must be that an aesthetic judgement is implied in it, and a subjective measure coming to found reflective judgments' (136). For Derrida, then, such 'preference' overwrites and undermines the borders of the mathematical sublime it is supposed to uphold, and operates to reintroduce comparability or comparison where it should, in fact, have no place (i.e., no preferentiality where mathematics is concerned). Here, then, the (mathematical) sublime is not merely subjected to its own, grand law of indetermination, but through the implicitly comparative process of preferentiality is somewhat brought down to size.

The colossus, the colossal, is, then, not just the column, the prop or support (although the *parergon* is no more wholly supportive of the *ergon* than the colossal is radically asymmetrical, absolutely free-standing, utterly self-sufficient, without-prop or *sans*-prop). The colossus is, however, neither simply the 'prodigious' nor the 'monstrous'. As Derrida observes, an object is 'prodigious' when, by means of its sheer enormity, it obliterates 'the end which constitutes its concept' (125). Whereas the sublime is resisted or diluted both by 'things of nature' whose concept 'already contains a determinate end' (for example, the horse, 'whose natural destination is well known to us'), and by the art object already endowed with aesthetic intention or purpose, the 'prodigious' aspires to that degree of superelevation (beyond degree, height, measure or coordination) with which one associates the sublime in its strongest manifestation (122–5). The 'prodigious' may be detected in 'raw nature' which, undomesticated by any sense of proportion, symmetry, or order, nevertheless overspills itself, deforms itself, taking on a monstrous or denatured quality (so extreme, in fact, that it is incapable of inspiring emotion or fear; incapable, that is, of human 'attraction' in any sense). Whereas the 'prodigious' or the 'monstrous', in their truest sense, work to annihilate utterly the 'end', determination, or purpose which might otherwise constitute their grounds, the colossal merely 'qualifies' the presentation of its concept, such that it is, in Kant's terms, 'almost too large' for the idea that it conveys. As Derrida puts it:

> Colossal (*kolossalisch*) thus qualifies the presentation, the putting on stage or into presence, the catching-sight, rather, of some thing, but of something which is not a thing, since it is a concept. And the presentation of this concept inasmuch as it is not presentable. Nor simply unpresentable: *almost unpresentable.* And by reason of its size: it is 'almost too large'. (125)

Here, the 'unpresentable' opens up (within) the space of presentation that it also exceeds, remarking it 'otherwise', according to a certain logic of the trace, perhaps. The colossal retains an affinity with the sublime to the extent that its appearance does not take the form of a 'thing' that is fully formed for the imagination or experience, but which instead puts conceptuality and thus reason itself to work. Yet the '*almost too*' of the colossus, rather than being just a pure excess, also amounts to a provocation of reason in the sense that it remains extremely difficult to arrest its 'category'. If it were just *too* large, the colossal would be absolutely unpresentable, and would thereby fall upon its own grounds. 'The pure and simple "too" would bring the colossal down' (125), just as much as the complete absence of this 'too' would effectively destroy the colossus by dint of a full adequation of the thing and the concept: colossus (cutting it back down to size, thereby reducing it to what it should not be). The 'almost too' thus plays against or upon the limit in a more complex way than the 'simple overspill' (125) that would seem to characterise the sublime. This is its 'singular originality', Derrida tells us. Hence, the 'almost too' at once invites reason's approach (in the form of the work of conceptuality); yet it also restricts, even confounds, its satisfactory completion (such that, for instance, the presentation of a concept is made difficult 'when the intuition of the object is "almost too great" for our "power of apprehension"', as Kant puts it (126)). Indeed, this to-ing and fro-ing of the 'almost too' threatens to unravel its trait in any kind of delimited form: 'Where are we to delimit the trait of the *almost too*?' asks Derrida (126).

Somewhere between the 'size' of the outsized or the always mis-sized, and the impossible logic of the cut (the limit, border, or frame), somewhere between the column and the colossus, we find ourselves in the midst of the 'sublime', albeit a 'sublime' that, like column and colossus, is not quite the same as itself, never quite the same. (And what is the nature or status of this 'between', this 'and', if neither simply an extension or protrusion, verging on a bridging-effect, nor simply a meeting at the edges, one limit touching another?)

> The colossal will perhaps be something, or rather the presentation of something which can be taken without being able to be taken . . . and which from then on crushes you, throws you down while elevating you at the same time, since you can take it in view without taking it in your hand . . . and since you can see it without seeing it completely. (139)

The Kantian sublime constitutes a movement away from empiricist or naturalistic theories of sublimity (for unpresentable 'raw nature' is ultimately a projection, the extreme or outermost limit of a sublimity which takes only its 'presentations' from nature). Thus, as Derrida writes, the Kantian sublime:

> can be encountered as such only in the mind and on the side of the subject. The sublime cannot inhabit any sensible form. There are natural objects that are beautiful, but there cannot be a natural object that is sublime. The true sublime, the sublime proper and properly speaking . . . relates only to the idea of reason. It therefore refuses all adequate presentation. (131)

Yet still, what is 'unpresentable' presents itself, the sublime is no more simply 'the infinite idea itself' than it is contained in a 'finite natural or artificial object' (131). Instead, the fundamental 'inadequation' or 'incommensurability' that characterises the sublime inheres in the fact that the 'infinite' is inadequately presented in the 'finite' as precisely the inadequation of the sublime itself. To complicate matters further, if sublimity is, for Derrida, 'only in the mind and on the side of the subject' it is nonetheless 'not just encountered in the mind'. For, in view of the preference which elevates the absolutely large over the absolutely small, the Kantian discourse of the sublime refers itself to the body, doing so at the point where the mathematical evaluation of size gives itself over to aesthetic evaluation of the sublime's enormity. Here, the 'primary (subjective, sensory, immediate, living) measure proceeds from the body. And it takes the body as its primary object . . . *It is the body which erects itself as a measure.*' This body is the 'body of man', says Derrida: 'It is *starting from* it that the erection of the largest is preferred' (140). Hence the presentation *in man-like form* of the Colossus in the painting attributed, now contentiously, to Goya, for instance – although with sufficient enormity and deformity to present a concept almost too great for its presentation. In Derrida's 'The Colossus', in fact, we find reproductions of two 'Goya' paintings of the Colossus, including the now-disputed one. This situation recalls Derrida's remark in the Hegel column of *Glas*: 'A scandalizing question traverses the text . . . how can one have two sons {*fils*}? How can one be the father of two phalli, erected one against each other?' (175). (Here, of course, he is also speaking of *Glas* itself.) In one of these images reproduced in *The Truth in Painting*, then, the Colossus sits amid a barren landscape under a slender crescent moon, part-man, part-animal, his head hairy yet his torso smooth and muscular, his back turned but his face looking towards us, though gazing upwards, beyond the space of both the composition and the spectator. In the other, perhaps the more famous – yet now disputed – of the two, the Colossus strides out across the shadowy wastes of a craggy landscape, leaving in his wake a desperate scene of chaos in which men and animals scatter in hurried confusion from their all-too exposed encampment. It is a sublime scene of darkness, violence and wild disorder. In both images, the Colossus seems intent on broaching the very bounds or borders of the picture that nonetheless confines him. Although Derrida does not offer an analysis of either of these paintings, their salient features recall his insistence that the colossal is always to be found between the 'monstrous' and 'man', between culture and nature, the infinite and finite, between enormity and the limit, the outsized and the 'frame'.

No sublime, then, without the emergence, the rising up, of man's body. Its monstration, one might say. This body is nonetheless a 'median place, an average place of the body which would provide an aesthetic maximum without losing itself in the mathematical infinite' (141). This body at once raised up and brought (or weighted) down a little, then, its apparent fixity (at mid-point) an effect, as much as a resistance, of the complex forces at work in its 'erection'. The colossus as that which, as in *Glas* and in glas (gl–), remains falling, slipping or sliding away, as it remains – somewhat like the decollated head or the droopy ding dong of an elderly man (244b).

This colossus is – these irreconcilable colossuses are – strangely like the circumcised Jew in Derrida's 'Circumfession', perhaps: '*the circumcised Jew: more naked, perhaps, and therefore more modest, under the excess of clothes, cleaner, dirtier, where the foreskin no longer covers, protects itself the better for being more exposed . . . whence my theme, foreskin and truth, the question of knowing by whom by what the violence of circumcision was imposed*'.[3] The colossus appears both strikingly naked and excessively covered, protecting itself all the better, maybe, for being more exposed ('fleeced', maybe): 'neither culture nor nature, both culture and nature . . . between the presentable and the unpresentable, the passage from the one to the other as much as the irreducibility of the one to the other. Cise, edging, cut edges, that which passes and happens, without passing, from one to the other' (143). In 'Parergon', while reading Kant, Derrida considers the clothes of statues, 'which both decorate and veil their nudity'. Tellingly, here, statues' clothing are termed 'hors-d'oeuvres stuck onto the edging of the work nonetheless, and to the edging of the represented body to the extent that – such is the argument – they supposedly do not belong to the whole of the representation' (57). Thus, perhaps, through the regaling of stone stumps, the problem or question of circumcision might be re-stitched or re-grafted, like the flower itself, onto that of the parergon. 'Fleecingly', one might even say.

Sexual Politics of *Glas*

I want to conclude with some brief remarks linking this ex-
pository reading of the Genet column of *Glas* to the Hegel
column that forms its counterpart. In Hegel's *Philosophy of Right*
the family plays a central part in the syllogistic reasoning that
connects marriage, education, property, capital and civil society.
The unification of the family through marriage and child-
rearing finds its external embodiment in the synthesis of the
civil sphere, education and capital. Indeed, the production of
free, educated and property-holding individuals through child-
rearing within bourgeois society itself brokers the transition
from family to civil life, and thus leads to the constitution of
the state. As *Glas* shows, the family therefore acquires pivotal
importance in the whole system of Hegel's philosophy of right,
notably in its relationship to his thinking of politics, ethics and
society. Yet it is not only that the family repeats intact the entire
dialectical system, but also that it renders that system problematic. For Hegel, the fundamental meaning of family is filiation. It
is that which defines Spirit, although at the exclusion or expense
of material, natural and animal realms. In the Christian faith
the family-ties between father and son connect infinite to finite
Spirit, God to man. The human family itself embodies the story
of a divine filiation which, indeed, incarnates itself in the figure
of Christ. For Hegel, Christianity inaugurates true filiation at
the point it overcomes and replaces the Old Testament rights
and duties prized by Judaism with an ethical paradigm of love
and freedom. In this (Greco-Christian) story of filial reproduc-
tion, not only is the Jew excluded as irredeemable within the
movement of dialectic synthesis that filiation itself seems to
name. The mother, too, is largely reduced to a material conduit

that remains extrinsic to the dialectical process to be found in the story of filiation. Only the father's image finds divinity in the filiation of infinite and finite Spirit (God and man) – Christ's (and man's) mother is merely 'actual'. The fact that the mother cannot be fully included within the divinely filiated family in which she nevertheless plays an inescapable part disrupts the movement of synthesis which hopes to reappropriate without remainder the circle in which are brought together marriage, family, education, property, religion, society and state. Thus, the ever-higher synthesis aimed at through the work of dialectical reason rests upon the violent exclusion/reduction of the otherness of the other that it cannot assimilate.

But, of course, that which is excluded from the system in fact assures the system's very conditions of possibility. As the Hegel column continues, Derrida turns to the story of Antigone which Hegel himself discusses in the *Phenomenology of Spirit*. In contrast to the masculine task of re-securing the polis after a period of internecine struggle (civil war but also family feud), in *Antigone* the feminine is associated with a work of mourning that fulfils its role within the family and community through ensuring burial rites for the dead brother. Thus, albeit at the 'other' end of life, the woman's function is once again merely to facilitate or actualise the masculine transition from finite to infinite Spirit. Yet the store Hegel sets by the brother-sister relationship problematises as much as secures dialectical reason. The sister-brother relation retains its purity in ethical and spiritual terms due to the absence both of conjugal desire and the parental sexual politics of the family romance. Freed from internal conflict, such a relation therefore establishes the basis for an unencumbered translation of family life into civil life. The bond between brother and sister thus communicates a positive image of filiation unspoiled by

longing or resentment, one that seems neither marred by lack
nor incapable of synthesis. Yet where Antigone is concerned it
also serves to displace the possibility of dialectical incorporation according to the prevailing logic of filiation, since by
resisting Creon as the state-substitute for the father she blocks
the pathway from the family to the civil paradigm. Antigone
represents the paradoxical conditions of possibility and impossibility for the synthesising universality of Spirit. One might say
she short-circuits the Hegelian system itself.

As internal 'enemy' possessed of an 'ethical' orientation
which the system can neither reduce, disqualify nor contain,
Antigone's appearance in the Hegel column of *Glas* prompts
certain connections with the Genet side of the page. Most of all,
perhaps, what Antigone's story tells us is that the system cannot
stably contain or 'sublate' its own figures – just as in the Genet
column the flower as poetic figure *par excellence* figures or allots
the entire field of literature or rhetoric of which it also forms
a part, according to a supplementing logic of 'transcendental
excrescence' which produces the flower as ungatherable gatherer
at the limits of philosophical conceptuality or dialectical reason,
rhetorical possibility or textual inscription. Antigone's story, in
other words, is also that of the deconstructibility of erection and
sexual difference, and therefore in a certain way of the limits
of a 'deciding discourse of castration' once more; it is the story
of what remains – what is spat out into our own mouths – as a
perhaps colossal edifice seems to begin to fall. (The 'deciding
discourse of castration' may even serve as an improper name
for that which assures the dialectical working of negativity in
the Hegelian system.) It is a tale, a tailored cut (*taille*) that also
fleeces us.

Notes

1 Jacques Derrida, *Glas*, trans. John P. Leavey, Jr. and Richard Rand (Lincoln: University of Nebraska Press, 1990). Page references will be given in the body of the chapter ('b' refers to the Genet column whereas 'a' is conventionally used to refer to the Hegel column in the bicolumnar layout of *Glas*).

2 Jacques Derrida, 'The Colossal', in *The Truth in Painting*, trans. Geoffrey Bennington and Ian McLeod (Chicago: University of Chicago Press, 1987), pp. 119–47. Page references will be given in the body of the chapter.

3 Jacques Derrida, 'Circumfession', in Geoffrey Bennington and Jacques Derrida, *Jacques Derrida* (Chicago: University of Chicago Press, 1993), p. 135.

5

The University and the Hysteric (after Derrida and Freud)

In 1999 Jacques Derrida's essay 'The University Without Condition' was first presented, under a slightly different, longer title, at Stanford University.[1] That same year, I helped to found the online journal *Culture Machine*, and a year later edited a special issue on the topic of the University institution, one that included Geoffrey Bennington's inaugural professorial lecture, given at Sussex University during the mid-1990s,[2] alongside other texts by Sam Weber, Hillis Miller and Derrida himself.[3] Bennington's lecture is as much about the always-divisible frontiers of the University (in other words, the University as, despite everything, the name we might still give to a yet undecided setting or situation), as it is inescapably the expression of a binding institutional 'context' (i.e., the professorial lecture). Bennington observes that the profession demanded of the professor – at once a solemn expression of vocation and a technical requirement of professional status – is itself 'divided' along an 'internal frontier' where free and faithful declaration, coming close to confessional mode, always comes up against the possibility of 'pretending or purporting', 'putting up a front'. For Bennington, this same undecidability is what, at every frontier, makes it difficult if not impossible to distinguish the legislator from the charlatan. If the professor's profession, perhaps most especially in its inaugural form, therefore aims to cross a frontier – connecting the speaker's discourse in all of its gathered-up solemnity and wisdom to a keenly expectant audience, but also 'transitioning' (as we are fond of saying in management circles these days) the professor from their previous University role to a wholly new institutional identity embodied in this conferred title – the fact that the professor may well always be 'fronting' suggests that the frontier problem of profession is not so easily traversed. (One online urban dictionary I consulted defined 'fronting' as 'acting like you are more, or you have more, than what really exists' – a definition that, depending on your point of view, might either be seen to ironically devastate the very idea of the professor, or instead to encourage an affirmative, deconstructive re-imaging of what a professor may actually be.) Bennington's talk on the deep duplicity of frontiers as itself perhaps the very problem of 'politics' is originally supplemented and complicated by just this difficulty of the double-dealing discourse of 'profession' in its always-divided sense. If, as Bennington rightly asserts, 'Of all institutions, the University is, traditionally speaking, unique in that its mission is one of rigorous self-understanding', this (ironically) not-always-recognised mission is inevitably complicated by way of the duplicitous frontier that double-marks the very discourse of the professor and indeed of the profession itself, although at the same time the 'formal impossibility' of resolving this situation is what may produce those forms of 'practical urgency' that Bennington wants to designate by way of the 'tired old epithet' of 'politics' that he nevertheless wants to renew or transform by means of the very thinking that is underway here. I wanted to begin by referencing Bennington's talk, not just to hint at my own undoubted charlatanism in making certain professions, here, about the University; and not merely to recall this issue of the mobility of those frontiers that traverse the University from its 'inside' to its 'outside'; but also to raise the question of *the frontiers of mobility*, a topic to which I'll have cause to return, as one that (so I'll wager) deeply connects politics, profession and the University 'itself'.

Bennington's lecture, as I mentioned, appeared in what was the second issue of the journal *Culture Machine* from the year 2000, where we all seemed to 'meet up' (as *Pulp* once sang) – Derrida, Miller, Weber, Bennington, and me – even if only according to a 'University' logic that, as I am describing it, somewhat puts into question what meeting together at one time in a single place might ever mean. In the first edition of the journal, meanwhile, I published a much longer text entitled 'Van Gogh's Shoes, or, Does the University have two left feet?'[4] In this essay I described how in 'Mochlos' Derrida suggests that, just as the founding of the law is not simply a juridical question, one either of legality or illegality, so the founding of the University cannot merely be treated as a 'University event'.[5] Rather it opens on to and is received from an otherness that conditions it as such. Thus the idea of the University as a unified institution with coherently defined characteristics and self-grounding borders *founders*, and the University is beset by a conflict or tension that is, for Derrida, 'interminable and therefore insoluble' (28). Insisting that 'there can be no pure concept of the University . . . due very simply to the fact that the University is *founded*' (29), Derrida, faced by this legitimation crisis of the University – a crisis of its own founding or *footing* – raises the question: How might we therefore orient ourselves in the modern University (within, in relation to: the question already faces in more than one direction)?

Through a close reading of Kant's *The Conflict of the Faculties*, Derrida suggests that Kant attempts to contain and control the violently disruptive energies of this crisis by insisting on its nature as mere 'conflict' as opposed to out-and-out 'war'. Thus, as Derrida puts it, Kant 'propos[es] for it a solution that is properly "parliamentary"' (28). Here, the University is reconceived as a 'faculty parliament'. The higher faculties (theology, law, medicine) occupy the right bench and defend the statutes of government, while the left bench is occupied by the philosophy faculty which offers 'rigorous examinations and objections' in the name and pursuit of truth. For Kant, the opposition that results from this 'parliamentary solution' serves the higher purposes of a 'free system of government' and therefore resolves conflict into a more fundamental image of polar balance, unity and accord. However, referring to Kant's 'What is Orientation in Thinking?', Derrida points out that right and left are not classified or recognised according to 'a conceptual or logical determination' but only from 'a sensory topology that has to be referred to the subjective position of the human body' (31). This means that the 'parliamentary' opposition between left and right into which the University's conflicts are ostensibly projected and resolved offers a no more reliable source of orientation. As Timothy Bahti, in his essay 'The Injured University'[6] (published alongside 'Mochlos' in the collection *Logomachia*), has put it: 'when we use corporeal directions we mean, "Be like me"' (62). Henceforth, we address the other's right as if it were a left, and vice versa. The resulting confusion between my left and another's right made possible by this situation can be located not just in the subjective position of the human body, but in the sensory orientation collectively of members within an institutional body politic. Thus, as Bahti points out, 'in the parliamentary situation, the left – the "opposition" – is located from the perspective of the president or the speaker, but the speaker's left is obviously the left's right' (62). From this somewhat disorienting point of view, leftness may be affirmed only by way of a certain repression of the right side, whereby a speaker, a president or some other arbitrarily erected figure of authority legitimates a repressive reorientation, recasting right as left.

Such disorientations between left and right suggest an image of an unbalanced body, a body off-balance or suffering imbalance. A body, like the University, disoriented because it is unsure of its ground or footing. In such a situation of imbalance, it is difficult to know how to proceed, what direction to take. Drawing on his own experience of undergoing therapy for a collapsed left lung, Bahti describes how, in order to restore balance, he was made by his physicians to adopt a position in which the weight of his body was shifted by means of leverage towards the healthy side (in this case, the right), 'inhibiting the free and strong use of the healthy lung, while forcing the injured side to do more of the breathing while it is also released of its "share" of the body's weight' (68). This example of leverage sets up a dialogue of sorts with Derrida's essay 'Mochlos' (*mochlos* is a Greek word for lever). In 'Mochlos', it is the leverage between inherited and newly founded laws, between conservation and invention, between 'right' and 'left' we might say, that in some way allows the body (the human body, the body politic, the institutional body) to walk, as it were, 'on two feet' (31). Bahti is keen, however, to 'ward off a possible misunderstanding that might arise with the analogy of injury as imbalance', that is, the assumption that 'a certain symmetry, verging on stasis . . . is perhaps being held out as either an original health to be restored, or an ideal state to be attained, or both' (72–3).

Rather, for Bahti, it is a question of 'recognizing imbalance as the condition within which leverage can and does take place'. Leverage – leverage within the University – occurs on condition of imbalance. To exert leverage within the University is, in the language of *The Chambers Dictionary*, to impart pressure, to facilitate motion, to gain advantage or power 'over a resource greater than one actually owns'. Recall our online definition of 'fronting' as 'acting like you are more, or you have more, than what really exists', and you may see why such a characterisation of profession in the University might as much reflect and affirm its originary or defining situation as worsen its predicament.

Now, this exposition was prefaced in my own essay by a citation from 'Mochlos' serving as an epigraph, which reads as follows:

> as Kant will have told us, the University will have to go on two feet, left and right, each foot having to support the other as it rises with each step to make the leap. It involves walking on two feet, two feet *with shoes*, since it turns on an institution, on a society and a culture, not just on nature. This was already clear in what I recalled about the faculty parliament. But I find its confirmation in an entirely different context, and you will certainly want to forgive me this rather rapid and brutal leap; I am authorized by the memory of a discussion, held in this very place some two years ago with our eminent colleague, Professor Meyer Shapiro, on the subject of certain shoes in Van Gogh. (31–2)

This passage obviously sent me scuttling in the direction of Derrida's 'Restitutions',[7] where I sought to trace the disorienting movements afoot in Shapiro's dispute with Heidegger over the attribution of certain peasant shoes in paintings by Van Gogh, in which, despite the strikingly oppositional tone of the debate,

Derrida detects a certain interlacing of *différance* that ties or binds as much as it differentiates the two combatants, not least in terms of their common assumption that the shoes in question formed a pair, or in other words that they could be separated and distinguished in such a way. (The history of shoemaking suggests that footwear was made in pairs, with a left and a right shoe, only as the nineteenth century progressed – and supposedly in the 'New World' of America first of all, as a result of industrial technology and also to serve the needs of the modern military. It is therefore to be supposed that there was a considerable historical time-lag before this innovation reached an impoverished European peasantry.) The resistance to what we might call un-pairing on the part of both Heidegger's and Schapiro's discourse represents, perhaps, their mutual blindness to some of the common ground, the shared assumptions or exchangeable positions which in fact inform ideas about aesthetics and representation over which they ostensibly differ. Though I didn't put things exactly this way, feeling authorised by Derrida's reference in 'Mochlos' to this other scene of apparent foot fetishism, I was able to get some mileage out of such analysis as one finds in 'Restitutions' in terms of what we might call the constitutive undecidability of 'fronting' and 'frontiers-manship' which, for Bennington, ties the legislator to the charlatan at the 'frontier' or 'front' of politics itself. Moreover, the curious 'with-against' movement of leverage stayed with me for a later book, *Counter-Institutions*, in which, via Derrida (both his writings and his institutional activism in relation to the GREPH and the Collège), I tried to analyse just such a counter-movement as the very condition of an institutional politics that could only be ventured or *risked* in a manner that was never simply *frontal*.[8] But I want to return, all these years later, to the motif of walking on two undecidably left/right feet, one which seems to characterise the precarious founding and footing of the University, while also establishing further the conditions of possibility of a certain leverage, whether for good or ill. As Bahti implies, injury or illness may not be the only context for such leverage; in fact, stasis or rest may on occasion be the unhealthier situation. If this is true, then in what ways might we analyse fear of movement, as itself epitomising a certain loss or lapse of control, in terms of a certain displacement or repression?

In Freud's writings on hysteria from the last decade of the nineteenth century, in particular the case history of Fräulein Elisabeth von R.,[9] difficulty in walking, leg pain, loss of balance and 'locomotor weakness' (142) led Freud – in his 'first full-length case study' of this particular illness – to endorse a diagnose of hysteria. Given the ultimately problematic locomotive image of the University derived from Derrida's reading of Kant, whereby the (institutional) project of walking on two feet is potentially jeopardised by the undecidability of the left and the right, would it therefore be possible speak of the hysterical University, of the University as itself hysterical or caught up in a case of hysteria? While it is perhaps difficult to immediately recognise in the University the hysteric's capacity to bear troubles 'with a cheerful air', as Freud writes of Fräulein von R. (he speaks of the hysteric's '*belle indifférence*'), the combination of such clearly feigned positivity with the intense 'hyperalgesia of the skin and muscles' which spreads over 'the whole of the legs', causing pain of an 'indefinite character' that nonetheless never goes away, does perhaps recall the obvious tension between the externally branded face or façade of many an institution and its inner woes. It is indeed this 'indefiniteness' of pain that provides one reason for Freud to concur with the diagnosis of hysteria in this case. The hysteric, unlike somebody merely suffering 'organic pains', is unable to describe them 'definitely and calmly', but instead usually 'gives the impression of being engaged in a difficult intellectual task' that tests to the limits their mental strength. The distress this brings about compounds and perhaps outstrips, one might even say engulfs, the original ailment – which, since the source of pain it is not just 'organic' but also psychological, is perhaps to be expected. The hysteric 'never tires' of venturing further descriptions of their symptoms, 'constantly adding fresh details', although this always-supplementing re-description is itself symptomatic of an inability to bring the analysis to a definitive end. Indeed, Freud writes that Fräulein von R.s 'confession' – her own telling of her story of suffering – 'seemed to offer even less help towards the cure of her illness than it did towards its explanation' (144). Let's recall that, for Bennington, one professes in the University in a way that comes 'perilously close to confession', or to a sincere declaration or admission. Yet is always possible, as he quickly reminds us, that such a profession or confession merely puts up a front, or puts a face on things. Here, then, one senses the possibility of a further connection between the discourse of the hysteric and that of the University, faced with the prospect of always-duplicitous frontiers on its intensely problematic mission towards self-understanding. Fräulein von R. confesses or professes her tale in a way that, far from alleviating her illness or shedding further light upon it, seems designed principally to discomfit and discourage her analyst in pursuit of progress in her treatment. In other words, it is as much the expression of an ailment that compounds itself at every opportunity, thwarting any efficacy that therapy might have, as it is the exposition of whatever sickens the analysand brought to a climax: an articulation of the illness, then, in precisely a double and highly conflicted sense.

The second reason why Freud sanctions the use of the term 'hysteria' in this case is because contact with the specific bodily area in which pain is concentrated produces a reaction that is far from straightforward, one that seems to suffuse suffering with a certain delight. Taking pleasure in one's pain is no doubt an extremely recognisable facet among the University community at large (as perhaps is the mixed and ambivalent reaction on the part of the hysteric to the shocking external stimulus provided by Freud's administering of electrotherapy), to the point at which one might be tempted to attribute Freud's notion of a 'hysterogenic zone' to the 'University' body itself. The disorder itself, then, is of a 'mixed kind', at once hyperalgesic and hysterogenic, the source both of genuine discomfort and partial relief of the kind granted by physical pains that are themselves just an 'accessory phenomenon', as Freud puts it, of a deeper or at any rate more complex malady. In fact, one might go so far to say that 'the hysterogenic body is a kind of prosthesis', as Ned Lukacher puts it in his introduction to Monique David-Ménard's *Hysteria From Freud to Lacan*, in the sense that such a body is never reducible to a physiological or somatic body but is itself constituted by repression and disgust of the body that David-Ménard interprets as not merely a psychic reaction to a 'real' body that is prior in some sense, but part of a linguistic or textual elaboration in which these relations are far more complexly entangled, at an always mobile frontier, constituting a movement that is at once painfully restless and somewhat functionally deficient.[10] (This recognition does not 'dematerialise' the situation, far from it; instead, for David-Ménard what we call 'language' must be refigured in 'material' terms, albeit ones that also refigure what we might mean by 'materiality'.) If it would be possible to describe the body of the University as prosthetic to the extent that it is originally self-supplementing rather than just artificially extended or developed (for example, manifesting itself as the instituted body of the spirit of reason) in the same way that the division of philosophy into origin and part of the University constitutes a situation of originary supplementarity, then this insight into the hysterogenic body forms another context in which we might analyse both the University's self-relations, and its interactions with its so-called 'outside'. Yet in this very context, we should note something else, too: in so far as they construct themselves through 'a signifying medium', such hysterogenic bodies may be capable of 'the power of thought', as Lukacher writes (xiv). What that may mean is, perhaps, the very question of the University. Meanwhile, to the extent that the hysteric's attempt to totalise the prosthetic 'part' aims at 'a totality that is also the signifier of a lack', as Lukacher observes (xvii), this very same predicament might be attributed a certain name, when it comes to the hysterogenic body of the University: Philosophy.

Freud attributes the onset of hysteria in the case of Elisabeth von R. to a succession of deaths and other departures in the family of his patient, which leaves her 'unreconciled to her fate' (even though her case is 'made up of commonplace emotional upheavals' (144)), and 'embittered by the failure of all her little schemes for re-establishing the family's former glories' (143). One might well struggle to better describe the psychic landscape of the twenty-first century University, or to resist the conclusion that, like Freud's patient, we are in the vicinity of a situation that is 'constitutionally' susceptible to hysteria in that hysterical symptoms are 'liable to develop . . . under the pressure of intense excitations *of whatever kind*' (144).

But why leg pain? Freud finds that the 'particular area of the right thigh' where the pain is most concentrated was the precise spot where during a desperate illness von R.'s father would rest his badly swollen leg while she applied new bandages to it. This transfer of pain – although not just straightforwardly pain – from the other to me on the strength of a comparable body part experiencing hurt recalls Lacan's understanding of the hysteric as someone who appropriates another's desire by identifying with them, although only on condition that such desire is not aimed at them, i.e., that the hysteric is not its primary 'object'. The transformation of paternal desire – the swollen leg – into a form of suffering (a hysterogenic zone) that might be appropriated in the interests of converting desire otherwise splits the hysterical subject as much as it divides her discourse. If the hysteric is the one who goads the master, demanding that they show their stuff, then Fräulein von R.'s 'cheeky' and 'ill-behaved' (145) narrative, which attempts to provoke Freud at the very point of analysis, daring him to prove his mettle by producing something serious by way of knowledge, is perhaps matched by her double gesture of at once exposing herself to the father's swollen leg, and protectively wrapping it anew. In both cases, the hysteric transfers something powerful from the master to herself while seeking to insulate herself from the source of that master's power. This is no doubt a brilliant strategic manoeuvre, but nonetheless it is also one that divides the hysterical subject anew – wanting what she refuses – as much as it conquers the 'other' she seeks to appropriate (by way of re-inscribing plenitude in terms of a certain lack or lapse). If Fräulein von R. proves herself able to cultivate pain in highly localised spots according to its supposed reference to particular memories or experiences (Freud finds that pain in her right leg connects to her feelings about her sick father, while the left brings up the suffering experienced at her sister's death), this endeavour – whether it is conscious or not – only partly mitigates against such double-movements as those that in fact structure or condition zonal hysterogenic pain in the first place. In other words, this zonal specificity is as much a symptom of that which renders the pain 'indefinite' (as Freud puts it earlier on) as it represents some attempt to overcome the very same 'indefiniteness'. Extreme zonality is ill-fated, of course, in just the same way that physical pain – however it may be delimited – is merely an 'accessory phenomenon' in relation to a much more complex illness that remains difficult to disentangle, precisely because it is by nature a form of *entanglement*, as the hysteric's relationship to both her father and her analyst amply proves. Equally, if one were tempted, as Freud is, to explain Fräulein von R.'s abasia by way of drawing a connection between her chronic loneliness and a fear of standing alone, or standing unaided upright, it should not be forgotten that, in Lacan's formulation, the perhaps inevitable loneliness of the hysteric is not the same thing as pure aloneness. As a hysteric, I appropriate the other's desires as my own, which aims to divest the other of any desire for me: if this means I will be lonely, it nevertheless also prevents me from ever being truly alone.

In the end, the pain in the right leg is not so different from the pain in the left, and cannot be so neatly compartmentalised. (Like the University, perhaps, the hysteric may have two left – or two right – feet.) For, in terms of this psychoanalytic conception of an hysteria that is based on the other's desire, it is important to note that Fräulein von R.'s hysterical reaction to her sister's death must be linked with the patient's own admission, after a severe episode of leg pain occurring while her sibling was still alive, that this was itself brought on because of the constantly painful 'contrast between her own loneliness and her sick sister's married happiness (which her brother-in-law's behaviour kept constantly in mind)' (151). As the case study proceeds, Freud becomes acutely aware that the leg pain occasioned by memory of the dead sister is indeed also a symptom of the guilt brought on by the analysand's desire for the widowed husband. From this point of view, the brother-in-law must line up alongside the father and Freud in the cast of male characters that take centre-stage in this case of hysteria. The frontier, in other words, turns out to be duplicitous: the zonality of the pain is breached by the double-movement that links desire and repression, revelation and concealment, truth and fiction – and in this sense the hysteric's discourse is marked by the structural ambiguity of *profession* as much as confession. (Indeed, in a way that reflects the non–self-identity of profession, Freud offsets his account of Fräulein von R.'s hysterogenic zones of bodily pain with a description of her repressed desire as a 'foreign body' within her (165), although of course not simply within her since the desire is unrequited, un-consummated or, as it were, not introjected as such.) If to grieve is also to desire – the mourning of the sister tells us as much – then the hysterical reaction to the other's desire when that other is a desperately ill father must be considered an extremely com-plicated thing. If Freud uncovers repressed guilty desire for her sister's widower as the origin of Fräulein von R.'s case of hysteria as a way to bring the analysis to a close, such closure is surely somewhat premature, and indeed highly peremptory on Freud's part (in other words, it may be as much a feature of the 'scene' of hysteria as its decisive overcoming).

In closing, let's recall once more that, as Timothy Bahti reminds us, leveraged movement such as walking depends on a certain situation of imbalance which, if it may be a little disorienting or destabilising, is nonetheless far from abnormal or unhealthy. Just as such leverage should not be limited to a situation of injury or ailment, as in Bahti's example, so stasis, as he also points out, is often not the ideal state. This is certainly true of Freud's hysteric, for whom movement is associated with pain only as the condition of a deeper or more complex malady that is itself not reducible to the sense of discomfort felt through movement. In other words, it is when his patient is still, at rest, bed-ridden that her illness is perhaps at its worst, no matter how much her physical pain abates.[11] And yet, equally, what ails Fräulein von R. is a series of unresolved psychic transactions or transitions – a psychic dynamic that is still in flux – for which the term leverage might still be appropriate, not least since, as *The Chambers Dictionary* tells us, to exert leverage is to impart pressure, to facilitate motion, to gain advantage or power 'over a resource greater than one actually owns' – whether this be one's father, one's family or one's analyst. To leverage against the other, or rather to receive leverage from the other, perhaps replicates the situation of desire in the case of the hysteric, who appropriates the other's desire, not least to gain just such an advantage where the other's arguably greater resources are concerned. If this is the condition of the University that, at least since Kant's time, walks on two undecidably left/right feet (or if it is the condition of profession at the double and duplicitous 'front' of the University itself), then perhaps we might do more than make a feeble joke about the Lacanian distinction between the discourse of the hysteric and that of the University. We would also do well to cultivate our own institutional politics by weighing them against both the advantages and the pitfalls of the hysteric's psychic strategies. In addition, if it is true to say that the repressed desire and divided subjectivity of the hysteric is received from an 'otherness' which calls forth the analysis that it also permeates or contaminates in some way, then such self-evaluation must to a certain degree assume the ironic conditions of its own possibility, conditions which always interrupt and disturb any 'strategy' we might care to imagine. In other words, just as the psychoanalytic discourse of the hysteric itself risks hysteria, something Lacan long ago taught us, equally our own discourse of the University, as much as that of the University itself, is bound to become hystericised to some extent. We might as well accept the fact, and do with it what we can. For David-Ménard, hysteria is produced by way of movements (difficult and resistant though such movements may be), and when speaking and thinking of the University, when acting within and outside the University, it is these movements we must negotiate with, in some way or other.

Notes

1 The original title of Derrida's lecture was 'The Future of the Profession; or, The University Without Condition (Thanks to the "Humanities", What Could *Take Place* Tomorrow)'. The lecture was subsequently published as 'The University Without Condition', in *Without Alibi*, ed., trans., and introduced by Peggy Kamuf (Stanford: Stanford University Press, 2001), pp. 202–37.

2 See Geoffrey Bennington, 'Frontiers of Literature and Philosophy', *Culture Machine* 2 (2000), http://www.culturemachine.net/index.php/cm/article/view/305/290.

3 See http://www.culturemachine.net/index.php/cm/issue/view/18.

4 See *Culture Machine* 1 (1999), http://www.culturemachine.net/index.php/cm/article/view/326/311

5 See Jacques Derrida, 'Mochlos', in *Logomachia: The Conflict of the Faculties*, ed. Richard Rand (Lincoln: University of Nebraska Press, 1992), pp. 1–34. Page references will be given in the body of the chapter.

6 Timothy Bahti, 'The Injured University', in *Logomachia: The Conflict of the Faculties*, pp. 57–76. Page references will be given in the body of the chapter.

7 Jacques Derrida, 'Restitutions of the Truth in Pointing [*pointure*]', in *The*

Truth in Painting, trans. Geoffrey Bennington and Ian McLeod (Chicago: University of Chicago Press, 1987), pp. 255–382.

8 See Simon Morgan Wortham, *Counter-Institutions: Jacques Derrida and the Question of the University* (New York: Fordham University Press, 2007).

9 Sigmund Freud and Josef Breuer, *Studies on Hysteria* (S.E. II) (London: Vintage, 2001), pp. 135–82. Page references will be given in the body of the chapter.

10 See Ned Lukacher, 'Foreword', in Monique David-Ménard, *Hysteria from Freud to Lacan: Body and Language in Psychoanalysis*, trans. Catherine Porter (Ithaca and London: Cornell University Press, 1989), p. xiv. Page references will be given in the body of the chapter. In fact, David-Ménard writes of the hysteric's pain that 'the body seems to be a pretext for language . . . the body is not so much the object of the hypochondriac's discourse as the territory or field in which that discourse operates', so that 'pain' is excessive 'information' that is not fully objectifiable or easily delimitable in given medical terms (18). Elsewhere, she speaks of Elisabeth von R.'s 'bodily positions' as part of an 'order of reality that makes the body a symbolic object, one that can never be defined solely by natural spatial coordinates' (40): precisely this question of its 'coordinates' may connect the hysteric's body to that of the Kantian University which walks on 'two feet', perhaps.

11 It is worth noting that on occasion Elisabeth von R. finds sitting intolerable, notably when retracing the paths along which she had once walked with her brother-in-law.

Part II Phobic Resistances

6

Detestable Residue: From Psychoanalysis to Blanchot and Lyotard

Freudian Phobophobia

Among some of his earliest remarks on phobia, found in a short paper on 'Obsessions and Phobias' from 1895,[1] we discover that Freud's attitude to Pascal's fear of abysses – which are themselves, tellingly, imposing psychic black-holes of a kind – is characterised by a paradoxical kind of resistance to the expression of phobic experience. Pascal, we are told, suffered from an intriguing illness: 'he always thought he saw an abyss on his left hand "after he had nearly been thrown into the Seine in his coach"' (74).[2] Knowing Freud as we do, one might have thought this example was a gift. One might have imagined that Freud would wish to dwell a good while on the salient features of such a case. One pictures the dizzying spatiality of a city very much still in the making, both as a site and as a concept (one might set such a Paris against the penchant for mathematical order or precision that characterised the Pascalian mind from an early age, tempered as it may have become – or strengthened, as Blanchot might have it – by less reassuring questions of probability and gambling); the thrilling yet daunting experience of speed, of movement, of accelerated time, sedimented nonetheless in recursive memory;

the constrictive interior of the carriage, sepulchral and claustro-phobic, reflecting perhaps Pascal's troubled sense of isolation; the deep, dark waters of the gigantic river and the rather weird impression of an abyss (one might refer here to Pascal's own studies of hydrodynamics and vacuums); Pascal's own litany of ailments, at once physical and emotional – all of these factors might seem grist to the Freudian mill. Indeed, since, for many, Freudian psychoanalysis allows us to think of agoraphobia – fear of place or situation – as a defining element in the making of the modern mind, confronting as it does the metropolis as a psychic terrain as much as a physical prospect, Pascal's case might even have been taken as somewhat inaugural. Freud was of course not given to overtly historicising psychological states as such, but nevertheless the case might have become a defining one in understanding the psychic conditions underlying the onset of a certain modernity. (In fact, Freud's own paper goes on to make several comments about agoraphobia, although this condition is hardly dignified in terms of the psychological attention it seems to warrant at this point. It is interesting, however, that he does ultimately locate the origin of phobia in enforced sexual abstinence, which is itself characterised as common to the experience of 'modern society', for women in particular.) But Pascal's phobia is quickly passed over as merely a hysterical reaction to trauma. Beyond this, it receives no direct analysis at all, and is ultimately reduced to a brief allusion in the opening paragraph (even if, for some readers, it may seem to linger over the entire essay, and perhaps beyond, not least since fear of the abyss – fear in want of an object, one might say – is effectively assigned a blank space in the analysis, perhaps uncannily echoing the symptom it downplays).

It is as if Freud comes across an apparent instance of what may be at stake in phobia (a word that he is prepared to elevate to a major term in the title of his paper), only to downplay its authenticity and perhaps its categorial validity as such. Phobias seem to spur his interest only to be set aside in favour of other psychic conditions of apparently greater importance. As if phobia is at best a faux-concept. For Freud, at this time, phobic response is largely 'monotonous' and 'typical' (80), no more than a predictable flight from traumatic experience (or, as he puts it in conclusion, a *'protective procedure* that seemed to relieve the fear' (82)). As such, phobia is deemed little else than a rather basic reaction to anxiety. (This is all the more interesting since to this day non-psychoanalytic treatments and therapies tend to proceed from this same assumption.) It is therefore to be regarded as a relatively minor psychic phenomenon, whereas obsession is richer in its emotional range, encompassing doubt, remorse and anger, thus proving itself capable of the deep relation of 'substitution' (rather than just repetitive anxiety) which phobia lacks (80). Indeed, even this distinction between the two 'is not of capital importance' (80), Freud writes, in the sense that, as he goes on to imply, phobia in its most common form is just a limited type of obsession in the first place. It may be little more than a preliminary condition, occurring prior to the onset of full-blown obsession in the same way that Pascal's complaint provides merely the (improper) pretext for the subsequent case studies of 'obsession proper' (82) that we find here.

This early theoretical confrontation with phobia is one that, if you read between the lines, hardly seems characterised by a confident certainty on Freud's part. For instance, Freud concludes with the assertion of a 'great difference' between obsessions and phobias, whereas previously he dismissively downplays the distinct identity of the latter (phobia) in regard to the former (obsession). Additionally, with a perhaps uncharacteristic capacity for crude assumption, Freud asserts that the phobic reaction is either simply 'an exaggerated fear of things that everyone detests or fears to some extent: such as night, solitude, death, illnesses, dangers in general, snakes, etc.'; or (an oddly opposed definition, this) it is a 'fear of special conditions that inspire no fear in the normal man; for example, agoraphobia and the other phobias of locomotion', of which Freud himself was known to have suffered, and with which he struggled, sometimes resorting to a form of denial that may not only have applied to his own personal situation but might even have affected his writings on the topic (80).[3] But who can say what 'everyone detests or fears to some extent'? (The vague gesturing towards death and snakes is almost laughable.) And who can isolate 'special conditions' of which it is safe to say that 'normal men' have absolutely no fear of them? The effort to produce clear distinctions (even those that oppose one another in seeking to define the very same concept or term) is so obviously problematic that it tends to overwrite the difference between the two types of phobia that Freud wants here to distinguish, in the process unravelling the very definition of phobia (in its various forms and in general) that he is attempting to offer. (Is phobia in the last analysis just a heightened version of what is 'common', or on the contrary is it 'special' in the sense that it may be characterised precisely by what falls outside of the norm? Who can say that what is deemed 'special' is not in fact much more common than one supposes, or indeed vice versa?) More to the point, perhaps, the normative assumptions that Freud brings to bear upon these alleged two types of phobia sound, in themselves, distinctly *un-Freudian*.[4] One almost suspects a flight from Freudianism in the early Freud, not dissimilar to the hysterical reaction to trauma that leaves Pascal with the rather weird and most disconcerting impression of an abyss, coming back time and time again. Pascal's case, in this sense, may be less the confidently excluded 'object', an isolated 'case' without much general interest, than a darkened – even abyssal – mirror in which Freud's own predicament might be dimly glimpsed. One might even wonder how Freud, should he have maintained focus on Pascal's phobia, would have allotted it in relation to the two types (the 'special' or the 'common')? Looking at its specific elements, is this particular phobia made up of 'common' fears – those concerning 'solitude' or 'death', for instance – or, on Freud's own terms, does it display 'special' characteristics – the fear of 'locomotion', say? How might one distinguish the fear of the abyss, into which one famously stares, in terms of obsession (which has the makings of a 'proper' psychoanalytic category) or phobia (which, it seems, does not), when the structure of the abyssal – if such a thing were indeed possible – implies here a sensing or vision of the insensible-invisible, a blank not-seeing of what is seen, which suggests as much the fixated yet un-self-knowing gaze of obsessionality as it does the tortured ambivalence of phobic sight, the inextricable attraction-repulsion of the phobic 'object' that causes the sufferer in a split-second to at once look and look away? To the extent that Pascal's phobia cannot itself be readily assigned a place in the schema developed by Freud, it threatens – like the coach veering off the road into the river – to violate its own boundaries, careering headlong towards an altogether murkier destiny. From such perspectives, it is far from easy to imagine what kind of protection might be reliably offered by the '*protective procedure* that seemed to relieve the fear' – Freud's own definition of phobia – that one may detect throughout this short text. In other words, phobia – too easily dismissed as merely a protective device – tends or threatens to return in a rather different and much less reassuring guise. Or, put another way, if Freud's reaction to phobia is itself, in a sense, phobic, the effects of this are at least double.

Phobia, then, is not merely trivialised or secondarised by Freud as an epiphenomenon of something else (in this case 'the recollection of an anxiety attack', or, rather, an 'anxiety neurosis' which is itself described as, in fact, having no 'psychical mechanism' or basis – and indeed no true origin in memory – arising simply through the build-up of sexual tension (81)). It is also perhaps *repeated* through its very denial. If phobia seems to produce something of a phobic reaction in Freud, one might even speak of Freud's *phobophobia*. As such, one wonders if phobia isn't from the very beginning – and even and especially through its repetition – scored through with the marks of its own (abyssal) enigma, its impossible doubleness or duplicity, or rather its impossibly divided and doubled possibility. Doesn't such a potentially phobic reaction to phobia on Freud's part involve a highly unstable, antagonistic relation that is far from simply external to phobia, constituting instead the mark of a certain resistance that is perhaps internal to phobia itself, part of its very structure or definition? Is Freud's phobophobia in the last analysis just another name for phobia itself?

Phobia of Little Hans

Despite – and perhaps because of – Freud's resistance to phobia, the story does not end there, of course. In 1909, more than a decade after the appearance of 'Obsessions and Phobias', Freud published his famous case study of phobia in a five-year-old boy, commonly known as 'Little Hans'.[5] The child – real name

Herbert – was the son of Max Graf, a music critic living in Vienna who met Freud in 1900 and went on to become actively involved in his circle during the first decade of the twentieth century. Freud treated Graf's wife during this period, and developed a close relationship with the family. Graf had shared with Freud a series of observations about the boy's childhood development, including speculations about his apparent concern with sexual matters, almost from early infancy. But in 1908, at a time when Freud's interest in children – and not just childhood memories – as a source of data for his theories was becoming more pronounced, Graf alerted him to a new turn of events in his son's psychological life. The tale is well known. During a walk in the park one morning, Hans suffers a striking phobic reaction on encountering a horse. Freud interprets this reaction in terms of fear of the father, which he construes as Oedipal. Underneath it all, Hans wishes for the demise of the father, the latter constituting a castrating threat to his desire for the mother. Freud discovers that Hans had previously witnessed a horse falling in the street, and this image – combined with a fear of the horse's biting teeth – offers the key to the Freudian interpretation of this case study, whereby the threat of castration and Oedipal desire are murderously projected like a psychic Molotov cocktail in terms of a death-wish aimed at the father. For Freud, Hans's terrible guilt at these secret desires, and the internal conflict they inspire, forms the origin of the phobia. (This complexity registers itself, for instance, in the fact that, as Freud notes, the falling horse represents not only the father's demise, but also the mother in childbirth.) More specifically, it is for Freud the blockage of the libido stemming from fear of castration that converts libidinous energy into (phobic) anxiety. This is perhaps his principal psychological insight in the 1909 'Little Hans' case study.

In 1926, however, Freud came to revise his interpretation of the case, although we should not be too quick to presume that the second interpretation merely trumps the first. (Again, just as in the time-lag between 1895 and 1909, one may wonder to what extent the problem of phobia gnawed away at him during the intervening years.) In 'Inhibitions, Symptoms, and Anxiety',[6] Freud suggests that anxiety is not simply a transformation of libido following repression, but a defence-mechanism of the ego when confronted by a threat. In other words, it is now Little Hans's ego, not his libido, which offers the key to unlocking the case's meaning. However, since the threat of the father still remains more or less irresolvably complex (albeit seen through the prism of the ego rather than the libido), the fear is projected elsewhere and through an inhibition is effectively contained and controlled, in the sense that avoidance of the phobic 'object' represents a practical response to the problem from which it itself emerges. In other words, the phobic 'object' here becomes less a fraught expression of the problem (an impossibly divided harbinger of danger, guilt, fear and repression) than the source of a (compromise) solution. Put bluntly, in the revised interpretation of 1926 the protective element of phobia is being rehabilitated, and given stronger psychoanalytic authority than in the rather dismissive account of phobic experience that occurs in 1895. If Freud's transition towards ego psychology was to have something of a fissuring effect, or after-effect, on the development of psychoanalysis (notably in terms of the split between Kleinian psychoanalysis and the work of Anna Freud), the changing fortunes of phobia in the 'Little Hans' case study may suggest what is at stake, here, for the father of psychoanalysis. For Freud, in 1926, it is perhaps a matter of becoming safer once more in phobia's vicinity – in other words, nothing more or less than another phobic reaction to phobia itself, one which may redouble as much as resolve the very problem of what we are calling Freud's 'phobophobia', turning its supposedly 'protective' dimension inside-out, as it were.

Such a suspicion is somewhat confirmed if one turns, for instance, to Gilles Deleuze's reading of Freud's 'Little Hans'. For Deleuze, what psychoanalysis wants is neither to uncover or release desire nor genuinely to understand its 'production', but merely to tame the beast – in a certain sense, a beast of psycho-analysis's own making, since psychoanalytic thought remains trapped within what Deleuze calls a 'personology', through which desiring can only be understood in terms of threat. In 'Four Propositions on Psychoanalysis',[7] Deleuze insists that psychoanalysis's very task is to intervene in and interrupt the revolutionary connectivity of desire. It thus 'reduces every con-nection and assemblage' (81). Paradoxically, perhaps, the principal means by which psychoanalysis blocks such desire and indeed restricts the formation of 'utterances' by which its production might be recognised is, according to Deleuze, by taking as its privileged object the *expressing subject* equipped with a proper name, a more or less self-identical 'I' extracted from the assem-blages that are productive of desire and turned instead into an isolable 'patient'. Such an 'I' as clinical subject is thereby located within a controlled framework of psychoanalytic relations and constructed in a predetermined way. Whereas schizo-analysis of the Deleuzian stripe wants to uncover the 'genuine production' (rather than the arche-origin) of desire, which it associates not with a subject *per se* but with multiplicitous 'machinic assem-blages', psychoanalysis is ultimately guilty of downplaying the array of forces that complexly traverse what we have come to call a subject, in favour of a reductive notion of the constitution of human relations that remains trapped within its own theoretical system. Even where psychoanalysis at the theoretical level seeks rigorously to depersonalise the family romance, Deleuze argues that its practice always returns us to a certain 'personology' over and above 'every assemblage of desire' (85). For Deleuze, this is certainly the case for Little Hans. Every utterance of this famous subject of Freud's case study is 'crushed and stifled', reduced to a passive and docile expression of 'a prefabricated and predetermined grid of interpretation', to borrow Deleuze's phrase from 'The Interpretation of Utterances' (89) – a bicolumnar piece in which, having worked collaboratively with Guattari and others, he presents a close reading of 'Little Hans' (supposedly unfettered by psychoanalytic prejudices) set against the strict Freudian interpretation. (Here, it must be said, Deleuze and company appear to focus much more on the original case study than on any aspects of its revised interpretation, even if the spectre of the latter is never far away.) While Little Hans in fact seeks a certain 'deterritorialization' (for instance, 'exploration of the street, each time in connection with a young girl' (98)), Freud misunderstands such desires in terms of 'the family-territory' (90), misattributing Hans's 'psychic' condition to the overwhelming presence of 'castration anxiety', 'Oedipus' and 'the family theme' (the mother, the father, the phallus) (95–6). Thus Hans is in effect violently 'reterritorialized' by psychoanalysis in terms of a family organisation (of its own making) which, far from opening onto machinic assemblages where relationality is more fully at play, imposes a fixed structure and a closed series of identities. And, needless to say, Hans's phobic 'object' – the horse – is denied the richness of 'intensive affects' and the singularity of its 'machinic assemblage' at just this moment of familial reterritorialisation. Psychoanalysis will not grant the horse its specificity either in relation to other animals, or for that matter in regard to other creatures of its own species, or indeed in terms of the kinetic particularity of the setting and series of events in which it appears or is produced. Put differently, psychoanalysis shows little interest in the horse's 'becoming' – or, for that matter, 'the becoming-horse of little Hans' (for Deleuze, Freud thereby *impossibly* anthropomorphises desire, turning it decisively away from the 'animal' or inhuman back towards the 'human' which is less its proper setting than the scene or symptom of a certain blockage). In other words, psychoanalysis forcefully reduces all the possible dynamism and unpredictability of the situation in question (that of Hans's encounter with the horse), in the interests of fixing the small boy, immobilising his desire along the frozen horizon of its manfully masterful gaze. As psychoanalysis reterritorialises the deterritorialising (desiring) impulse, then, Hans is ultimately turned away from the horse (the shock, affect, connectivity, desire of the 'outside') and back towards the family (the home, the father, the mother, the phallus), in a way that refuses to tackle what is perhaps most intensely significant – and perhaps most unsettling – about the confrontation, interaction or mutual 'becoming' of these two 'beings'. For Freud, the horse is merely a pretext for something else, the false or faux centre of the whole tale, one that, correctly understood, leads from the immediate 'case' in hand – the street-scene of phobic dread – back to the 'study', the safe home and hearth, of the psychoanalyst. And yet it is as if Hans's phobic reaction – his repulsed recoil from the object of otherwise dangerous fascination – is more properly that of psychoanalysis itself. Here, the second interpretation creeps back in, in the sense that psychoanalysis's security-measures look like the defence-mechanism of a threatened ego. But is it possible that the comforts of the drawing room do little more than offset, and yet also underscore, the phobic reaction to the out-of-doors from which psychoanalysis feigns to shy away? Is it as if Freud doesn't so much solve or domesticate Little Hans's phobia, as re-inhabit it 'otherwise', in a way that is both a safety-measure and yet, perhaps, far from safe at all? As if Deleuze's text ultimately points towards the following complexity: while the second interpretation of the case study might in fact be found lurking here behind the first, nevertheless through the return of a certain Freudian 'repression', the repressed original may return (and vice versa – the original 'text' of 1909 may not only return through the psychoanalytic mechanism of repression, but it may in fact condition that repression's repeatable possibility).

If, for Deleuze, psychoanalysis – far from aiming to uncover or liberate 'the essence of libido and sexuality' (98) – seeks to immobilise such an 'essence' by arresting every moment of de-territorialisation, endeavouring at each turn to quash both desire and its utterance, then we might add that the Freudian (double) encounter with 'Little Hans' might not take us in the direction of a certain resolution or arrestation of phobia; rather it seems to compound phobic experience itself, folding psychoanalytic inquiry back into the very same problematic it seeks to address. (How far phobia is symptomatic of impending danger and how far it is the harbinger of relative safety remains a question that is itself dangerously unresolved, as the two Freudian interpreta-tions of the case study intersect one another in a complexly non-linear manner.) In this sense, while Deleuze may be right to depict the psychoanalytic impulse as one of 'closing all exits' (98) – something that represents a certain solution to Little Hans's problem, if Freud's 'Inhibitions, Symptoms, and Anxiety' is to be believed – nevertheless the comparatively stable opposi-tion that Deleuze so forcefully sets up between Freudian fixity or closure, on the one hand, and desire's 'becoming', on the other, is somewhat opened and unsettled by the revisitation of phobia 'otherwise', or in its double sense, upon the supposedly safe interior of the psychoanalytic *chez moi*.[8] In fact, one might go so far as to say that Deleuze himself unwittingly (phobically?) reproduces rather static strictures (reflected by the columnar walls of his own text), to which (phobic) psychoanalysis cannot possibly conform – try as it might. Psychoanalysis may well wish not only for Little Hans's silence – the repression of his every utterance, the blockage of each deterritorialising instance of 'becoming' – but also, in a certain sense, for the suppression of its own fear or terror, its own pain, its own 'desire', its own 'becoming' (all of which it plays out through the projected other of its own 'case study'). But this 'phobia' on psychoanalysis's part is only partly protective, since what Deleuze unwittingly portrays – and perhaps re-performs – is perhaps nothing other than the double, unstable nature of Freudian phobophobia. To put this rather differently: Freud is far more phobic than Deleuze thinks, and this deficit in thinking may point to a certain phobic residue that characterises the Deleuzian relationship to psychoanalysis. Meanwhile, the phobia that would seem to close off, shut in, or shut down, turns out actually to destabilise, de-securitise, deterritorialise, to throw out-of-doors – from Hans, to Freud, to Deleuze, and no doubt beyond. All the way from his first flinching, his initial recoil in the presence of phobia, occurring in 1895, to his subsequent attempts to make phobia 'safe' in 1926, Freud displays unmistakable signs of phobophobia, phobia *of* phobia, and it is the intricate (non-linear) doubleness of this situation that would seem to confound every attempt – not just Freud's – to reckon up or reckon with the 'phobic' once and for all.[9]

Lacanian Little Hans

For Lacanians, the Little Hans case study is as much about the absence, lapse or failure of fatherly authority as it is about the recuperation of psychoanalytic power, although whether one is possible without the other – whether psychoanalysis can exist without the threatened demise and recuperation of the father operating in tandem – remains an open question. Hans is phobic because the father is lacking (not just the person of the father, but more properly speaking the function or structure of paternity).[10] Little Hans's horse phobia thus constitutes a way in which the paternal metaphor, as Lacan would put it, may be reestablished after a fashion. It shores up a decisive element of the (paternal) Other by offering a substitute for (in Lacanian terms) the Name-of-the-Father, and thus allows repression's return, blocking an excessively intimate correlation with the 'object' of desire (the mother) on the part of the subject (the child). Since, for Lacan, it is the paternal metaphor that functions to enable an explanatory principle for the child's existence, it must be reinvented somehow. (Noteworthy here is Freud's observation of a suggestive linkage between the 'because of' in Hans's exploratory discourse – 'wegen' in German – and the possible transfer or indeed harnessing of linguistic and semantic weight to 'wagen', the wagon or horse-and-cart; this harnessing being more originally an operation of language than a tethering of animal to vehicle. The 'wagen', in other words, substitutes so as to provide the 'wegen' that Hans is in need of.)

If the father cannot find a place in the mother's desire, for Hans that desire goes nameless, and this unfocused and so potentially all-consuming desire is the source of his anxiety, whereas it may become a possible source of enjoyment if the paternal barrier is re-established. The horse therefore takes on this role, endowed as it is with attributes that the child associates with a fatherly attitude, thus beginning the work of remaking the mother in the image of both conjugal procreation and paternal prohibition. This particular solution is a partial and temporary one, however, and not the only form of separation Hans will attempt over time (including imagining new family genealogies – his own family tree – by which the separation could be reproduced anew). Moreover, he seems destined never to arrive at a name for his mother's desire, and thus cannot confront it directly. He may well endure and indeed address her demand for him as 'object', not least by imagining substitute 'objects', but properly speaking he cannot appreciate her desire in terms that exceed this more narrow 'demand', or in other words in relation to a desire that is more complexly constituted than through the simple prism of his status as its solitary 'object'. The phobia hardly gets him beyond this, not least in the sense that, in the way that the Freudian narrative works, it does not equip him with the capacity to convert a sense of 'demand' into a fuller acknowledgement of 'desire', to switch his thinking from one register to the other. Here, then, phobia may give way only at the point a certain perversion sets in. Once again, phobia – even if it can't be avoided – is merely *on the way to* something else, and not necessarily something good, or something conclusive. Its appearance mixes reassurance with foreboding – precisely the complexly double phobic 'effect' that psychoanalysis, whether it means to or not, invites us to ponder, but of which it also perhaps inevitably partakes to some extent.

For Lacan, phobia – by shoring up the Other – prevents the onset of psychosis. It keeps psychosis at bay, albeit precariously, in the sense that its own resources are far from secure. In the wake of Lacanianism, psychosis itself may be thought of as accompanied by certain key characteristics. The psychotic quickly relinquishes doubt, and is capable only of forms of certainty. Equally the psychotic's discourse is largely devoid of metaphor or inventive figures of any kind, mortgaged as it is to a crude and hasty conception of the 'real'. Unlike the neurotic, the psychotic is less strongly drawn to conflict with authority figures (psychosis arising on condition of a lapse in the paternal function), but instead focuses hostility on rivals (we might say, those caught up in a nexus of 'demands'). The psychotic violently refuses symbolisation, so that psychotic foreclosure represents a catastrophic, near irreparable disturbance of the symbolic order, becoming quite different from the comparatively functional repressions that accompany neurosis. Rather like the discourse of the sadist as understood by Deleuze, psychotic language tends towards grinding repetition rather than illuminating explanation (albeit that phobia and perversion do not exist in the same relation to the Name-of-the-Father that must somehow be propped up). In particular, psychosis denies itself opportunities for self-questioning. It is given to delusions of grandeur, placing the psychotic centre-stage in a delusional world of his own making. If psychosis violently dispenses with doubt, the phobia which supposedly blocks psychotic experience is sufficiently double or duplicitous in nature, indelibly marked as it is by an internal resistance to itself, that its ultimate effectivity must remain highly doubtable. And yet, at the same time, its very doubleness may be what impedes the passage to psychotic certainty. Phobia, in other words, resists psychosis by means of its own resistance to itself, a resistance that at the same time threatens its power of resistance in relation to psychotic becoming. Phobia resists itself – it is *phobophobic* – so as to maintain or, rather, risk this double possibility. Whether or not such a conclusion is in itself entirely Lacanian, it is one I'd venture as a consequence of reading the 'text' of Little Hans as it traverses both the decades and authors in question here.

Pascal's Abyss

But what of Pascal's abyss? Are we to have done with it, as quickly and dismissively as Freud himself? Have we begun to understand anything about it? Do we yet appreciate why Pascal's experience of the abyss should have been reduced to that of a trivial phobia unworthy of genuine psychological interest, only for its inaugurating presence (presence-as-absence) to cast a persistent if oblique shadow over the psychoanalysis to come?

In a short text entitled 'Pascal's Hand',[11] Blanchot suggests that the *Pensées* are not just a sincere record or personal diary, offering empathetic insight into the author's religious and emotional life. The text does not serve simply to convey with tremulous immediacy the passion and pathos of the author, as is so often assumed, so much as it constitutes a deliberate and calculated gesture on Pascal's part. For Blanchot, the tormented impression of the *Pensées* is merely the effect of a meticulously planned demonstrative discourse, intended not so much to express anguish on the part of the writer as to revive or provoke it on the reader's behalf. Hence the *Pensées* arise not from a surfeit of fear. Instead, in a certain sense, they derive from its absence or lack. A stranger to torments, the intended reader languishes complacently in the lap of reason, satisfied with the 'worldly life'. Meanwhile, despite all appearances to the contrary, the author in fact shuns the 'anxiety' with which the text seems palpably to tremble, since for him the latter must surely constitute a form of 'impiety' or 'forgetfulness' of God (257). The *Pensées* seek to demonstrate that 'the claims of intelligence' or reason alone lead to 'false certainties' and therefore to what is actually 'absurd, incomprehensible, grotesque . . . terrifying, heavy with menace' (257). For the sake of their souls, Pascal therefore feigns passion in order to disturb the peace of others.

Yet if Pascal's text is not an exercise in terrified 'stammering' but a masterful instance of reflective discourse, a highly assured linguistic performance well in control of its own effects, the 'absolute distress' it inspires in others is as much the result of a certain 'nothingness' that thereby confronts them, as it is a product of the 'great resources' and 'logic' of the *Pensées* (258). Paradoxically, in other words, the text is richly equipped in terms of a range of philosophical and linguistic techniques capable of inducing a sense of just that 'nothingness' beyond reason or intelligence that ultimately could never support or sustain them. Pascal's 'lucidity' serves a 'bewilderment' that must remain totally alien to it, as a sort of 'abyss' that lies entirely beyond its reach. If Pascal's own phobia of abysses captures perfectly the sense of the phobic object as 'non-object' or object in want of an object, here the abyssal limit of philosophical and linguistic 'resources' does not merely paralyse the subject of Pascal's demonstrative discourse, but instead contrives anguish in order to invite salvation, albeit a salvation made possible by a devastating sense of 'emptiness', of vertiginous groundlessness, of a perhaps 'eternal silence' and 'infinite space', as Pascal himself writes. Nevertheless, if the pathetic tone of the *Pensées* is intended to communicate the 'authority' of 'fear' inspired by such groundless images of infinity or eternity, leading other 'selves' into desperate torments, this very same discourse – since it forms part of a rigorous strategy or 'formal argument' on behalf of an impersonal and perhaps unfeeling 'I', a self already beyond the hopes and fears that must awaken the self to itself – stems from an austere 'emptiness' whose profundity echoes that all-redeeming 'nothingness': a redoubling abyss of sorts. As seeming 'confession' thereby transmutates into 'an abstract instance of a completely general proof' (260), an implacable reason beyond reason takes hold: reason beyond the subject, one might say, or reason's impersonal 'soul'.

Freud may have been right to dismiss Pascal's so-called phobia of abysses since, on the basis of this reading, the abyss is less the phobic 'object' that saves the subject from want of the paternal function, forcing them to recoil from prohibited desires, than it is that (non-)phenomenon which in fact converts the subject into the wholly other-of-itself. Indeed, since the onset of the abyssal is only made possible on the strength of the always-already abyssal (the reader may be led towards the 'absolute distress' of 'nothingness' only because the 'I' or author-function of the text already resides in its abyssal condition), the very grounds of the subject seem to be put into question. The abyssal 'I' of Pascal is neither desiring nor lacking, neither wanting nor fearful, but radically impassive even beyond the machinic operations that seem to lead us to the threshold of 'nothingness' without ever being able to cross its borders. Constituted by or within a language that renounces itself in this very same act of constitution, such an 'I' – as 'soul' rather than 'subject' – is thus the 'impossible' of language, its 'silence' (262). Yet in this way, Blanchot argues, 'the language of the *Pensées*, to be true, must be a language overwhelmed by existence' (264). (Here, as in many places in his writing, Blanchot seems to be making his own distinctive, idiomatic intervention in debates concerning the existential and linguistic turns of the twentieth century.) But how exactly may 'existence' overwhelm 'language'? Isn't the demonstrative text of Pascal doomed to failure, or to its own limits as such, if all of the linguistic and philosophical techniques or 'resources' of the *Pensées* cannot guarantee passage to salvation? What might in fact take us over the threshold, if the 'nothingness' beyond is quite alien to those 'resources' that draw us towards it? Borrowing and adapting terms from Brice Parain, for Blanchot it is the 'poet' who 'stuffs' himself into the gaping hole, 'not to stop it up but to become a gap himself, sometimes to the point of actually disappearing, like Empedocles, in order to make this whole real, to realize this void' (264).[12] Ultimately, here, it is not language that is demonstrative (that of Pascal or the *Pensées*), it is existence itself. Yet such an existence overwhelms language and its limitations not simply by remaining beyond its grasp, but by opening a 'hole' in its very space, through a performative or demonstrative gesture – a leap or 'gap' – that happens not beyond all linguistic frontiers but precisely within the space or spatiality of those 'gaps' that mark the conditions of possibility of textuality itself (what Derrida might call the trace-structure of the text); or as Parain puts it, 'the gaping hole around words' (264). (Hence the allusion to Empedocles, whose death has inspired many a literary treatment: seemingly in pursuit of an immortality utterly beyond the embodied life, Empedocles hurled himself into an active volcano, although according to some versions of the legend the volcano spat out one of his sandals, casting some doubt on the 'poetic' thinking or philosophising for which he is remembered. In other words, Empedocles may well have profoundly communed with the void, but not without trace . . .) In this sense (that of 'the gaping hole around words'), existence doesn't just overwhelm language, but overwhelmingly 'becomes' language, as it were, in its very becoming. Language, then, is from this point of view as much 'abyssal' as it is the limit of the abyss. The abyss names those conditions of impossibility which project existence 'outside of its conditions' as its very condition of possibility, or which subject it to a 'trial' in which 'it discovers its truth' (265). Language, writing, is not barred from these conditions of impossibility, but might be just another name for the very 'form' they may take. Blanchot names this Pascal's 'joy', 'limited, moreover, to two hours of life, "from about ten-thirty in the evening to about twelve-thirty"' (265), during which time – the very time of writing – such 'joy' communes with 'absolute distress', so as to acquire its extreme or abyssal authority (266). Filling the void by deepening it, Pascal's writing 'does not stop giving value to the fictive deficiency of words by the reality of its deficiencies' (268) but, on the contrary, affirmatively re-marks such writing's gaps or gaping 'holes' from its own abyssal perspective (if one might call it that). For Blanchot, then, while it is a 'living Pascal who projects and arranges the work' – who marshals all of its techniques and resources in the interests of a certain demonstrative strategy or 'formal argument' – it is nonetheless 'a Pascal already dead who writes it'. It is only a radically empty, impersonal, impassive, impossibly pious Pascal, already beyond all hope, fear, want or desire, who is capable of writing as such – 'writing' in the sense that Blanchot wants to bestow on Pascal's text. (A writing that in the end overwhelms any simple sense of capacity or capability, that is of active 'living'.) Thus the *Pensées* are entombed: 'peace is peace only in the tomb . . . reconciliation can happen only in the abandonment of the tomb'. The always abyssal tomb, like Hegel's Holy Sepulchre, is 'hidden'. It registers an emptiness so profound as to mark the tomb's 'absence' beyond itself – 'this absence of the tomb that is the tomb' – in which salvation and death, solitary anguish and joyous communion with 'nothing-ness', vertiginously intermingle (268). One thinks of Pascal in the dark, sepulchral confines of his carriage hurtling towards the abyssal waters of the Seine:[13]

> This hand of Pascal that Valéry thinks he sees at work is so little visible, so distanced from the work, that it is dead; and what it traces is the sign of its own disappearance, the proof of its incognito, this absence by presence in which 'the strange secret' of God would also be revealed. And undoubtedly even this trace is too much. Detestable residue. (270)

Such a 'detestable residue', of which 'even this trace is too much', may indeed be that of the Pascalian abyss which proves just too much for a certain (phobic) Freud. If it is 'forever ir-reducible with regard to a truth that is without sign and without trace' nevertheless the 'fault' of such an abyssal 'disappearance' is indeed 'inscribed in language', and, correspondingly, 'to seek to surmount it, even in vain . . . alone justifies language'. Pascal is at once the most 'guilty' and the most 'justified' in this regard. Blanchot concludes that the experience of the impossible (whereby the abyss must be abyssally met) thereby echoes that of the true prophet who confronts the demand to decipher holy meaning: '"A book is given to someone who knows how to read, and he will say I cannot read"' (270). For Blanchot, we might say, such a 'reader' is closer to Pascal than to a certain Freud that we inherit in the wake of 'Obsessions and Phobias'.

Mutic Matter

In a short text first published in French in 1993, and subsequently collected in *Postmodern Fables* under the title 'Music, Mutic',[14]

Jean-François Lyotard argues that what is truly artful about works of art, including music and painting, cannot be reduced to an 'object' of cultural production, historical classification or academic knowledge. Neither is art simply the creation of an author as the engineer of artistic forms. Rather, art depends essentially upon a somewhat enigmatic 'gesture' that fundamentally exceeds both the 'content' and 'form' of the work. Such a gesture cannot be adequately registered within any history of art, since the latter ultimately restricts itself to knowledge of 'cultural products'. Lyotard suggests that affect constitutes the critical medium or condition of art's always singular gesture, and that this must be sought – however impossibly – in the 'emotive power' of art works, or, more complexly still, through art's paradoxical capacity to 'affect sensibility beyond what it can sense' (218). (One senses that for Lyotard historians of art continually flirt with the idea of artistic sensation as a characteristic element of their discourse and posture in the world, but never really take it seriously, which would entail – as it does for Lyotard – working through post-Kantian aesthetic philosophy in the most rigorous way possible.) Indeed, since the intricate and perhaps irrecuperable temporality of such affect cannot be assimilated within any chronological schema of time, 'art' is in essence bound to elude art history.

In music, therefore, 'art' must labour to affect sensibility beyond what may be readily sensed by generating audible traces of that which is constitutively inaudible as such – although, since it is the irremissible heart of *music*, such an inaudible origin is nevertheless is some sense '*already* a sound' (218). This, then, is art's paradoxical gesture: to translate the 'other' of itself (both less and more itself than itself) in a way that acknowledges the innate divisibility – the tension, but also the traction – of such otherness from the outset. Such an operation is never, and could never be, simply the 'doing' of a 'conscious subject'; it involves instead a radical passivity or inoperability on the artist's part that may allow art's gesture to somehow take hold. Or, put differently, art's appearance as such constitutes an event made possible only through an excess of the artist in him- or herself, its very possibility channelled through the artist only by way of a with–against movement taking profound hold of the artist's subjectivity (just as must happen with the audience, the listener or spectator). Even though the conditions for such a happening are no doubt elaborately developed each time of asking, nothing can prepare for this. Even at the height of its experience, no one may know definitively what this 'event' may be.

At this point in the discussion, mindful perhaps of the super-ficial affect so dear to art experts and consumers alike, Lyotard is keen to qualify 'what might seem to be an overly romantic way of raising the question' of art (219). Lyotard makes clear that his aim is not merely to celebrate some ineffable essence of art, through which the art work proper might be feted as a spectacu-lar incarnation of pure spirituality, but rather to trace out the problem (inherited in a certain way from a Kantian philosophy of aesthetic judgement) whereby art – if we are to consider there is any such thing – must distinguish itself from other cultural products susceptible to (and reproducible in terms of) deter-minate or objective knowledge. Put differently, in the wake of Kant, Lyotard is trying to think art's affect from a more rigor-ously philosophical standpoint. (Here, we should point out, it is not simply the case that philosophy may be wheeled in to resolve or even dignify the question of art beyond the purely poignant and affecting discourse of art lovers; rather, in the vicinity of art's 'gesture', the import or value of the 'philosophical' cannot be reliably confirmed as a self-identical 'given', since the 'event' of whatever art may be profoundly jeopardises whatever intactness we might want to accord the 'philosophical' as such, albeit opening anew the very possibility of philosophy.) Thus, Lyotard writes:

> The musical masterpiece cannot remain unknown to the ear. To open up a passageway for the sonorous gesture is necessarily to inscribe something of it in a language that speaks to the hearing, that affects auditory thought. The gesture may be an enigma, but its actualization within a human body sensitive to sounds does not signify the mystery of an incarnation. (219)

Since art's paradoxical gesture as a somewhat enigmatic source of affect cannot adequately be dealt with in terms of, say, the opus as 'finished object', it constitutes an unconcludable movement for which the musical motif is probably rather apt. In many ways the opus may come to us as an archive of sorts (this is unavoidable and not necessarily to be scorned), but the musical work takes fresh flight not as a static deposit or monument but rather in the sense that archival traces register or remark their significance only as singular inventions of the 'other' without simple end, or in other words in terms of the possibility of an 'event' that may happen beyond any horizon of expectation.

If the affecting sonority of music is made possible only on the strength of an essential quality that is to be deemed extra- or rather ultra-sonorous, one that cannot simply be 'composed' through technical mastery or form, Lyotard continues to worry that 'the implication seems suspect, a metaphysical proposition, and pretty hazy'. If such thinking risks acquiring 'poetic value' without philosophical 'credit', nonetheless the conceptual grounds or limits of philosophy may be tested at the threshold where its discourse meets with literature or musical 'language' (220–1). In other words, this thinking of art's gesture may not only provoke philosophical suspicion or scorn but forces philosophy to reconsider its position in relation to an 'enigma' with which it may or may not be equipped to deal. (Once again, we are in the midst of the problem of aesthetic judgement bequeathed to us by Kant.) It may even be that the 'worry' that this enigma causes philosophy may be better explained in terms of the very structure of the resistant 'object' (or non- or partial object) of what we are calling 'art', as through recourse to philosophy's own conceptual toolkit in the interests of objectival cognition on philosophical grounds of the matter in question. (Although this possibility may tell us more, rather than less, about philosophy than we might at first imagine.) Here, Lyotard turns to one of the *Petits Traités* by Pascal Quignard, titled 'Language', in order precisely to question the motives of the philosopher when confronted with art's enigma. For Lyotard, what we find here is not some discourse on the primordial origin of 'language' (whether that of literature or music), but a text which instead helps us attend to the 'characteristics proper to the element of sound' or even 'sound matter' (224). As should be clear by now, through his discourse on music Lyotard is obviously less interested in succumbing to a 'romantic' or 'metaphysical' excess easily spurned by philosophy, than he is in venturing to ask the question of sound's materiality – albeit linked to an enigmatic yet powerfully affecting gesturality not readily susceptible to conventional materialisms – in a way that perhaps provokes philosophy's movement into potentially new domains of thought. (Once again, music is perhaps a very apt choice when trying to think the *matter* of art, as it were, in a way that intricately negotiates a pathway between metaphysical haziness, on the one hand, and crude materialism, on the other. That said, near the end of the essay Lyotard insists that 'matter is not heard, it is the sorrow of being affected' (230), so that from this point of view music's materiality, such as it is, has less to do with sound as such than with affect itself, which intensifies at the limits of what may simply be audible in music, or in other words through what may be 'lost' in music.)

On the strength of his reading of Quignard, Lyotard suggests that the very 'element of sound' – the basis of languages of all kinds – is the inspiration of a sublime terror. This might itself be inaudible as such, but it is not mute. It may still somehow speak to us. Or else, if the 'element of sound' is mute, this would only be in terms of 'the old root *mu-*, *mut*' (225). In its very element, then, sound is perhaps *mutic*. This means several things, possibly. It means it lacks defensive parts, such as claws or teeth. It is toothless. It is, in other words, blunt, which may also mean it lacks pointedness, or a point. If Blanchot writes of Pascal's text as a highly orchestrated and strongly motivated venture in demonstrative discourse which nevertheless ultimately gives itself over to an abyssal 'other' of itself – risking a salvation made possible only by a devastating sense of 'emptiness', of vertiginous groundlessness, of a perhaps 'eternal silence' and 'infinite space' that in a very complex sense overwhelms the existence of the subject – here Lyotard evokes music as mutic in a similar sense. In Blanchot's essay on Pascal, we might recall, redeemed existence doesn't just overwhelm or supersede language, but overwhelmingly 'becomes' or inhabits language, through and through, in its very becoming. This, indeed, is precisely how existence becomes overwhelming. Language, then, is from this perspective as much 'abyssal' as it is the limit of the abyss. Blanchot thus names writing Pascal's 'joy' – at once passionately creative and passive-impassive, both a source of renewed life and the upshot or outcome of a certain death. To be worthy of its vocation, artistic form must give way to the 'other' of itself – an 'other', in Lyotard's terms, it 'awaits' and indeed 'violently wishes for' but cannot truly foresee (219) – and yet this 'other' does not simply transcend or dispense with the artistic medium that makes possible its translation or appearance in some way, but instead constitutively transforms, inhabits, engulfs it *otherwise*. If, when we follow Pascal's hand in its most singular sense, we trace nothing but the 'detestable residue' of its own disappearance, this strange left-over matter may not be far removed from the (sublime) 'sound matter' that Lyotard calls upon us to think.

Abyssally enigmatic and yet materially inscribed or endowed somehow (thus not reducible to full conceptual objectivisation or empirical objectification), in haste we might thereby characterise the art work as a faux or partial 'object', one of fear or detestation as much as fascination, a phobic object perhaps. And yet we saw how Blanchot's treatment of the Pascalian abyss may, ironically, explain its inassimilability in relation to the psychoanalytic field. For, here, the abyss is not so much linked to a phobic 'object' that recuperates a subject in want of the paternal function, than it is that which – however enigmatically – transforms the subject into the wholly other-of-itself. Indeed, because the advent of the abyssal is in fact potentialised by nothing less than the always-already abyssal – i.e., the reader may be brought to a state of 'absolute distress' and 'nothingness' only since the 'I' of the text already dwells in its abyssal condition – the very grounds of the subject seem to be put into profound question. Once more, a comparison with Lyotard's mutic music suggests itself: the mutic overwhelms music not in the sense of its violent displacement or transcendence, but as an overwhelming condition of possibility. Tellingly, then, Lyotard writes:

> Such is, in summary, what Pascal Quignard imagines in the form of a 'language beneath languages' and which I hijack in the name of a mutic beneath music. It is not said that music *would express* or *translate* a phobia among the living for whatever evokes their death. The terms of expression and translation are inappropriate. (226)

It may seem that music – like language or writing (Pascal's or any other) – may present us with a phobic (faux or phoney) object, one that both conveys and suppresses profound distress, only ever bringing to life (albeit in substitute form) the terrifying prospect of destruction or oblivion. And yet comparison with Blanchot's commentary on Pascal helps explain why 'Music, Mutic' is not readily susceptible to a phobic logic, which is of course also one of *expression* or *translation* (to borrow Lyotard's own words). Ultimately, these terms are inappropriate to either Blanchot's 'detestable residue' or the 'mutic' matter of Lyotard, not only in the sense that such writers want to think about exposure to rather than defence or recoil from what is seemingly abyssal, but to the extent that the abyssal in their case is as much brought out (however enigmatically) in all its transformative power as it is covered over and converted by the work of what might otherwise be called 'translation'. The very mode or manner of mutic music or Pascalian writing may have to do with fearful inspiration, but is not phobic as such.

This non-phobic 'relation', if it may be called that, between 'art' and 'work' can be further glimpsed in Lyotard's subsequent remarks, complex as they are, concerning music and the mutic. The 'lamentation' that inspires art 'breathes forth' yet without 'striking a blow', 'it does not echo like a vibration that has just struck an obstacle'. In other words, it is not in search or want of an object (whether desirable or prohibitory), it seems to elude or obviate the objectival quandary of psychoanalysis in its various forms. Unlike the horse that inspires phobic fear on the part of Little Hans, it is toothless, with no possible bite. It does not seem to *go after* anything, or any thing, to threaten or attack *as such*; nor has it any defences to speak of. It thus seems to be outside the phobic 'game'. Toothless (and also without 'vocal chords' or 'phonatory cavity'), its 'lack of articulation' is also a lack of pointedness or point. It does not 'echo', 'resound' or 'percuss' since it seems not to strike at a resistant object. It asks 'nothing' (230). It is merely 'an empty wind' that blows through (226–7).

Yet this 'breath' of affect, whether it becomes a sharp intake or not, 'never stops passing through all the obstacles that engender the audible', perhaps passing through them precisely as if they were not obstacles (and thus eschewing the audible in one sense) in order to engender the audible otherwise, by dint of a by-passing movement that at once 'passes and does not pass', that passes through in the interests of another 'sound', or that attends to the matter of sound's affect in a way that is not re-stricted to notions of resistance construed musicologically in the customary terms of percussivity or vibration. If what 'puts you out of breath' is the 'precariousness' of 'passibility', of passing/ not passing – a 'master shakes your hand, and grabs you, let's you go, and holds you back' – the accompanying 'disconcert-ing rhythm' that here might recall (phobic) resistance is, still, overwhelmed by 'the breath of nothing' itself, 'naked affection', which can only ever be modalised, organised or 'shaped' after the fact (phobically, one might say), but which, still, constitu-tively animates or inspires – whether pleasurably or painfully

– through sheer affective power. Affection may be termed 'distress' since for Lyotard it entails a (passing) movement which is also 'immobile' or, at any rate, that cannot 'pass', in the sense that it is without direction, point or 'object' – thus constituting a form of passing/not passing that is not easily reducible to the play of phobic resistance that is always, precisely, in want of an object. However, since as Lyotard reminds us from the beginning we are dealing with matters that are essentially paradoxical, what this 'breath of nothing' comes to inspire is, still, 'audible sound', that which promises 'something rather than nothing', if only 'other sounds'. For Lyotard, the sublime inspires a terror roughly akin to the possibility of nothing rather than something happening, yet also gives us the question of 'is it happening?' which itself tasks philosophy with something new each time of asking. (This is a theme he dwells upon at greater length in his essay, 'The Sublime and the Avant-Garde'.) And yet if it provokes such a question to 'philosophy' as its purported addressee, nonetheless this 'terror' is, more fundamentally, 'continuous, inarticulated, addressed to no one' (228). It cannot be reduced to audibility as such, whether of language, the 'question' or any other articulation. Music struggles to set the mutic into 'phrases', each of which announces most of all another. Such phrases, in Lyotard's own terms, are less normative than they are prescriptive: while a normative phrase tends to control its own performativity in advance, formulating or effectuating by itself the legitimation of those obligations or effects that it demands, a prescriptive phrase always entails a further phrase that is more fundamentally left to another. Thus music surely betrays the 'inaudible' by giving it 'form', but doesn't so much close around it as offer it an opening, the 'honour' of a further phrase, always: 'The honor so rendered is sufficient to prevent the beast from floundering in fright and from being suffocated by the scent of sound' (229). Music thus finds a way to echo itself 'in nothingness' – perhaps beyond the percussive or vibrational possibilities of a resistant object – in that its echo is not just self-enclosing but instead, phrase by phrase, radically exposed to 'the future of what is'. A community – and not just a musical one – may be founded on the promise music thereby offers, but this far from eradicates or effaces the inspiring, affecting power of the mutic. Instead, the whole *matter* of the mutic and music – its strange material impression beyond any vulgar conception of materiality – comes down to 'the nothing which *estranges* the affected body and breathes the terror of being abandoned into it' (231). Since music cannot much outlast such estranging affection, its promise cannot ever break free of what it must always still inherit. That, indeed, is its promise, of sorts.

If affective estrangement occurs because the body is 'passible' or is composed of open 'doors', its very sensation is, at bottom, of the 'nothing' of affection: 'What enters through the blazon of the body, sensations, *aesthesis*, is not just the form of an object, it's the anguish of being full of holes' (231). It's because of the holes, not because of an 'object', that affectivity comes to *matter*. Mattering comes down to 'the various ways, all contingent, the body has of being threatened by nullity' (232). Mutic, toothless, art's gesture is not to threaten and yet we are of course deeply threatened by the absence of such threat (which we expect, want, hope for, dream of, dread, phobically or otherwise). Threat of nothing, not threat of threat but threat of no threat. Thus, while for Lyotard music does not simply 'express' or 'translate' a phobia or succumb to a logic of the phobic, still paradoxically enough: 'Aesthetics is phobic' (232). It risks organising itself phobically. In terms of the creation as much as the reception of works of art, fear in want of an object may always return, and is probably ineliminable in the course of aesthetic practice. For instance, to 'paint *for* not seeing', as Derrida teaches us one must, may involve the production of 'phrases', as Lyotard puts it, that are 'equivalent to a remission from pain', remission of just the kind that the phobic sufferer in one sense aspires to. Thus, artistic practice 'forgets the terror, which nonetheless motivates it' (232). But this is not the whole story of art's gesture, which as we have seen is at any rate far from reducible to a 'phobic' aesthetics. The very 'element' or 'matter' of art – the 'nothingness' of affect – overwhelms the logic and strategy of phobic resistance, even as it invites phobic practices or phobic activity.

Pulling Teeth

In a section inserted into the text more than a decade after its original publication, Freud devotes a passage of the sixth chapter of *The Interpretation of Dreams*[15] to a comparatively lengthy commentary on dreams 'with a dental stimulus', notably dreams about losing teeth or having them pulled. Freud's discussion is prefaced by the observation that such 'typical dreams' may be divided into two types: 'those which really always have the same meaning, and those which, in spite of having the same or a similar content, must nevertheless be interpreted in the greatest variety of ways' (385). Given Freud's declared distaste, in the previous chapter, for 'dream books' that offer simple and reductive explanations of the meaning of typical dreams, such a distinction perhaps provokes the desire for further explanation or clarification. Be that as it may, Freud leaves it relatively unclear how dreams 'with a dental stimulus' might themselves be classed. This is instructive in itself, since throughout *The Interpretation of Dreams* we are offered comparatively decisive accounts of the significance of apparently ondontophobic dreaming which nonetheless differ in important ways. For instance, several passages earlier, Freud writes that the dream of teeth falling out, alongside those about hair-cutting, baldness and decapitation, might be interpreted in terms of castration (357).[16] Like the horse's teeth in the Little Hans case study, biting teeth that may be lost, or that may fall (out), provide a clue that we are closely in the vicinity of a certain Oedipality at work. However, elsewhere in the text (as in the passage inserted in 1911, to which we will now turn), such dreams are associated with 'the masturbatory desires of the pubertal period' from which they are seen to derive (385). To support this interpretation, Freud resorts to the colloquial German phrase for masturbation – 'pulling one out' or 'pulling one down' (in English, the closest parallel is perhaps 'knocking one out') – which suggests an obvious affinity with the image or idea of teeth-pulling. While a phallic dimension seems to persist in both interpretations, in the first – the 'castration' explanation – the classical interplay of prohibition and desire would seem to be at the root of object-formation, albeit the phobic dimension of the dream would suggest that the paternal function or metaphor is still insufficiently strong and the dream itself may be working to re-establish its prohibitory terms (i.e., to restore the positive possibility of 'object' and 'subject' alike). In the second, meanwhile – the 'masturbation' explanation, which Freud derives from the analysis of several dreams, including one he is told of by Otto Rank – we are informed that a nocturnal emission arising from such dreaming in fact occurs in a purely 'auto-erotic' way: that is, it is 'not, as it usually is, directed to an object, even if only an imaginary one, but had no object, if one may say so' (392). The first interpretation, in other words, suggests a subject in (phobic) want of an object, while the second – just as firmly asserted – seems to present us with the image and idea of a subject capable of dispensing altogether with the object, auto-erotically as it were (which might in turn suggest a troubling and questionable connection between masturbation – which in this form is linked to a 'trace of homosexuality' (392) – and the potential onset of psychosis). Whether or not such a possibility is entirely convincing, it is telling that Freud offers two inter-pretations which are presented with equal force,[17] as if dreams with a 'dental stimulus' flout the very distinction by which they might be classified (are such dreams stable or variable in their meaning?), or as if their point is pointedly blunted at the very point such classification tries to take hold. Mutic, without sharp point, without convincing defence or defences as they contend with their own double interpretation, dreams of tooth-pulling or of toothlessness therefore complicate the phobic explana-tion towards which they nevertheless seem to gravitate in their complex relation to the 'object' (whether 'objectless' or in want of an 'object', or undecidably both/either). In other words, dreams of tooth-pulling become, themselves, toothless, without (equine) bite. One might think the whole passage should have been pulled like a bad tooth, unless of course the somewhat blunted object or objective of these inserted paragraphs comes down to a case of a highly indulgent, near masturbatory gesture on Freud's part, especially given that one of the dreams he cites is that of a colleague of Otto Rank, who himself struggles to interpret it by referring heavily to Freud's own discussion of dreams about teeth in the earlier version of *The Interpretation of Dreams*. Thus the declared 'object' here (namely, a further contribution to the analysis of dreams with a 'dental stimulus') may turn out to be a non- or pseudo-object, having as much to do with self-loving self-congratulation on Freud's part (inserting references in his own book to that very same book) as it has to do with the pointed explanation of dental dreams. Whether a pseudo-object that suggests, once more, Freud's phobophobia, or a mutic matter that troubles phobic analysis, the onset of toothlessness causes Freud's text to drift back towards the contested field of interpretation that we have been seeking to track throughout this chapter.

Notes

1 Sigmund Freud, 'Obsessions and Phobias: Their Psychical Mechanism and Their Aetiology', in *The Standard Edition of the Complete Psychological Works of Sigmund Freud*, Vol. III, ed. and trans. James Strachey (London: The Hogarth Press and the Institute of Psycho-Analysis, 1962). Page references will be given in the body of the chapter.

2 Anthony Vidler, in *Warped Space: Art, Architecture, and Anxiety in Modern Culture* (Cambridge, MA: MIT Press, 2001), has an interesting reading of this Pascalian 'myth' and its afterlife in the cultural imaginary of the eighteenth and nineteenth centuries, especially in France, and notably in terms of the fortunes of what might be termed abyssal thought. Vidler pays particular attention to this 'myth' in the context of both the rise of medical pathology and the architectural imaginary of the period in question. See especially pp. 17–24.

3 This is noted on several occasions in Vidler's *Warped Space*: such phobia (notably agoraphobia) may be projected and displaced in Freud's own work, for instance in the way it is treated in the Little Hans case study.

4 Melanie Klein, for instance, writes that by 1909, in his famous analysis of childhood phobic reaction, Freud 'thinks that Little Hans's phobia differs from extraordinarily frequent phobias of other children only in that it was noticed', in fact providing the boy with some degree of advantage in dealing with psychic repression. Here, then, Freud blurs the distinction between the phobic and the non-phobic not merely by asserting universal fears. Rather, he moves beyond the terms of a simple choice between

phobia as either exceptional or common to all, as set out in 1895, locating its specificity instead in the particular combination of 'disposition' and 'experience' (as Freud himself puts it) that defines Little Hans's case. (Of course, as we shall see, the subsequent reception of Freud's case study, including that of Deleuze, contains criticism of the reductive interpretation of phobia in terms of castration.) See Melanie Klein, *Contributions of Psycho-Analysis 1921–1945* (London: The Hogarth Press and the Institute of Psycho-analysis, 1948), p. 66.

5 Sigmund Freud, 'Analysis of a Phobia in a Five-Year-Old Boy', in *The Standard Edition of the Complete Psychological Works of Sigmund Freud*, Vol. X, ed. and trans. James Strachey (London: Vintage Books, 2001), pp. 77–178.

6 Sigmund Freud, 'Inhibitions, Symptoms, and Anxiety', in *The Standard Edition of the Complete Psychological Works of Sigmund Freud*, Vol. XX, ed. and trans. James Strachey (London: Vintage Books, 2001), pp. 1–149.

7 This essay, and 'The Interpretation of Utterances' to which I subsequently refer, may be found in Gilles Deleuze, *Two Regimes of Madness: Texts and Interviews 1975–1995*, ed. David Lapoujade, trans. Ames Hodge and Mike Taormina (New York and Los Angeles: Semiotext(e), 2007), pp. 79–88 and pp. 88–112 respectively. Page references will be given in the body of the chapter.

8 In his essay 'Reading and Writing – *chez* Derrida', Samuel Weber offers a fine analysis of the linguistic and etymological resources of *chez*, demonstrating in the process (if we may borrow Deleuze's language) that as a product of a certain assemblage which remains far from closed, the word deterritorialises itself at every turn: *chez* does not so much lead back home (to itself), but instead constantly risks casting us (and itself) out-of-doors. See Samuel Weber, 'Reading and Writing – *chez* Derrida', in the expanded edition of his book *Institution and Interpretation* (Stanford: Stanford University Press, 2001), pp. 85–101.

9 As a note to this section, it is worth recalling that Anna Freud takes the Little Hans case study as the occasion to dispute some aspects of her father's reading of child psychology, noting that in the context of paternal rivalry some male children develop not a defensive phobic reaction but forms of fantasy through which the question of the father is tackled without recourse to neurosis. See Anna Freud, *The Ego and the Mechanisms of Defence* (London: The Hogarth Press and the Institute of Psycho-Analysis, 1966), Chapter VI: 'Denial in Phantasy', pp. 73–88.

10 See especially Jacques Lacan, *Le Séminaire. Livre IV. La relation d'objet*,

1956–57, ed. Jacques-Alain Miller (Paris: Seuil, 1991), as yet untranslated into English.

11 Maurice Blanchot, 'Pascal's Hand', in *The Work of Fire*, trans. Charlotte Mandell (Stanford: Stanford University Press, 1995), pp. 256–70. Page references will be given in the body of the chapter.

12 It may be interesting to note, here, that in Paul Carter's *Repressed Spaces: The Poetics of Agoraphobia* (London: Reaktion, 2002), which I discuss in Chapter 8 of this book, mention is made of Mettius Curtius, 'the self-sacrificing youth who, in 362 BC, threw himself into an abyss that had opened up in the Roman Forum, thus satisfying the soothsayers' declaration that the hole could only be filled up by "throwing into it Rome's greatest treasure"'. Carter cites this tale because 'if the agora was a coming together born of a violent spreading apart' – an idea I myself try to develop – 'then it's reasonable to expect evidences of that original violence to survive *within* the agora/forum' (137). As such, the proximity of these two tales from antiquity may provide a way to connect the question of the abyssal in Blanchot to what might be termed the originary crisis of the agora discussed in Chapter 8 of the present book.

13 In his essay 'Tragic Thought' (in *The Infinite Conversation*, trans. Susan Hanson (Minneapolis: University of Minnesota Press, 1997), pp. 96–105), Blanchot suggests that Pascal's 'literary' reputation stems from his capacity to practise and authorise 'diversion', which has perhaps bequeathed to 'the literary art of the future one of its privileged categories' (97) – not least, we might assume, in the wake of modernism. Pascal veers, so it would seem, like the carriage towards the Seine. If one might presume that Pascal would write in order simply to condemn diversion of the type that characterises 'inauthentic existence', as Blanchot puts it ('senseless . . . half awake, half deceitful'), which causes life to merely 'slip away', nevertheless Blanchot observes that Pascal resists this temptation 'because he knows that the thought explaining and judging this movement already belongs to the vicissitudes of a diverted life'. In other words, 'knowledge of diversion' is, as it were, already 'the very essence of diversion'. This thinking seems to be the corollary of what Blanchot sees as Pascal's somewhat feigned passion in the *Pensées*. It is as if, in order to earn the right to analyse or critique, one must first not only have participated in the phenomenon in question, but have gone beyond demonstrable participation, practising a subtler (though far from unconnected) art which seems to hide the 'essence' from 'knowledge' while at the same time enduring its trials without the reassuring compensations of 'knowledge'. This, in turn, converts writing

from analysis, critique or even pedagogy into something else. For, if it is to avoid the worst possible 'ruin', diversion can no more be 'known' than 'nothingness'. This might be another way of saying that you can never know where diversion will take you – as Pascal's close shave with the abyssal waters of the Seine amply demonstrates. In 'Tragic Thought', indeed, reflection on 'diversion' leads to the ambiguity of appearing and disappearing, presence and absence, and to a certain confusion of surface and depth, clarity and obscurity, this-worldliness and other-worldliness (detachment or refusal of the world in which one must nevertheless learn to live), which recalls many of the themes found in 'Pascal's Hand'.

14 See Lyotard's *Postmodern Fables*, trans. Georges Van den Abbeele (Minneapolis: University of Minnesota Press, 1999), pp. 217–34. Page references will be given in the body of the chapter.

15 See Freud's *The Interpretation of Dreams*, in *The Standard Edition of the Complete Psychological Works of Sigmund Freud*, Vol. VII, ed. and trans. James Strachey (London: Vintage, 2001). Page references will be given in the body of the chapter.

16 It is interesting that this explanation is considered to arise on condition of the interpretation of dreams in terms of their symbolism, to which Freud devotes several critical passages. In the fifth chapter of *The Interpretation of Dreams*, for instance, he offers a critical response to Scherner's theory whereby dreams give 'a *symbolic* representation of the nature of the organ from which the stimulus arises and of the nature of the stimulus itself', leading to a kind of 'dream-book' serving as a guide to the interpretation of dreams 'which makes it possible to deduce from the dream-images inferences as to the somatic feelings, the state of the organs and the character of the stimuli concerned' (225). Here, dreams with a dental stimulus occur in terms of a symbolic representation of the body as a house: 'an entrance-hall with a high, vaulted roof corresponds with the oral cavity and a stair-case to the descent from the throat to the oesophagus' (225). Freud goes so far as to suggest that the revival of dream-interpretation by means of symbolism represents mere regression to antiquity, wholly lacking in scientific validity or technique. Indeed, it is his persistent interest in dreams about teeth and teeth-pulling that urges Freud 'to find an explanation of another kind for the supposed symbolization of what is alleged to be a dental stimulus' (227). Nonetheless, at other moments he is prepared to endorse certain symbolic interpretations of particular dreams, compounding the confusion that, I am arguing, somewhat blunts the point of the distinctions and classifications Freud wishes to offer more generally.

17 Or, equal provisionality, given that Freud's reservations about symbolic interpretations of dreams – the context in which his evocation of the 'castration' explanation arises – might be seen to be matched by his statement, when discussing the 'masturbatory' interpretation, that the latter is not yet 'entirely cleared up' (387) but that 'I have given what explanation I can and must leave what remains unresolved' (388). Indeed, Freud suggests that dreams 'with a dental stimulus' are perhaps especially resistant to interpretation since, unlike other body parts which allow an obvious displacement upwards from the lower bodily region of the genitals (the nose representing the penis, the facial and labial lips, etc.), the 'structure' of the teeth 'affords no possibility of an analogy' in such a direct way, although in another sense this also makes them the ideal representational tools of sexual repression. Such a double resistance places teeth, perhaps, in an interesting relationship to phobia, which we have characterised in terms of its own resistance to itself.

7

Something (or Nothing) to be Scared of: Meillassoux, Klein, Kristeva

Quentin Meillassoux: Correlationism Against Itself

For Quentin Meillassoux, philosophical thought since Kant has been defined by a principle of correlation between thinking and being, whereby neither may be contemplated outside of the other.[1] In seeking a departure from pre-critical dogmatism, such philosophy disputes the idea of a world 'in itself', a 'world' that might be available in any way other than 'for us'. Thus, post-critical thought remains trapped in a correlationist circle in which objects emerge only as a function of their subjective representation, and in which subjects are only ever constituted as an effect of their object-relations. Since all that is thinkable – all that remains to think – is the correlation itself, no chance is left to access what Meillassoux calls the Great Outdoors (that which exists in an uncorrelated relation to my thought). Instead, philosophy is trapped in a situation in which, since consciousness is always consciousness of *something*, or some *thing*, it seems beckoned by an 'outside' that can never be experienced in terms of full or proper exteriority, but which arises instead as an expression of a certain interiority of thought, albeit an interiority which can never be reconciled with itself to the extent that it dreams relentlessly of an 'outside' that it is bound never to reach. Thus, the 'world' as merely correlate of our own existence impoverishes thinking in the sense that it signals not just philosophy's sophistication or advancement, but the catastrophic loss of philosophic possibility beyond correlationist repetition.[2]

For Meillassoux, however, the formulation by contemporary science of 'ancestral statements' – that is, statements about material realities that predate human existence and are thus prior to any human relationship to the world, or in other words events and phenomena that were not manifest to *anyone* – serves to challenge the correlationist paradigm in the most provocative of ways. The correlationist may well argue that the truth-value of such statements depends as much upon present-day experimentation, and thus retroactive evaluation, as upon direct reference to an ancestral past. But for Meillassoux to impose upon scientific knowledge such a human 'correlate' amounts to denying science its very *sense*. As he puts it, scientific enquiry does not exist simply to refine its own methodological conditions *ad infinitum*, but principally seeks to improve the reliability of its experiments 'with a view to external referents' without which such experiments would be, effectively, senseless or meaningless (17). Thus the ancestral statement must always, in the end, be oriented towards a literal or realist sense, or otherwise for Meillassoux it tends towards non-sense. 'There is no possible compromise between the correlation and the arche-fossil: once one has acknowledged one, one has thereby disqualified the other', he writes (17). Correlationism does not simply moderate or qualify scientific ambition, or provide an alternate testing-ground for its findings. For Meillassoux, if left unchecked its ultimate effect would be to reduce science to mere illusion.

(Meillassoux goes so far as to compare the correlationist impulse with the licence taken by creationists.)

The provocation offered by the arche-fossil therefore concerns the question of the origins of 'givenness' in the world, or in other words how to conceive of the passage from non-givenness to givenness, from the non-being to the being of the 'given'. Thus, 'the problem of the arche-fossil is not the empirical problem of the birth of living organisms, but the ontological problem of the coming into being of givenness as such' (21) – a problem that simply cannot be thought from the vantage-point of the correlationist 'circle'. The event of such a passage is, henceforth, the very problem of properly scientific thought today: 'To think science is to think the status of a becoming which cannot be correlational because the correlate is in it, rather than it being the correlate' (22). The onset of givenness cannot be explained from 'within' correlationism, since it constitutes the very conditions of possibility for correlationism's taking-place. Thereby, science – or more properly mathematics – is alone capable of confronting the enigma of how to 'manifest being's anteriority to manifestation' (26). Although the question of the legitimacy of science's ancestral statements would seem, at first glance, to be a transcendental one, it can proceed only on the strength of relinquishing the transcendentalism bequeathed to us in the post-Kantian era. The challenge of ancestrality must therefore be faced through rejecting both 'naive realism' (which merely dismisses the correlationist mind-set, rather than seeking to overcome it as such), and 'correlationist subtlety' (which always seeks its own recuperation in view of alterities of any kind, of which ancestrality is here absolutely paramount) (27).

But how is one to resuscitate some form of the absolute (i.e., the 'uncorrelated') without lapsing into absolutist dogma?

187

Meillassoux approaches this problem first and foremost by working his way back into the correlationist circle, in order to expose the fault-lines or, perhaps better, the uncontainable supplements within its own make-up, those that permit some possibility of exposure or opening beyond its seemingly closed repetitive sequences.

From the perspective of correlationism (in the stronger sense it has acquired over the time that separates us from Kant), no reason can be given to justify the disqualification of the most irrational discourses about the absolute, including the most strident forms of religious fundamentalism. If no truth is 'uncorrelated', there is no essential ground from which such a disqualification would draw its authority. For the correlationist solely interested in the fact that there is for us a 'world', rather than in the facts of the world, and thereby restricted to analysing the conditions and limits of thought, rather than any referent as such, it is '*conceptually* illegitimate to undertake such a refutation' (44). This is because today's philosophers largely subscribe to a brand of correlationism so radical that it deprives its proponent 'of any right to rule out the possibility of there being no common measure between the in-itself and what thought can conceive' (44). In other words, strong correlationism must accept not only that thought and being are inextricably entangled, but that they might intersect one another according to a relation that may be wholly without reason. For Meillassoux, then, post-Kantian thought's resistance to dogmatism has perhaps unwittingly let in 'unreasoned' fanaticism by the back door.

Correlationism abjures absolutising thought, but by what principle can it be renounced? Isn't there in fact an absolute principle at work in correlationism's remorseless anti-absolutism? Meillassoux's project is therefore to grasp 'why the very source which lends its power to the strategy of de-absolutization' also 'furnishes the means of access to an absolute being' (52). The resources of this 'absolute' are to be found in the very facticity that characterises the correlationist gesture. It is thus, for Meillassoux, *'the facticity of the correlation that constitutes the absolute'* – an absolute that no longer stands outside the correlationist circle as its ideal, its incapacity or its lack, but which establishes itself in terms of the very knowledge offered by facticity. As Meillassoux puts it:

> facticity will be revealed to be a knowledge of the absolute *because we are going to put back into the thing itself what we mistakenly took to be an incapacity in thought.* In other words, instead of construing the absence of reason inherent in everything as a limit that thought encounters in its search for the ultimate reason, we must understand that this absence of reason *is*, and can *only* be the *ultimate* property of the entity. We must convert the facticity into the real property whereby every world *is* without reason, and is thereby *capable of actually becoming otherwise without reason.* (53)

The decisive move of strong correlationism towards a seemingly illimitable principle of 'unreason' therefore allows for the emergence of an 'anti-absolutist' absolute (facticity),[3] the latter arising, paradoxically enough, on condition of correlationism's de-absolutising power. Correlationism cannot simply re-establish its terms by arguing that 'the apparent unreason of the world' may be merely an unreason 'for us' rather than an unreason 'in-itself' (54) without of course conceding the possibility of a reason 'in-itself' not available 'to us' – something its strong form seeks to denigrate, although in fact makes 'philosophically' possible once more. Thus, either correlationism must accept contingency in its 'absoluteness' or necessity (a position it implies or tends towards,

but nevertheless cannot fully embrace), or it must expose itself
to the possibility that correlationist circularity in its seemingly
most radical guise might re-empower dogmatism as something
more than just one 'world-view' among others. Put differently,
the very 'facticity of the correlation' that serves to disqualify pre-
critical forms of philosophy must be based, however awkwardly,
on the 'absoluteness of the contingency of the given in general'
which, if de-absolutised as a mere correlate, opens the circle to
the radical possibility of its destructive 'other' (55). Either way,
it begins to look as if the circle *must* have an outside, whether it
be a de-absolutising absolute that necessarily forms its condition
of possibility, or an absolutist one – however illusory it might
actually be – that defines a frontier beyond which it must not pass
(but which nonetheless cannot be dismissed without restoring
the 'absolute' of de-absolutisation or 'unreason'). While in the
latter case the 'outside' is conceivable as a limit against which
the correlationist circle re-draws and defends itself, however
impossibly (i.e., in auto-immune fashion, reacting to a part of
itself it nevertheless refuses to recognise), in the former it constitutes the very medium of correlationism's possibility, without
which its logic might implode, even though the correlationist
argument is at the same time deeply threatened by it. In either
situation, of course, correlationism cannot come full circle, and
not least since each version of itself must partake of the other
to some extent in order to resist correlationism's own collapse.
That said, such a system of thought thereby remains trapped
in a potentially catastrophic situation in which it must always
either de-absolutise the correlate at the cost of absolutising (its)
facticity (i.e., the correlate is not an absolutist proposition per se,
but merely the upshot of 'unreason' for all of us and for everything); or de-absolutise facticity at the cost of absolutising the

correlation (facticity may only be true for me, for all of us, as an absolute proposition), therefore never ridding itself of the absolute it seemingly abjures.

Up to this point, then, Meillassoux's argument proceeds as much on the strength of a deconstruction of correlationism as a critique of it. That is to say, while much of *After Finitude* concerns itself with Meillassoux's critical – indeed, often polemical – assessment of the effects of correlationism not just within philosophy but implicitly in terms of post-Enlightenment culture more generally, nevertheless the decisive step in the philosophical procedure of the book comes at the moment Meillassoux seeks an opening beyond the seemingly closed system of correlation by exposing that system to the very limits of its own systematicity, albeit limits that are constitutive (rather than being merely hazardous flaws) in that they simultaneously permit such a system to institute and operationalise itself, in however provisional a fashion. To acknowledge the 'event' that is Meillassoux's engagement with correlationism as a deconstruction as much as a critique not only provides the grounds to dispute the assumption many might leap to, namely that deconstruction is correlationism *par excellence*, it is also to observe a double movement within Meillassoux's writing, whereby an opening onto the 'Great Outdoors' comes at the price of a deconstructive procedure which, while far from returning us to the correlationist paradigm, may not itself straightforwardly license the subsequent philosophical decisions he makes. That is not to say that Meillassoux is not free to make them, according to a trajectory that would not be that of a thinker like Derrida (here, we could spend quite some time demonstrating why Derrida's reading of Meillassoux might not simply be oppositional in terms of his own philosophical inclinations, but more complexly provocative with regard to the pathways Meillassoux chooses to follow). But it does prompt the feeling that there is some degree of tension between the deconstruction, as I am calling it, of correlationism, which is brilliantly done, and the subsequent steps towards a philosophical 'proof' of the 'Great Outdoors'. Let me spend some time explaining why I think this is so.

If the correlationist circle opens in two ways – in the direction of a new thought of absolute facticity, on the one hand, or back onto the ineliminable vestiges of metaphysical absolutism, on the other (mutually implicated though they may be) – Meillassoux chooses the path of facticity over that of any possible return to some dogmatic or idealist absolute. (Indeed, one might well ask, since each of these 'options' is made up *in part* of the resources of the other, whether this choice might be presented as more complicated than Meillassoux allows.) The counterpart to 'the absence of any reason for my being' as the unavoidable upshot of correlationist logic is, says Meillassoux, 'the possibility of my not being', in the sense that the one makes the other thinkable. Or, to be more precise, 'even if I cannot think what it would be not to be', it nevertheless remains possible to think about it, even if only in terms of such a paradoxical 'thesis' – it is not unthinkable as such (56). Meillassoux therefore concludes, 'I can think the possibility of the unthinkable by dint of the unreason of the real' (56). Put another way, the 'unreason of the real' entails a 'capacity-to-be-other' (there is no necessary reason why an entity is what it is) which cannot be conceived purely and simply as a correlate of thought since its very proposition is based precisely on the possibility of our non-being (which may then, nevertheless, be thought in a different manner). The idealist alternative – to assert the sheer impossibility of conceiving of one's non-being *post-mortem* – amounts, for Meillassoux, to an insupportable aggrandisement of a certain conception of thinking over facticity itself: even if 'death', like everything else, were to depend on its correlate in 'thought', this cannot mean that thinking will stop death, so that it must be granted that 'my possible annihilation is thinkable as something that is not just the correlate of my thought of this annihilation' (57), but rather as something ultimately indifferent to thought (and, paradoxically, thinkable as such).

Facticity thus opens onto or opens up an absolute which nevertheless remains resistant to any idea of an absolute entity, depending as it does upon the necessary possibility of a being's being other-than-itself even to the point of its non-being as such (as we saw above). This absolute is therefore 'the absolute impossibility of a necessary being'. It is opened up by strong correlationism's exposure to radical 'unreason', and is the counterpart of the absolute necessity of contingency. If it is 'absolutely necessary that every entity might not exist' (60), if everything is pervaded by a wild and gratuitous 'unreason' that ultimately undoes all hope of correlationist recuperation, for Meillassoux this proposition grants us the non-metaphysical absolute which arms science with the capacity to produce valid ancestral statements not constrained by the correlation-ist conundrum. Chaos lends itself to science at the point one converts correlationist ignorance ('everything is possible') into knowledge of the necessity of contingency, ridding us of the sense of the necessary entity and thus providing us with the means to overcome dogmatic or idealist metaphysics while making possible progressive inquiry into the 'norms or laws to which chaos itself is subject' (66), those norms and laws which do not control it from the outside or above (which would be to re-introduce a metaphysical absolute) so much as make its 'internal' operations possible. Whereas correlationism increasingly finds itself trapped in a discourse of 'everything is possible', the proof of contingency's necessity and thus the disqualification of any necessary entity puts an end to metaphysical truths and thereby harbours 'the principle of an *auto-limitation* or *auto-normalization of the omnipotence of chaos*' (66). From this point of view, science is not destined to repeat 'everything is possible' *ad infinitum*; it is tasked instead to uncover the determinate conditions that in fact stop something from being 'anything whatsoever', even if only provisionally or temporarily.

On its own terms, this is all well and good, perhaps. But in a subsequent chapter of *After Finitude*, entitled 'Hume's Problem', Meillassoux confronts one possible objection to his thesis, namely that physical laws appear manifestly stable and consistent despite their radical contingency. Meillassoux seeks to refute the probabilistic logic that he detects behind the reasoning that finds this situation impossibly problematic (to wit, 'if physical laws *could actually change for no reason*, it would be extraordinarily improbable if they did not change *frequently*, not to say frenetically' (98)), by disputing the related assumption that contingency must be allied to chance. It is on the basis of this idea of chance that probabilism is able to make its arguments, and yet for Meillassoux such a conception of chance presupposes a pre-existing set of laws without which probabilistic calculation could not get going in the first place. Resorting to Cantor's set theory (which suggests, since the number of possible groupings of a set A is always greater than A itself *even if A is infinite*, that we have 'no grounds for maintaining that the conceivable is *necessarily* totalizable' (103)), Meillassoux challenges the idea of the 'totalizability of the possible' (105) upon which conceptions of chance must, for him, rest. Thus, he insists, the necessity of contingency is not inconsistent with the manifest stability of laws; rather, to detotalise the possible is to potentialise a new thinking of the conditions of such stability that is not constrained by ideas of chance and probabilism which, for him, emanate from metaphysical reasoning and concepts that remain hostile to the constitutive 'unreason' he wants to think. Here, it seems to me, the philosophical 'proof' part of the case that Meillassoux makes for speculative materialism or realism (the determination of facticity, etc.) is not as strongly compelling as the 'negative' demonstration of the limits of the ('Humean-Kantian') thesis that reduces contingency to an argument about chance. I think this also applies to his argument about death, outlined above, in the sense that the 'proofs' Meillassoux wants to offer at decisive moments in his thesis seem more disputable philosophically than the demonstrations he attempts of the limits and pitfalls of certain philosophical configurations. In any event, there does seem to be an unreflective assurance that egress from the confines of correlationism in the direction of speculativism can be accompanied by adopting different philosophical techniques at different moments, swapping out one for the other, without asking whether the passage between them genuinely permits the direction of travel in which Meillassoux's thesis takes us, or whether instead such a miscellany of philosophical procedures puts in question as much as authorises the book's trajectory. Does the deconstruction of systematicity in respect of correlationism simply clear the pathway for speculativism to make its case, providing a firm basis to initiate and perform Meillassoux's subsequent arguments? Or as a philosophical gesture does it ask us to pause for thought before acceding to Meillassoux's 'proofs'? To say that correlationism implies an 'outside' of itself that can never be fully recuperated, because correlationism is always heteronomous, double, or constituted by the non-closeability of its system, does not immediately license other sorts of argument about the 'outside' (like Meillassoux's) in which the highly complex effect of the double genitive – 'outside *of* itself' – is wholly expunged. To say this is not just to maintain a certain degree of correlationist reserve at the point Meillassoux's argument radicalises itself, far from it; it is simply to suggest that the decisive procedure he adopts, that of a deconstruction of correlationism, makes possible different vantage-points on the question of how to theorise such an 'outside'. (Indeed, it may also imply the possibility of some healthy scepticism about the centuries-old unbreakable hegemony of so-called correlation-ism with which we are presented in *After Finitude*, which might be read in less uni-dimensional ways than Meillassoux allows. How does the story of its extreme intensification square with the divisible resources implied by its originary deconstructibil-ity, for instance? Isn't the narrative of its historical trajectory complicated and perhaps problematised by its divided temporal-ity, caught between tropes of advancement and regression or retroactivity?)

As Meillassoux contends, the objection to the thesis about the necessity of contingency offered by those continuing to confuse the latter with the question of chance or probability is that it would condemn us to a constant fearfulness of the world:

> However, the objection continues, anyone who accepts the foregoing thesis would have to expect objects to behave in the most capricious fashion at every moment, and thank the heavens that this is not the case, and that things continue to conform to everyday constants. Those of us who endorse this claim would have to spend our time fearing that familiar objects could at any moment behave in the most unexpected

ways, congratulating ourselves every evening on having made it through the day without a hitch – before worrying about what the night might hold in store. (83–4)

Such persistent trepidation is, of course, not that of the speculative thinker, who understands contingency better (it is the principle by which we must acquire knowledge of determinate conditions, and not that by which we should expect random effects). And it is hardly part of the mind-set of the correlationist, whom it does not trouble as a problem partly because the thesis about the 'unreason' of the universe is only one among a number of possibilities for thought in its connection to being, even – and precisely – to the extent that each and any such correlation may be quite without reason (for the strong correlationist, at least). In other words, even though ultra-correlationism accepts that there may be no reasonable basis for the correlate joining being to thought, this does not cause the severe trepidation Meillassoux describes above, because 'unreason' constitutes only the principle governing our relation to the world, not necessarily that dictating the world's relation to itself (although it may well do). Even though (correlational) 'thought' may have no 'reasoned' connection to the world that it thinks – indeed, precisely *because* this is the case – it seems able to stem the panic, a panic whose origin may be deemed as potentially fictional or illusory as any other attitude to the world. Thus is extreme consternation transformed into inert complacency, although without disqualifying the possibility that occasions such dread, far from it (since it is in a certain sense by radicalising rather than refuting 'unreason', as not just a principle of being but of thought's relation to being, that its terrors are pacified somewhat). Within this view of the world, then – which may indeed be a 'phobic' view according to many of its salient features – fear of the world itself is once more ripe for mockery and derision. But, for Meillassoux, such fear-fulness would presumably be the reaction of those who at once misconstrued the realist thesis about necessary contingency, yet failed to be reassured by the correlationist sleight of hand ('of course everything is possible, but in a certain way that surely makes chaos less not more likely'). In this light, if for the specu-lativist the first of these responses leading to dreadful fearfulness is based upon an absurd misunderstanding, the latter does not just constitute a straightforward mistake (since correlationism cannot legitimately muster the authority to denigrate such fearfulness as simply misplaced). Instead, the fear-stricken in-dividual described by Meillassoux negotiates differently among the divided resources that correlationism has to offer, accepting an element of its core reasoning while failing to adopt the overall attitude that its compromises encourage. Put differently, such a person shuns speculative materialism or realism and correlation-ism alike, albeit she falsely rejects the former (as Meillassoux would have it), and only adopts an (ineliminable) part rather than the (heteronomous, divisible) 'whole' of the latter. Which, in another sense, is all one could ever do, to the extent that to accept certain key aspects of correlationism is inevitably to deny others, as Meillassoux himself teaches us. For that matter, Meillassoux himself does just this – he precisely spurns correla-tionism as a 'whole' while re-using some of its (integral) parts, with a view to conceiving of the possibility of the 'world' absol-utely otherwise. There may be a world of difference between Meillassoux and the deluded fictional person we encounter in 'Hume's Problem', yet my point here is that the relationship of those who wholly embrace speculative thinking and those who (falsely) reject it may not be merely oppositional in the sense that they display certain telling similarities in their response to the correlationism which is realism's adversary (although not just its adversary). If here I seem to be wilfully practising a certain style of what is sometimes called deconstructionism, surely such a practice only extends the possibilities opened up by Meillassoux's own 'deconstruction' of correlationism? To practise such an 'extension' is not so much to disqualify Meillassoux's subsequent arguments in any intrinsic way as it is to highlight the fact that, at a certain point, in order to make his philosophical 'proofs', he has to discard the very techniques that supposedly open up their horizon. (On this topic of 'proof' – a term that in his preface to the book Badiou asserts on Meillassoux's part – we could say that since Meillassoux posits as axiomatic the truth of a formally mathematisable domain receptive to science, his conclusions occur not via correspondence with the 'world' and are in this sense less a matter of proof than assertion.)

Melanie Klein: Between Correlationism and its Other

How might any object-orientation that would seemingly remain recuperable in terms of the correlationist paradigm in fact practise what I am calling the 'deconstruction' of correlationism that Meillassoux suggests is critical to its philosophical resistance as such? A good place to begin might be the forms of psychoanalysis that prioritise their interest in the 'object' or object-relations as such.

If 'Hume-Kant' and Meillassoux alike evoke the spectre of a deluded and fearful 'other' (he who imminently expects the most 'capricious' behaviour from worldly objects) only to deride their viewpoint as uncommonly absurd, we should not forget that such characters aren't always to be thought of as simply fictional – merely a figment of the scornful philosopher's sarcastic imaginings – even if the question of their 'staging' stubbornly persists. For other forms of analysis, that is, they are encountered rather differently. In Melanie Klien's 'Infantile Anxiety Situations Reflected in a Work of Art and in the Creative Impulse',[4] for instance, early sadistic impulses directed towards the parent are analysed by way of the elaboration of the infant's sense of danger in terms of an 'anxiety situation' that is susceptible to psychoanalysis. The analytic scene here is the libretto written by Colette for Ravel's *L'enfant et les sortilèges*, where for Klein the nursery-bound child rages against the parental regime. Projection of destructive wishes corresponds to the extreme sense of threat experienced by the child in early infancy, but through the pleasure in destruction those maltreated things that convey certain human representations strangely come to life. Objects live, they radically transmute, and are in capricious revolt. Broken crockery begins to jabber, torn wallpaper 'sounds a heart-breaking lament' as if it were the very 'rent fabric of the world' (85), mathematical instruments abused during a much-resented lesson are transformed into a perplexing dancing figure, 'the spirit of mathematics' (86). Furniture inside the house and the small animals just outside spring into anthropomorphised action. In short, the child has created a world with which to convey sadistic resentments; but also, ultimately, with which to sympathise, or at any rate to 'pity' (89). This world, which in its domestic context is for Klein an expression of the mother's persecutory body, is within an initially hostile natural setting suddenly transformed, so as to provide the circumstances for reparation to be made to the mother ('"That's a good child, a very well-behaved child," sing the animals' in response to the child's astonished whisper, 'Mama' (86)). Thus, as this world comes to life, the attack directed on his parents (ink spilt in childish defiance of mathematical learning represents excremental soiling, the sharp shards of broken objects represent both the penis and that which may threaten it, and so forth) is converted in reparative terms into a scene of 'love'. The anxiety situation that provokes sadistic aggression also permits destructiveness of a creative and transformative kind. The child actively seeks, indeed deliberately provokes, punishment only so that he may play out his transgressive wishes with full licence, with a view here to addressing the anxiety creatively. Yet it is far from certain whether the world of objects brought to life by creative negotiation with one's own infantile anxiety may not just as quickly revert to its original persecutory form. Infantile anxiety, focused on the mother's breast as exemplary, takes particular forms: fear of persecution, the projection of destructive impulses, a desire to raid what is 'good' and violently exteriorise what is 'bad' about the now–split 'object', wherein such violent intention may manifest itself, nevertheless, in terms of the wish to *consume* the 'other', and so on. Thus, the Kleinian breast is constituted, in Kristeva's terms, as an '*amalgam* of representations . . . a diverse array of internal objects',[5] the ambivalence of which is reflected in the instability of psychic identity as it develops, always bordering on the possibility of destruction. Thus, reversion to a persecutory and destructive state is the fragile and precarious condition of any relief the ego may obtain. Animated initially by human projections, the half-living things that gambol in the nursery may nevertheless enjoy a zombie or even 'anthropocenic' afterlife, surviving beyond the scene of love and reparation that they occasion, constituted as they are by complex relations or states that may well outlive the ego's attempt to thwart destructive forces. (I allude to the term 'anthropocene' here to refer in a particular sense to the idea of the persistence of human markings in a world where the human may have become extinct, and which therefore could not be humanly witnessed. Such an uncorrelated 'outside' would doubtless appeal to Meillassouxian thought, but here it is opened up by an 'object-oriented' psychoanalysis of the Kleinian type.) If, as in the tale Klein subsequently tells of the reparative value of painting in the case of Ruth Kjär, works of art may creatively address anxiety, including infantile guilt and the anxiety of lone-liness, it is nevertheless also in this sense that our creative works may in the end not just turn upon us, exploiting the darker side of our natures, but may actually outlive us more fundamentally still. Objects that demonstrate the capacity to become suddenly and vividly 'other-than' themselves – broken crockery, torn wallpaper, mathematical instruments – are not simply projected anthropomorphically in the image of the infant's woes, so as to be recuperated uniformly into the drama of subjectivity that is under way; instead, they harbour *in their very object-form* the potential for an 'otherness' that no identity can simply survive. If the psychic theatre of the Kleinian subject seems to conform to the correlationist paradigm in which every being is correlated to a thought, and every thought to an 'object', nevertheless it is curious that what is taken conspicuously *seriously* within this self-same (quasi-comic) theatre is the capacity of objects to become inordinately 'other' than themselves (and 'other' than us, other than 'for-us'), up to the point of quite outlasting the ego that, indeed, only ever acquires a provisional or makeshift foothold upon this particular stage. Like the fear-stricken in-dividual of 'Hume's Problem', the anxious child who features in Colette's libretto could never fully succumb to the (false) reassurances of correlationism. Nor, one suspects, would they ever downplay the violence harboured by contingency as just a matter of (bad) luck, something that might be overturned on a different spin of the coin. The Kleinian child, beset by infantile anxiety, doesn't simply correlate thought and being; neither may their fear of the capriciousness of objects be dismissed as some absurd error. In other words, such an infant exposes the deconstructibility of correlationism, and their reaction is therefore one which realism or materialism of the speculative kind is not properly justified in deriding and externalising.

Julie Kristeva: Psychosis Beyond Correlation

In her essay 'Something to be Scared Of',[6] Julie Kristeva reconsiders the Oedipal tradition of psychoanalysis. Here, while the mother figures as 'first object' (both of desire and signification), the father as 'the mainstay of the law' intervenes so as to separate and thus distinguish 'subject' and 'object' as such (32). In these terms, the psychoanalytic object arises on condition of the inextricable interplay of desire and prohibition.

Drawing on the interpretative resources of Klein, Winnicott, Bion and others, Kristeva is quick to problematise this Freudian tradition of analysis. The movement towards the differentiation and separation of the maternal 'object' is marked by a series of transitions, transformations, gradations, and therefore *semi*-objects that complicate the simple set of identifications one might otherwise derive from the Oedipal situation. Here, the 'object' – such as it is – is always constituted by tortuous processes bound to produce anguish. (Klein brilliantly teaches us this.) Hence, psychic pain occurs not just at the point at which the father intervenes so as to separate the (maternal) object as such, but at prior stages in the life of the object as 'pre-object', or, rather, as a series of 'pre-objects'. Such thinking sets in motion a psychic dynamics one might describe in terms of a pre-history of the Oedipal triangle. Kristeva therefore asks us to think a relation between fear and the object that may be more original than hitherto allowed by the Freudian discourse of Oedipality. Here, Kristeva revisits Freud's 'Little Hans' case study in order to argue that the 'signifier of the phobic object . . . calls attention to a *drive economy in want of an object*', showing up at the place of 'non-objectal states of drive' where drives are just 'mishaps', 'diverted' or 'disappointed' desires (35). The phobic object, then, has to do with pre-objectal '*want itself*', not want oriented towards an existing object. From this point of view, to endure a phobia is to experience the persistence of a certain confusion both about the 'world' in which objects may appear for us and about the 'self' itself, since 'something remains blurred in the Oedipal triangle constituting the subject' (35). That 'something' is precisely the function of the father as 'mainstay of the law'. If phobia names the more original relation of fear and the object, prior to the constitution of the object as such, then it follows that phobic sufferers experience just this 'blurring' where the Law of the Father is concerned. (Perhaps no wonder, then, that 'a certain handling of the analytic cure runs the risk of being nothing else but a *counter-phobic* treatment' (36), redeploying itself in terms of a constitutive misrecognition of the phobic situation put into analytic practice: probing for objects that fear is in want of.)

If, for Kristeva, phobia might be considered the very 'metaphor of want', it is equally possible that the phobic person is 'a subject in want of metaphoricalness'. Phobic sufferers are 'incapable of producing metaphors by means of signs alone' – put differently, they cannot make metaphors signify properly, and so aspire to metaphoricity through the 'material of drives' that is capable only of a rhetoric of affect 'projected, as often as not, by means of *images*'. Here we find between the 'primary process' and the 'signifier' little more than a 'void' that equates to fear (37). Thus, phobia 'slides beneath language', although not only to oppose or resist language but to re-mark its own resistances. Kristeva argues that if, by standing 'at the place of want' that founds his fear, the phobic person may be deemed a fetishist, nonetheless language itself is in principle based on just such 'fetishist denial' – it is in want of the object – so that in its very constitution the 'phobic object' is less an anti-writing than a writing in the making. To the extent that the phobic object may be deemed 'proto-writing', writing itself (in the enlarged sense it is given here) always comes down to a language of want and fear, the subject of which can name such a 'world' as he lives in only 'backwards, starting from an over-mastery of the linguistic and rhetorical code' that is far from proper to the fear that defines him.[7] Thus, each writer is a phobic in want of metaphors to keep 'himself from being frightened to death' (38). He himself is always at a crossroads, poised between (phobic) writing – that which hangs over a certain linguistic abyss, stricken by a fear of nothing – and the 'over-coded' discourse of objects through which one might recognise counter-phobic construction taking place. The phobic 'object' – in so far as it is one – is itself precisely this 'avoidance of choice', Kristeva observes (42).

Fear entails an aggressivity that, whether or not it precedes aggressive drives, want cannot dispense with. As Klein has taught us, this is another feature of those transitions, gradations and semi-objects that occur on the way from paranoid-schizoid to depressive states. 'Phobia literally stages the instability of the object relation', Kristeva says (43). Narcissism may be deemed not just the 'opposite correlative' of the object relation, but a better platform from which to raise the question of the 'psychotic structures' that may derive from such 'instability' (43). Nonetheless, this begs the question of what such 'narcissism' may mean, given that we are dealing with a situation that is pre-objectival or pre-linguistic in any proper sense, to which it is therefore difficult to assign a subject without a certain 'forcing of thought' (43). Since, when speaking of fear in want of an object (phobia), we are in the midst of a 'failure of the triangular relationship', it is not only difficult to posit an 'object', but to establish its correlate in terms of a 'subject'. Nonetheless, for Kristeva, narcissistic drives continue to dominate precisely when this failure pertains so as to prevent the subject from finding their place 'within a triadic structure giving an object to their drives'. In other words, narcissism prevails where the subject leaves off; narcissism surpasses and falls short of the subject (doubtless, for many, a strange narcissism indeed, narcissism going beyond or outside itself as such). Here, in fact, 'the object relationship of drives is a belated and even nonessential phenomenon' (44). The phobic situation, marked by the failure of the paternal agency to create a 'strict object relation' by introducing the 'symbolic dimension' between object (mother) and subject (child), is for Kristeva the evidence of drives without object, of drives that precede and exceed both subject and object, which indeed threaten their identity with dissolution, obsolescence, annihilation. Here, psychoanalysis determines those forces that persist outside of correlation's ambit – even if such forces meet with counter-phobic resistance at the crossroads between correlation and its other – and assigns to them a name for their 'unreason'. But, here, we are not merely in the presence of science. 'We are then in the presence of psychosis', writes Kristeva (44). It is as if this entire analysis leads us to the punch-line of a rather cheap joke: He who, like Meillassoux, advocates mathematics of a Badiouist stripe in order to totally overcome correlational thinking advocates what is 'psychotic'. I will forgo such a jibe, although it is not without some theoretical justification (especially when one recalls that, for Meillassoux, 'facticity' is not proven as a fact but instead holds its ground as a theoretical 'necessity' on the way to overcoming necessary entities).

At any rate, for Kristeva, fear-in-want-of-an-object – always experienced at a crossroads for which phobia is as good a name as any – leads not just to the 'borders of psychosis' but also to the gates of symbolicity's 'structuring power'; yet the choice this seems to present to the subject is in effect little choice at all, to the extent that in either case 'we are confronted with a limit that turns the speaking being into a separate being who utters' (46). Whether one is confronted by a 'scattering of objects' that necessarily remain somehow 'false', or whether one beats a 'secret' retreat into 'archaic narcissism', one faces a near-abyssal 'walling in', a terrible incarceration. This is bad news for any oversimplified critique of correlationism that imagines its overthrow in terms of an escape from prison. For, here, the psychotic who cannot 'correlate' seems just as horribly trapped as anybody else. Moreover, if flight from the borderlines is possible for the patient only through 'a slow, laborious production of object relation' – aided presumably by psychoanalysis – through which 'pseudo-objects' are superseded by those that are somehow 'good' or properly 'desirable', nevertheless we must surely recall (alongside both Kristeva and Klein) that every scene of object-formation is beset by abyssal traps. In this sense, the borderline patient may cross the border only at the cost of re-drawing its

207

battle-lines, thus surviving them in a far from unharmed way. As Kristeva writes:

> The absence, or the failure, of paternal function to establish a unitary bent between subject and object, produces this strange configuration: an encompassment that is stifling (the container compressing the ego) and, at the same time, draining (the want of an other, qua object, produces nullity in the places of the subject). The ego then plunges into a pursuit of identifications that could repair narcissism – identifications that the subject will experience as in-significant, 'empty,' 'null,' 'devitalized,' 'puppet-like.' An empty castle, haunted by unappealing ghosts – 'powerless' outside, 'impossible' inside. (49)

If such a ghost-ridden 'empty castle' recalls Meillassoux's evocation of the correlationist's transparent cage, it also brings to mind the theatre of *L'enfant et les sortilèges*, in which correlationist reassurances are as much spurned as is contingency's necessity beyond chance. For, in the text of Colette's libretto, the sense of reparative work being done – as Klein would have it – vies uneasily with what 'Hume-Kant' and Meillassoux alike might deem merely delusional, suggesting the onset of madness or, as Klein might concede, the return of those destructive forces experienced in the paranoid-schizoid state. Here, one senses that the infant's 'pursuit of identifications that could repair narcissism' may be quickly superseded by those that are '"empty," "null," "devitalized," "puppet-like"' (perhaps even anthropocenic, in the sense that we are confronted with a theatre that is so constituted as to potentially obliterate the integral perspective of protagonist and audience alike). Amid these various echoes, then, one might view the 'walled in' borderline patient as not simply the victim of a dominating correlationism, but, in flight from psychosis, as the victim of correlation's deconstructibility too (that is to say, as much a victim of its 'other' as of 'itself'). And all of this complicates the stakes of any straightforward opposition where correlationism is concerned.

I said a moment ago that I would refrain from the jibe about speculativism and psychosis. But if one wanted to extend such a joke, one might point to Kristeva's observation that the border-line patient seeking flight from psychosis 'is often abstract, made up of stereotypes that are bound to seem cultured; he aims at precision, indulges in self-examination, in meticulous comprehension, which easily brings to mind obsessional discourse' (49). Could one recognise in this description any glimmerings of the quasi-Cartesian method or style of Meillassoux?[8] Earlier in the text, Kristeva remarks that an 'extreme nimbleness' and 'a vertiginous skill . . . traveling at top speed' typifies the speech of 'the phobic adult' (41). Since the phobic adult is always to be found at the very crossroads of psychosis – forming the phobic 'object' as a wanting object in order to elude psychosis's grip – one might speculate further on speculativism's style as symptom. We might even venture the following proposition, one that is deceptively complex in both grammatical and semantic terms. Speculativism is characterised – in ways it may not yet fully understand – by both a certain symptom and style: it is indeed in want of an object to be scared of.[9]

At the Ragged End of Everything

At the close of the slender volume *In the Beginning Was Love*,[10] Kristeva includes a short essay that asks whether psychoanalysis should be considered a form of nihilism. Kristeva begins by clarifying Nietzsche's famous declaration, 'God is dead'. Here,

Nietzsche is not to be found merely 'echoing the cry of un-believers' (59). Instead, in Heidegger's terms, he is to be taken as announcing the fundamental erosion of the suprasensible Ideal. What this means, for Heidegger, is that the suprasensible world no longer enjoys the power to oblige or gratify.[11] Kristeva notes that Christianity itself may be considered a consequence of this decline, and is thus as much an expression of nihilism as its contrary. Descartes and Leibniz are singled out as major thinkers in this tradition that points in nihilism's direction, one that has the more general effect of reducing Being to 'an object of sub-jective thought', as Kristeva puts it. Here, then, correlationism is the upshot of nihilism, and must be understood in such terms (while the 'will to power' arises on the strength of a craving for the value of the absolute – a situation about which Kristeva need take no instruction from anybody).

It would seem that the counterpart of Nietzsche's dreams about the transvaluation of all values is Freudian psychoanalysis as, in one sense, the pinnacle of nihilism. For it is psychoanalysis's signal achievement to 'subvert the subject's being by viewing it as a psychic "object"' (60). Thus, the 'effort to objectify man's being' is 'part of the nihilist effort'. The nihilist 'program' therefore includes both the correlation of each 'existent' in terms of the 'immanence of subjectivity' (through which it is objectified), and the subversion of the subject through its trans-formation into psychic object. In a further twist, however, the object-form imposed on the subject by psychoanalysis falls short of 'objectivity' as such. Structured in terms of an 'unfolding' language that 'resonates' as one subject intersects another, the analytic situation – in which, we might say, *nihilism overcomes itself* – cannot partake of simple relations of 'unification, distanti-ation, and objectification'. The very possibility of psychic life is received from an 'other' that is neither a 'subject' nor an 'object' in any simple sense, just as psychoanalysis is both the end-point of nihilism's departure from the suprasensible Ideal in the direction of the 'immanence of subjectivity' and the radical subversion of this 'immanence' (radical, in that it does not simply reverse or invert such 'immanence' in favour of a polarised 'objectivity') through which we witness nihilism's self-overcoming. Psychoanalysis can therefore be thought to stand 'in a new relation' to both the 'Ideal' and the 'physical' realm, to the extent that it remains complexly poised in regard to those same demarcations within the field of thought from which its possibility nevertheless arises. (This would perhaps be another way to describe 'the role ascribed to language' in the psychoanalytic field.) Psychoanalysis thus represents 'the extraordinary effort to recast our whole intellectual tradition' from 'inception' to 'annihilation', encompassing an extraordinary recasting of these same terms. In fact, the psychoanalytic subject experiences himself as (analytic) object in a very particular way: he is 'submerged . . . in the immanence of a significance that transcends him' (61). Kristeva assigns a specific name to this 'significance', that of the *unconscious*. Through the unconscious – that is, through the 'unfolding' of language in Kristevan terms – the analysand undergoes both objectification and immersion. There is nothing but the subject / the subject is nothing but that which it is not ('the subject derives from an alien significance that transcends and overwhelms it, that empties it of meaning'). Psychoanalytic nihilism – if there is any – allows us to rethink the subject as an object beyond (subjective) objectification. Yet at the same time psychoanalysis is, for Kristeva, one possible antidote to a certain nihilism (not just in its 'vitalist' but in its 'scientific' cast). This is because psychoanalysis finds within itself the resources to check metaphysical drift towards both 'ideality' and 'objectification' as the two poles of our 'whole intellectual tradition',[12] making possible a 'fragile equilibrium' whereby objectival desire is transformed by the other: 'Only the meaning that my desire may have for another and hence for me can control its expansion, hence serve as the unique, if tenuous, basis of a morality' (63). Kristeva calls this antidote a 'modest if tenacious' one, a protective shield where the 'superman' is concerned, at least for the time being.

Notes

1   See Quentin Meillassoux, *After Finitude: An Essay on the Necessity of Contingency*, trans. Ray Brassier (London and New York: Continuum, 2008). Page references will be given in the body of the chapter.

2   Meillassoux concludes *After Finitude* by highlighting the seeming irony that the Copernico-Galilean revolution, through which science proved itself capable of a profoundly decentring and indifferentist gesture in relation to dogmatic theocentrism, was accompanied or followed by a 'Ptolemaic' counter-revolution in the field of philosophy, whereby all being was effectively recuperated as a correlate of (human) thought. As he puts it: 'Even as thought realized for the first time that it possessed in modern science the capacity to actually uncover knowledge of a world that is indifferent to any relation to the world, transcendental philosophy insisted that the condition for the conceivability of physical science consisted in revoking all non-correlational knowledge of the same world' (118). Of course, this is not simply a matter of contradiction or tension, to the extent that both 'events' result from a crisis in the human relation to 'God', thereby constituting different yet related reactions to religious dogmatism. Nonetheless, Meillassoux describes such developments in philosophy, as opposed to those in science, as catastrophically counter-revolutionary. My argument, in engaging with Meillassoux here, is that the deconstructibility of correlationism that he himself proposes may well problematise such a simple opposition between what is revolutionary and what is counter-revolutionary, so that the complex connection (as much as the contrast)

between scientific and philosophical reactions to modernity remains of interest.

3 It is important to note that Meillassoux's argument acknowledges that 'facticity cannot be thought of as another fact in the world – it is not a fact that things are factual, just as it is not a fact that factual things exist' (75) – in the same (or similar) way that contingency is not itself contingent. Indeed, for Meillassoux it is this argument which forces us towards a 'strong' interpretation of the principle of factuality, whereby factual things can be said to exist not as a fact but rather as 'an absolute necessity' (bearing in mind that 'necessity' throughout *After Finitude* means the necessity of contingency, so that the 'necessity of the contingency of the entity' is what 'imposes the necessary existence of the contingent entity' (76) – for Meillassoux such radical contingency therefore deflates or de-dramatises the age-old philosophical question: 'Why is there something rather than nothing?' through a specific understanding of the interplay between being and being-otherwise or non-being).

4 See *The Selected Melanie Klein*, ed. Juliet Mitchell (London: Penguin, 1986), pp. 84–94. Page references will be given in the body of the chapter.

5 See Julia Kristeva, *Melanie Klein* (New York: Columbia University Press, 2001), pp. 63–4.

6 This essay may be found in Kristeva's well-known book, *Powers of Horror: An Essay on Abjection*, trans. Leon S. Roudiez (New York: Columbia University Press, 1982), pp. 32–55. Page references will be given in the body of the chapter.

7 It would be interesting to consider this situation in reference to the material I include in the previous chapter of this book, on Blanchot's reading of Pascal, where linguistic and rhetorical expertise on the latter's part grant access to abyssal fears they can nonetheless never hope to master.

8 Indeed, it might be as fitting to discuss the Meillassouxian 'text' in terms of obsession as phobia. If the phobic is the most radical neurotic, in some ways as disruptive as the hysteric, the obsessional is the most conformist, whose repression entails introversion, retreat into the life of the mind and a delirium of thoughts placed under the governance of (Cartesian) doubt as a repetitive process.

9 One thing held in common among several of those influenced by the speculative turn is the Lovecraftian nameless Entity of Terror, which is taken to stand for the weirdness of the 'outside' upon which one speculates. This might translate as the figure or structure of a phobic (non-)object,

and as such licenses in another way the move from a 'philosophical' to a 'psychological' treatment of Meillassoux's thought.

10 Julia Kristeva, *In the Beginning Was Love*, trans. Arthur Goldhammer (New York: Columbia University Press, 1987). Page references will be given in the body of the chapter.

11 Kristeva's text alludes to Heidegger's 'Le mot de Nietzsche "Dieu est mot"', in *Chemins qui ne mènet nulle part* (Paris: Gallimard, 1962).

12 Although it is also within psychoanalysis's very character to all but succumb to these same temptations.

8

Fear of the Open:
Resistances of the Public Sphere

Lapse of the Object

For Freud, writing in 1887, agoraphobia seems to stem from 'a romance of prostitution'[1] – a striking description of the perhaps rather nebulous fear of what might be exchanged, or possibly exchanged, in a more or less public place.[2] Albeit that, at the same time, the phobic state itself complicates the separation or distinction of the 'public' and the 'private' in the first place. Not only in the sense that, even when triggered by exposure to what is 'public', phobia still calls up the notion of a special condition, or, as Adam Phillips has written, 'a private language . . . a secretive exemption from shared meanings';[3] but because the *want* of an object that for psychoanalysis characterises phobic behaviour points simultaneously to an 'outside' to be internally appropriated in some sense, even through fear (and whether or not such an 'outside' feels intimidatingly empty), and to an 'inside' that must be defended or consolidated at all costs (regardless of whether it seems hollow or bereft) even if only by faux recoil from the world *as such*, or from some of its parts. As Phillips himself writes, 'phobia reveals virtually nothing about the object except its supposed power to frighten' (16).

215

Whether or not this is strictly true from a psychoanalytic viewpoint (Freudian, Kleinian, Lacanian, etc.), nevertheless such a statement does convey the sense that phobic fear – even and perhaps especially that of the *agora* or of public places – is indeed *in the first place* fear of an emptiness or a voided spatiality – of the possible *lapse* of the object, or of a fake 'object' without genuine content or consistency as such – that is far from just external, being instead conjointly a fear of inner desolation, hollowness, or perhaps even vacuity. Not just fear of open spaces, then, but also of a 'space' which opens perhaps infinitely, as Pascal feared, not just to threaten us at its ever-advancing limits, but to engulf us, radically, abyssally. A space beyond all possible space. Perhaps the agoraphobic projects this fear 'outside' (and to the outside as a 'place' of sorts) as a way to ameliorate such feelings. Or perhaps, to the contrary, fear of relatively formless or at any rate inadequately delineated and thus always potentially dynamic, transmutable 'objects' – manifest to an important extent in the agoraphobic's fear of *situation* – constitutes a realism of sorts, or at any rate a distorted recognition of the relational object or of object-relations that never fully permit the separation of 'inside' and 'outside', 'public' and 'private' in the first place, but instead continually conjure their interactions in ways that are bound to remain unstable and sometimes deeply troubling. (Here, perhaps, psychoanalysis is at its best when it recognises that the problem is not just how to defend oneself from the onslaught of such forces, but how to deal with the fact that one is constituted by them, for good or ill.)

It is no wonder, from this point of view, that agoraphobia is often taken as a defining phobia, or the phobic condition *par excellence*, since it seems to strike at the very heart of what phobia is mainly about: the distressing possibility of exchange (a

216

possibility that may be unavoidable, whether or not it is desired or dreaded) *where more terrifyingly still there may in fact be nothing to exchange.* (The 'romance of prostitution' may capture just this fear of an exchange in which, for all its crudeness as an exchange, it is far from clear exactly what is being exchanged, or what may be the risks of exchange: indeed, perhaps all sex is precisely an exchange beset by the same uncertainty.) In other words, one may think of agoraphobia in terms of the potential lapse of the object in at least a double sense. Through exchange-relations the object loses its self-constitution, which might in a certain respect deepen the alarm of the phobic in want of an object; but, equally, exchange-relations may well prolong the fiction of exchangeable objects, and might therefore revive the object in something like phantasmic form (which may, indeed, be the object's 'proper' condition). Such a 'revival' of the object in its very spectrality may happen against the backdrop of a yet more horrifying (and possibly psychotic) sense that there might finally be no objects at all – or at any rate no ground for figuring the subject/object in the way the phobic (i.e., everybody) wants to do. If, as Phillips writes, 'one has to become phobic' in order 'to become what Freud thinks of as a person' – a becoming that is itself dependent upon the belief that 'there is an external and an internal world that are discrete' (19) – then nevertheless, as he himself remarks, Kristeva teaches us that the phobic 'object' arises on condition of a certain avoidance of choice, a constitutive hesitation or a deep suspension of the capacity to decide. If, as I am suggesting, one way to interpret this avoidance is in terms of a *double* lapse or want of the object, then the phobic sufferer (i.e., every person in general) constitutively hesitates between two fearful possibilities: the possibility of an object that might always slip away, or lose its place; and the possibility that every object is itself just a symptom of a 'ground' (or a 'place') that has already gone or was never really there. The phobic object, in other words, as best hope and worst nightmare rolled into one, placing and unplacing us at every turn. So that the ostensibly redemptive aspect of phobic life is always darkly hollow – not merely fragile yet provisionally or pragmatically effective, but wildly and no doubt degradingly ironic.

Public Parts

In his book *Repressed Spaces: The Poetics of Agoraphobia*, Paul Carter, writing of metropolitan cultural experience after modernity (particularly from the late nineteenth century onwards) observes that, for many commentators of the day, it was to be 'the rationally grounded public whose influence holds in check those *unconscious seething excitations* that so easily fuse individuals into an uncontrollable crowds'.[4] Such commentators presumed, of course, that a sustainable opposition might be put to work between, on the one hand, the perceived advent of mass hysteria, mob rule or other forms of 'irrational' collective behaviour, and, on the other, the calming influence of the 'rational' public sphere. (Here, of course, the fraternal model of modern political society is, whether tacitly or not, supplemented by the assumption of a certain paternalism.)

Classically speaking, the concept of the public sphere as the arena of open political debate or exchange, permitting the free expression of public opinion, although regulated by reason as its first principle, is based on a conception of civil society that developed alongside the very idea of the modern nation-state. The authority of the public sphere in helping to shape national politics and policies was granted historically by this model of statehood, a model which in turn received much of its historic legitimacy from the public realm that supposedly supported or grounded it. In this model of the public sphere, then, the rationality of the state and of the citizen-subject were brought into a specular or circular relationship, no doubt in the interests of an entire array of ideological and political functions, but nonetheless to secure the idea of reason's more or less pure self-articulation, or in other words (mirroring the tripartite constitution of the 'People' in the canonical text of US 'government') its expression *of* itself *by* itself *for* itself. Carter contextualises historically different forms of mass behaviour – for example, during the Paris Commune – by tracing ways in which their emergence as social phenomena occurred alongside the rise of various discourses which, paradoxically enough, strove to lend distinctive shape, colour, texture, and sometimes meaning, to what was often depicted in terms of sheer chaos and caprice. As Carter suggests, the production of such images of 'irrational' behaviour on the part of the multitude (described, for instance, in terms of mass hallucination, collective estrangement, or the hystericisation of the social body) not only prompted the re-inscription of a seemingly secure distinction between the onset of such terrifying 'madness', on the one hand, and a reassuring and often nostalgic recollection of the profound 'sanity' of the rational public sphere, on the other. It also pointed to something less straightforward, namely a rather complex interplay in which the seeming opposition between these two forms or conceptions of public experience begins to break down.

Carter asks us to 'suppose that the public is a *phantom*' and that 'public *space* is a phantom' (37). For him, this is mainly because the democratic ideal that would seem to found the modern conception of the public realm continually erodes as much as it defends received certainties. As Jacques Derrida noted on several occasions, the 'demos' is itself nothing less than the expression of a certain *aporia*. At its classical root, the 'demos' conjures and demands both the irreducible singularity of anyone (even before any subject, citizen, state or people) and yet also a fundamental equality (one that finds expression, for instance, through the law that defines and defends citizenship or subjecthood, but which at any rate requires some conception of equivalence). Thus, the 'demos' permanently confronts us with the unavoidable yet always ultimately incommensurable encounter between what in human life is preserved in its incalculability (in other words, what remains 'free'), and what in that life must be conserved or upheld on the strength of universal ratiocination or calculation according to a general law (i.e., that which establishes the measure of equality to vitally supplement freedom itself). Yet this impassability is also the very possibility of democracy since if the aporia of the demos were to be fully reconciled, put to an end once and for all, far from heralding the advent of democracy in pure and finished form this would undermine the democratic ideal or spirit in a profound way. It would resolve and thus terminate the very play of forces that give it life. In other words, democracy must have a *future*, and an uncertain future at that, if the 'demos' is to survive in the here and now. From this point of view, if images of irrational collective behaviour spur wistful (and doubtless false) memories of, as Carter puts it, 'a democratic citizenry formerly representing a coherent body of public opinion' (37), such nostalgia is as much *anti-* as it is prodemocratic. For to pine for a public sphere (with its very image and idea fixed in the past) that is conceived of as unwaveringly stable, remorselessly functional and serenely rational is not to dream of democracy but, perhaps, to wish for its nightmarish 'other'. Since the aporia of the 'demos' will in fact not succumb to a 'rational' outcome (nor should it, if the democratic ideal is to survive), one must find ways to reason differently with reason in the very interests of democracy. This does not amount to giving oneself over to wild irrationality, far from it; it suggests, rather, that a certain (perhaps 'reasonable') supplement to the purely 'rational' is needed if the chance of democracy is to be kept alive.

While the 'rational' public sphere requires a measure of that which is resistant to itself as precisely an antidote to itself, then, the 'public' (like the 'demos') is always phantasmic in the sense that it can never be fully constituted as such. It is as much made of dreams as those visions of mass hallucination, of the somnolent torpor of the crowd or the frenzied hysteria of the mob, that so preoccupied writers and thinkers of the late nineteenth and early twentieth centuries. Yearning to wake up, then, communicates not only the desire to be set free from nightmarish monsters but also the deep agitation that must always accompany democratic dreaming. Carter wonders whether we might consider such shrinking from the call of the 'demos' to be itself a form of agoraphobia: not just a fear of public spaces, but of the open space of the 'public' itself ('open' in the sense of being forever irresolvable, irreconcilable or unconcludable). Such an agoraphobic may not be a (democratic) visionary, but is instead a fantasist, one who evokes a 'citizenry formerly representing a coherent body of public opinion'. Meanwhile, whether the 'public' is reduced to the falsely serene image of rational exchange, or whether it is subjected to the more authentically democratic 'dream' that both engenders and unsettles it, the fact that a phantasmic element is always present means

221

that neither 'perspective' (the retrospective nor the futural) can be fully constituted as such. And this leaves no space outside of the 'open', no exchange that can be undertaken with complete satisfaction, and probably no way to avoid agoraphobia in some form or other.

To put this another way: what, if anything, the nostalgic fantasist and the dreamer of the to-come have in common, despite the political differences that actually underlie their allusions to the 'demos', is something like the *as if*.[5] There is no space outside the *as if*, whether one wishes to mount a defence of the public realm by way of an effectively anti-democratic attitude or, contrariwise, open the public sphere to its own self-resistance in the interests of a democracy that is always in the making. As Carter notes, in Greek 'agora' shares a family relationship with the word 'ago', which refers to acting and actorship on the public stage. Indeed, he contends that, here, as Stanislavski teaches us, 'the core idea of action is a *leading out* or *drawing together*' (73). It seems as if to act upon such as stage involves, then, a double and perhaps undecidable movement of both inward concentration and rather forceful egress, dispersal, or dissipation; a careful and concerted gathering-in and at the same time a wilful, perhaps even capricious, breaking forth; a certain gesture of assembly oddly coupled with a powerful driving out or leaping away (or, put differently, a driving together that is far from simply an act of conservation). If this double situation defines stage-acting it profoundly disturbs the frontiers or limits of the 'theatrical' space in which action is so configured. Rather than safely or securely hemming in an enclosed domain, and so effectively delineating its identity as such (i.e., as recognisably a 'place'), the action which itself gives definition to this theatre at the same time exposes its borders not just to an 'outside' but to an 'other' of itself.[6] Such a theatre, in other words, is not just confronted with an exteriority that lies identifiably beyond its own boundaries, but is instead made to face its own lack of self-identity in each (double and divisible) performative gesture through which it nevertheless acquires its specific character.[7] If for Stanislavski this makes theatrical acting potentially 'explosive', it also suggests that the 'ago' permanently verges on implosion, perhaps not least in its complex yet intimate relationship to the 'agora'. Once again, where public space and action are concerned, it is possible to appreciate an abiding fear of the 'open' that nonetheless also supplies the very conditions of possibility for a democratically oriented public sphere. Agoraphobia is not, then, just about recoil or retreat from public or open spaces; strangely enough, it cannot help but open them anew, for good or ill. To go further: gathering at the marketplace as much as political assembly – themselves potentially antagonistic yet no doubt interconnected activities (and not only historically) – therefore depends on the force of a supplementary movement which they simply cannot integrate or contain. This may, indeed, come between them as much as connect them, perhaps helping to explain the always agitated and potentially implosive yet still undoubtedly proximate relationship of politics and the market – something which surely intensifies with 'the growing cohesion of the agora's articulation' (129), to borrow Carter's own terms.

That said, as its form or 'articulation' develops, the 'agora' encourages not just actorial 'leading out' - powerful (political or economic) agency heightened to explosively theatrical levels - but also a certain clearing away, the expulsion of marginalised and unwanted groups that becomes a more and more concerted and extensive process, although almost with its own momentum (strangely echoing the image of irrational mass behaviour onto which, perhaps, its own drives are projected).[8] This clearing away intensifies to the point of inducing 'dread' in many. As Carter puts it: 'As its unity depends on banishing the many from it, the resulting space looks rather empty. It might . . . induce a sense of dread, a foreboding of violent expulsion' (134). The double movement of the agora – that which produces its very possibility – is here explained in terms of the expropriation upon which its supposed unity and identity rest. To gather together, the agora must cast out; to defend its integrity (indeed, its very form) it must expel from itself, violently if needs be; and yet in the end this process becomes so all-consuming as to threaten self-evisceration. Agoraphobia is therefore as much the fear of forcible ejection that accompanies any possible sense of belonging, as it is the uncertain receptivity to openness that re-founds the possibility of the 'demos'. Perhaps the two are not entirely unrelated, although of course agoraphobic dread of the 'rather empty' space of the public square can face both ways, politically speaking. It can fuel reactionary paranoia as much as fire political dissent. As much as provoking speculation or some new wager, it can license retrenchment, as if all bets were off.

The 'dread' of 'empty spaces' suggests that fear of what may have been driven out is also fear of one's own drives as they threaten to turn upon oneself, and at the same time a projection of this fear upon an 'outside'. The agoraphobic drive turns itself upon the 'other' in a variety of ways, not all of them immediately or obviously consistent, so that the agoraphobic often fears crowds as much as open spaces. Fear of the 'irrational' collective behaviour of a supposedly undifferentiated mob sees this drive project itself in terms of *drift* – Carter notes a Germanic etymological connection between the two (148) – giving rise to the question of what connects this particular pair. Is such 'drift' just the resistant opposite of the 'drive', the threshold or limit through which its force is in fact renewed? Or does it involve, instead, the projected displacement of an intrinsic yet unwanted or unrecognised element of the drive, hinted at by the etymology to which Carter alludes? When does the drive come adrift? If in the Freudian sense the agoraphobic fears public spaces (or meeting places, where approaches can possibly happen) because she fears illicit sexual temptation, agoraphobia is also, as Carter notes, the fear of being alone (hence the need for an escort, or for other props like a cane or a hat to make bearable the experience of public settings, particularly those that seem vast or expansive). These two fears – which themselves suggest a certain degree of tension or inconsistency of wants – may, one might think, be resolved through masturbation as a sort of double 'prop'; although we should recall from our earlier chapter that in *The Interpretation of Dreams* the 'masturbation' explanation of dreams with 'a dental stimulus' presents us with the idea or image of an auto-erotic subject who feels able to dispense with the 'object' altogether, constituting at once, perhaps, the resistance of drives connected to phobic anxiety and the possibility of onanistic 'drift', which, given what we have said above, may or may not prove to be ultimately pleasurable. This would be one way, indeed, to think of the 'obscure economy' (to borrow a phrase from Derrida) of drive and drift, one not simply defined by their mutual exclusivity, resistance or opposition. Such complex relations, in fact, may be no more recuperable from the perspective of a 'single' theoretical discourse (such as psychoanalysis) than they are exhausted by etymological explanation. In other words, the question of the drive coming adrift is perhaps not a question that psychoanalysis or any other 'theoretical' perspective would be fully resourced to answer since it might take hold at the very borders of theory's possibility. If, in fairness, this is something that psychoanalysis is capable of recognising, perhaps it is no wonder that Freud was himself known to be agoraphobic (albeit somewhat invested in a certain repression of his own agoraphobia).

In another section of *Repressed Spaces*, Carter notes a further etymological interplay between 'agora' and 'agros', the latter referring to 'the wilderness where the shepherd goes with his flock' (113). But is not long before such 'shepherding' of the flocked-together comes adrift or gives ground to 'hunting' and 'raiding' (148), as if the two are linked, whether obscurely or not. (The very problem of 'psychoanalytic' agoraphobia, of 'drift' and of 'drive', may once more be detected here.[9]) If such a locale as the 'agros' stands at the frontiers of civilisation itself, we are soon in the vicinity of questions about the 'human' and the 'animal', where such interrelations are not readily reconciled in static or sterile terms, by way of self-identical categories or established hierarchies, but are subject to both potential drift and violent, driving force. Carter writes, then, of a connection made in antiquity between 'agora' and 'agra':

> In the *agra*, one both seizes and is seized, one is both the hunter and the one who, responding to the call of the hunter, is killed. At the *agra*, an accident occurs, a gathering that can mimic extinction. The *agra*, on this account, is the other scene that haunts Levinas, the 'other "other scene" beyond the psychoanalytic unconscious'. (162)

In the last part of this paragraph, Carter is in fact citing John Llewelyn's book on Levinas, *Emmanuel Levinas: The Genealogy of Ethics*.[10] Throughout his own writing, Carter is keen to evoke

Levinas in terms of what he calls an 'ethical agoraphobia' at odds
with the 'marketplace of self-interest', testifying to a sense of 'responsibility' that 'transcends any rules of exchange' (161), a sense
of responsibility from which there is no hiding place, whether
in the country or the city. This would seem to imply a certain
sensitivity or receptivity to the 'open' that, whether or not it is
always site-specific, cannot be confined to one particular type of
locale.[11] Perhaps this is because such an openness corresponds in
some way to what Pascal means by the infinite, but at any rate
it is important to appreciate that such an 'ethical agoraphobia'
would be complexly structured, as the foregoing discussion
indicates. Sensitivity would no more entail merely complacent
toleration of a more or less assimilable 'other' than receptivity
would be reducible to a form of welcoming issued from the safe
and secure place of a 'home'. Instead, (Levinasian) responsibility is complicated by a deeply unsettling foreboding, by fear,
suffering, hatred, persecution, horror of the 'other' − a complexity that cannot just be traced in terms of the unconscious
construed as the 'other', deeper part of our selves, but which
arrives asymmetrically, as it were (the very 'other' of the 'other'),
to violate one's own desires or drives from the outset. If such a
situation is not totally unknown to (or at any rate unsuspected
by) psychoanalysis, the point here is that it cannot be reduced
to the psychoanalytic paradigm without that paradigm selling
itself short. (Such dealings would come under particular scrutiny,
needless to say, in precisely the vicinity of the 'agora' where
questions of exchange and the marketplace are strongly at issue.)
Or, put differently, in Llewelyn's terms 'absolute ethical agoraphobia' is 'a phobia of the "unconscious" beyond therapy' (202).

In the chapter of his book entitled 'Ethical agoraphobia',
therefore, Llewelyn writes: 'But we have taken Levinas to say that

in extremis there is no suspicion of a rational ground upon which my responsibility to the other can be required as the correlative of a debt' (201). The (agoraphobic, crowd-fearing) appeal to the 'rational ground' of a public sphere is thus resisted by this notion of Levinasian responsibility, or 'ethical agoraphobia', particularly if such a realm is construed in terms of the debts we owe to, in Carter's terms, 'a democratic citizenry formerly representing a coherent body of public opinion'. There is no single under-lying rationality that can contextualise, calculate, moderate or economise with such a responsibility, which nevertheless comes to us, as we have already seen, *in extremis* of such a 'ground' where it seems to exist,[12] at the point where all good sense drifts or is driven towards senselessness as perhaps precisely the 'other "other scene"' we have remarked upon. And, here, perhaps – through the 'obscure economy' (or economy on the very cusp of aneconomy) that we have been trying to describe – such responsibility has its chance, or takes its risks. Out in the open, one might say, even if at the (extreme) point of a 'phobia of the "unconscious" beyond therapy'.

Outside, Outdoors

In the final chapter of *Otherwise than Being*,[13] 'The Outside', Levinas puts in question the philosophical tradition that ties essence to subjectivity, and he seeks to identify its highly prob-lematic historical effects, not least in the twentieth century. While philosophy is certainly capable of higher and more excep-tional thought, it has mainly regarded being in terms of a certain homeliness or inwardness to itself – a position which for Levinas connects powerfully to European histories both of conquest and defence.[14] In turn, such a philosophical tradition posits itself in relation to the 'other' only where this relationship is itself regarded principally in terms of the possibility of 'disclosure'. By disclosure, Levinas means subjective access to entities, the spatial conditions of which reduce space itself to the mode of representation by which such entities are given or presented to a subject (so that space is itself converted into place or site). Kant is singled out here as the philosopher *par excellence* of such a position that objectifies essence by connecting entities to subjective consciousness via such forms of representation (themselves committed to ever more 'transparent' conditions of disclosure). Responsibility to (or of) the other, if there is any, must therefore be thought as a profound challenge to this particular configuration of object, subject and space (one that is in a certain way always impossible or at any rate never fully possible, and thus prone to a recursive and perhaps even intensifying violence that for Levinas must be lessened). The 'outside', in these terms, must not be reduced to merely the outside of my 'home' or the 'homely', since this would risk reinscription not only of an existing binary but of the larger set of relations that produce it, which is precisely what is to be put in question and indeed transformed here. Still, the 'openness' of which Levinas speaks is far from de-spatialised as such, if only because his allusions to a utopianism that in all probability no thought can escape suggests the persistence of the 'topic' even in the midst of a certain a-topical or u-topian turn.[15] Here, freedom is not so much freedom from space but rather freedom that entails insistent and unconcludable enlargement of what otherwise seems closed or enclosed.[16] In turn, this is not so much a movement 'outwards' (*à la* 'conquest') as one that traces and extends openness within what is supposedly 'inward' where such a tradition of thinking being is concerned.

Levinas's critique of 'disclosure', taking Kantianism as its high point, suggests certain affinities with the analysis of correlationism offered by Quentin Meillassoux. As we have seen, if Levinas's thinking of the 'outside' turns more upon a disorientation of the 'inwardness' he critiques, rather than simply an escape from it, the 'ethical agoraphobia' that writers like Carter and Llewelyn associate with Levinasian responsibility entails a step into the open that is taken, paradoxically enough, in the seeming depths of a 'phobia of the "unconscious" beyond therapy', taking us to a 'place', if it may be called that, that may be construed in terms of the 'other "other scene" beyond the psychoanalytic unconscious'. If such a step opens anew onto the agora, and its perhaps undomesticatable family of terms, it is one that cannot be faced without severe trepidation, indeed which seems to depend on a strongly phobic reaction for its very possibility. Since, as we have argued, Meillassoux's evocation of the 'Great Outdoors' proceeds as much from a deconstruction as a critique of correlationism, one might be tempted to claim a strange and perhaps surprising kinship between the complex movements of Levinasian thought of 'the outside' and the deceptively non-simple aspects of Meillassoux's own philosophical procedure. But, leaving that a little to one side, it is interesting to contrast this idea of agoraphobic fearfulness as the very condition of getting out into the open and our preceding analysis of speculative materialism as *in want of an object to be scared of.* While in the former a fearful doubleness or redoubling lapse of the object (it has gone/it was never there) serves as a provocation to the 'out-of-doors', in the latter it is as if the 'object' in want of a subject or of subject–object relations themselves provokes a drift towards psychotic certainty rather than fearful doubt. As we have already suggested, Meillassouxian thought may do well to be more afraid than it is (or than it *says* that it is) – not least if it is correct to say that any access to the 'outside' (however complexly constituted it may be) depends upon this. It may be that some such trepidation might be detected in Meillassoux's argument about facticity itself. By writing that 'facticity cannot be thought of as another fact in the world – it is not a fact that things are factual, just as it is not a fact that factual things exist',[17] he is impelled towards a 'strong' interpretation of the principle of factuality, whereby factual things can be said to exist not as a fact but rather as 'an absolute necessity'. This is not so much a recoil from the 'outside', of course, as an attempt at philosophical consistency in support of Meillassoux's argument about the 'Great Outdoors'. Yet it may still be ironic that this confident assertion of the integrity of his philosophy – of its self-sufficiency, even – is accompanied by an indispensable double movement, one that does not just lead immediately or straightforwardly 'outwards', but that turns itself outdoors only once its own domestic order and hygiene have been attended to and assured. (Perhaps this is all the more ironic given that, for Meillassoux, getting out of the circle or cycle of correlationism involves precisely an affirmation of the impossible consistency and thus ultimate disorder and impurity of its 'inner' space.) Does a certain agoraphobia in all its doubleness and complexity drive every wish for exteriority, however radical or fundamental it may be, causing it some 'drift', turning it inside-out (and outside-in) at every turn? Are such wishes to be feared, or (to turn this around) is fear itself the very condition of such a wish?

Notes

1 This phrase is cited by Anthony Vidler in *Warped Space: Art, Architecture, and Anxiety in Modern Culture* (Cambridge, MA: MIT Press, 2001), p. 38, where it is tracked to 'Draft M' of 'The Architecture of Hysteria', enclosed in a letter to Wilhelm Fliess in May 1897.

2 Vidler, in *Warped Space*, discusses the connection in Freud's thought between agoraphobia in women and the repressed desire 'to walk the streets' and to engage in the illicit pleasures of streetwalkers. He also comments on Freud's analysis of the urge to defenestrate in young women in terms of the connection between sexual repression and the spatial dynamics of public, metropolitan space. Here, the transgressive desire to beckon up a man from the streets is accompanied by anxiety and guilt that forms the basis for a wish to 'fall' that itself may be interpreted in at least a double sense (38–9).

3 Adam Phillips, *On Kissing, Tickling and Being Bored: Psychoanalytic Essays on the Unexamined Life* (London and Cambridge, MA: Faber and Faber, 1993), p. 16. Page references will be given in the body of the chapter.

4 Paul Carter, *Repressed Spaces: The Poetics of Agoraphobia* (London: Reaktion, 2002), p. 35. Page references will be given in the body of the chapter.

5 The question of the *as if* arises from the Kantian distinction between determining and reflective judgement. In the latter, judgement is unable satisfactorily to determine individual phenomena simply by treating them as a case or example that can readily be subsumed under a more general category, rule or concept. Instead, in the absence of a fully determining law that might accord objectivity to the process at hand, Kant suggests that aesthetic judgement treats phenomena (to cite Samuel Weber's translation) 'in accordance with such a unity as they would have if an understanding (although not our understanding) had furnished them to our cognitive faculties so as to make possible a system of experience according to particular laws of nature' (see Weber, *Mass Mediauras: Form, Technics, Media* (Stanford: Stanford University Press, 1996), p. 18). Here, reflective judgement involves itself in a highly complex procedure to the extent that, in order to arrive at its judgements, it must project and understand nature as purposive; and yet, in regarding nature as the product of an 'understanding', reflective judgement must view this 'understanding' as different from, outside or beyond its own, since its own 'understanding' is precisely incapable of bringing the phenomena at hand to satisfactory judgement. Deconstructive writing has of course made much of this *as if*, tracing its dislocating effects in a number of fields that are far from limited to the

figurative, linguistic or aesthetic domains which, of course, could never contain it.

6 Elsewhere in the book, as we shall see, Carter notes the 'etymological constellation' that includes 'agora' and also 'agros', or, in his terms, 'the wilderness where the shepherd goes with his flock' (113). Whether or not Carter's various etymological linkages are tenuous, the latter certainly conveys a sense of a gathering-together, a 'flocking' of sorts, that is somehow dependent on journeying to the very wildest outdoor locations or the most faraway of places. It is not long before such 'shepherding' or 'gathering' gives way to 'hunting' and 'raiding', needless to say (148), as if the two 'actions' are far from unrelated. Furthermore, in the sense that such a locale perhaps defines the limits of human civilisation, we may find here highly interesting questions of the relationship of 'human' to 'animal', relationships that are not so easily resolved into static identities or fixed hierarchies.

7 Regarding the idea of theatrical space as non-self-identical or dislocated space, the work of Samuel Weber is especially instructive. For Weber, theatricality is what happens when the deconstructive problem of the parergon is restaged. As Derrida shows in *The Truth in Painting*, the Kantian problem of aesthetic form requires a consideration of the contour, boundary, border or frame of the art work. If art's borderline is that which allows 'form' to be established, then it is as much an enabling or constitutive limit as it is an 'outer' or terminal edge. If that which effectively frames art turns out to participate in the very constitution of the work, then this not only troubles the hierarchy which sets aesthetic 'form' above 'frame'. It also means that, as Weber puts it in his influential essay, 'The Unravelling of Form', 'just this participation would require another frame' (see Weber's *Mass Mediauras: Form, Technics, Media*, p. 23). Presumably, this frame would in turn partake of its constitutive function in delineating or demarcating the art work, calling for yet another, and so on. Thus, for Weber the Kantian problem of aesthetic judgement connects to the dislocating effects he associates with theatricality (limited neither to painting, theatre or indeed any art form), with highly ambivalent and unstable yet dynamic consequences for a range of fields, encompassing questions of technics, media, politics, institutions and so on. For a fuller account of Weber's thinking on these topics, see my own *Samuel Weber: Acts of Reading* (Aldershot: Ashgate, 2003), especially the chapter on theatricality (81–102).

8 But here the question of drive and of drift raises itself, in the sense that this projection of drives constitutes itself in part through the anxious image of

a drifting mass, of an undifferentiated mob that sprawls or spreads without clear direction or purpose. The present chapter will return to this issue. As we will see, the question of the relationship of drive and drift thus becomes far from just an etymological one – and perhaps not only a psychoanalytic one, either (or, at any rate, perhaps a question that psychoanalysis or any other 'theoretical' perspective would by definition not be fully equipped to answer, but that might instead trace out the very limits of 'theoretical' possibility as such).

9 This idea is pursued in the following chapter of the present study, in the sense that the Vienna Circle of the early twentieth century sees Freud's flock come adrift due to the agency of complex drives that both constitute and deconstitute it.

10 John Llewelyn, *Emmanuel Levinas: The Genealogy of Ethics* (London: Routledge, 1995), p. 202. Page references will be given in the body of the chapter.

11 See the footnote below – the question of agoraphobia's precise relationship to the site-specific, on the one hand, and to its 'excess', on the other, would doubtless be unanswerable outside a consideration of the complex dynamics of agoraphobia itself, to which the present chapter attends.

12 Thinking of the 'dread' that 'Pascal felt before the eternal silence of infinite space', Llewelyn writes that 'the space of the world, incessantly expanding though it may be, remains a place in which I am incessantly immured' while 'ethical agoraphobia' is endured in an 'open space . . . without walls and without place, a u-topic exteriority' (204). When thinking about agoraphobia, the interplay between the infinite (space) and the particular (place) is a complicated one that no doubt cannot be resolved without recourse to the complex and indeed impossible dynamics that we have begun to trace of agoraphobia itself.

13 Emmanuel Levinas, *Otherwise than Being, or, Beyond Essence*, trans. Alphonso Lingis (Pittsburgh: Duquesne University Press, 1998).

14 See the note below: in his essay 'Place and Utopia' Levinas aligns such a double appropriation of space as place with Christianity. In general this essay is usefully read alongside 'The Outside', not least in terms of Levinas's complex and ambivalent evocation of utopianism, which here veers towards the more critical end of the spectrum.

15 In an essay included in *Difficult Freedom: Essays on Judaism* (London: Athlone, 1990), entitled 'Place and Utopia' (99–102), Levinas shows himself to be sharply critical of the Christian participation in Europe in contrast to the achievements he discerns in the Jewish contribution to

it. (In a way that resonates with some of the analysis in 'The Outside', Christianity is aligned historically with both conquest and conservativism in a double appropriation of space as place.) Here, Levinas is sceptical about Christian utopianism, arguing that its rejection of the world can foster otherworldly tendencies that often obstruct worldly change, or alternatively that may encourage partisan dwelling which answers, with not inconsiderable danger, the sedentary call of the 'village' (as Levinas puts it in 'A Religion for Adults', also found in *Difficult Freedom* (11–23)).

16 The evocation of freedom in conjunction with Levinas's thought obviously requires extensive development. A detailed and complex account can be found running throughout Howard Caygill's *Levinas and the Political* (London and New York: Routledge, 2002). In broad terms, Caygill offers a cogent demonstration of Levinas's philosophically hard-fought commitment to the notion of freedom, especially during the earlier part of his career (albeit that responsibility takes centre-stage over freedom later on, at any rate as the context in which freedom needs to be rethought). For Caygill, Levinas's interest in freedom stems initially from the Bergsonian notion of creative spontaneity (although this was revised by the sense of a difficult freedom after the Second World War), rather than from a liberalistic identification with autonomy. But it is also a view of freedom that eschews the pagan concept of fate which may itself be used to contrast the cultic particularism of a Hitlerian philosophy with the universalist resources of Western civilisation (albeit a 'particularism' that sought universal expansion for itself). Caygill shows how Levinas's concern with freedom powerfully affected his relationship to both Heideggerian and Husserlian thought.

17 Quentin Meillassoux, *After Finitude: An Essay on the Necessity of Contingency*, trans. Ray Brassier (London and New York: Continuum, 2008), p. 75.

9

Lupus (Adler and Freud)

In 1929, Alfred Adler, noted one-time follower of Sigmund Freud, published a book-length case study of 'Miss R.' which commented in detail on the life story of the young daughter of a Viennese tailor.[1] The book itself – a record of Adler's improvised engagements with the girl's diary in front of a select group of psychiatrists and educators – was meant as an introduction to his Individual Psychology. Of the many difficulties faced by his subject that were discussed in this volume, one chapter was devoted to her lupus phobia. Lupus is in fact the name given to a chronic auto-immune disease taking several different forms. As the human immune system becomes dysfunctional and hyperactive it attacks normal, healthy tissue, potentially affecting a number of systems of the body including the lungs, heart, kidneys, blood cells, joints and skin. It is estimated that women are nearly ten times more susceptible to lupus than men. In one form, common in tuberculosis skin infection, painful lesions with an inflamed, nodular appearance form on the nose, eyelids, lips, cheeks, ears and neck. The lesions are often hard and cracked, and can create unsightly pock-marks. They spread virulently across the face, paying little heed to its natural curves and patterns. They are sometimes dry, sometimes weeping, and they are red raw or dark purple to look at. Without proper treatment, these sores can develop into disfiguring skin ulcers, leaving permanent scarring. Such lupus, then, is a continual source of fear for Miss R.

While use of the term 'lupus' dates to the thirteenth century, it was in the nineteenth century that the specific skin diseases in question were medically classified under this name. Lupus may often result when pre-existing tuberculosis is not tackled effectively, and so perhaps unsurprisingly it reached a high point in nineteenth-century industrial and metropolitan Europe. The bacillus causing tuberculosis was not isolated until the early 1880s, while risk of transmission was claimed to be reduced dramatically by the invention of the pasteurisation process, milk being thought of as an important source of infection. If one might be tempted to attribute lactaphobia, of which Deleuze was known to suffer, to a fear of mother's milk, the latter being no doubt susceptible to classic psychoanalytic interpretation (e.g. Oedipal repression), nevertheless the auto-immune risk posed by unpasteurised or 'raw' milk might differently nuance such enquiry.[2] Miss R. herself veers wildly between a childhood love of mother's milk, from which she refuses to be weaned (this and other eating disorders are linked to her attempts to exert control in the family setting, to which her lupus phobia also relates), and revulsion and distrust of milk in other contexts, for example when offered sickly sweet milky drinks at a children's party (of course, since such horror and loathing of milk is undoubtedly part of her lupus fear, it's a thin line between Miss R.'s love and hate where milk is concerned). In terms of the treatment of lupus, meanwhile, sufferers were condemned to decades of agony, due to the chronic and progressive nature of the disease, until, as the century drew to a close, photobiomodulation – a form of light therapy – was found to be an effective form of treating the condition. If the incidence of lupus began to decline thereafter, the fact that well into the twentieth century Adler was writing about lupus phobia suggests that the disease still existed to a significant degree. What is also clear is that its persistence, as one might expect, was largely among the poor and, of course, women. Mention in Adler's text of hospitals or homes specifically for lupus sufferers dotted around the town suggests a kind of subterranean afterlife for the disease, hidden away as it was in dark, dingy, near-phantasmic places, quarantined so as to generate relief and dread in equal measure, echoing perhaps the terror of leprosy in earlier times.[3] Indeed, the very fact of this afterlife – both in real and psychic terms – suggests the difficulty of lupus's containment in at least some important senses. Such gloomy 'hospitals' bear an uncanny (rather than simply demarcated) relationship to the bright sanatoriums devoted to the treatment of psychological ailments, which, given her condition (though perhaps not her relative poverty), Miss R. herself seems always on the verge of gravitating towards.

Although the origin of the designation is not clear, the term 'lupus' – connected to the word 'lupine' (meaning wolf-like) – may have originally been used to indicate the fearful speed and voracity with which the disease can develop and spread. Lupus is, indeed, hungry like the wolf, as one sixteenth-century commentator put it. Adler himself notes the connection between the two terms, calling this terrible condition 'a devouring disease whose name in Latin means wolf' (196). In fact this remark comes, perhaps pointedly, at such an early moment in the chapter on lupus that one cannot fail to register the implied connection between Adler's own study of phobia and the case of the Wolf Man in Freud, which the latter worked on during the period that immediately followed Adler's split from the Freudians (penning the text, in fact, in the same year that Jung was effectively driven out of the group).[4] It could be, then, that the question of lupus phobia, and indeed of lupine terror (threat of the hungry wolf), might need to be addressed by way of the complex dynamics of the Freud–Adler relation, in which phobia may therefore play its part, as much as in terms of Miss R.'s own neuroses. (For Agamben, of course, the wolf or rather wolf-man is intimately connected in European culture and memory to the figure of the outlaw, while for Derrida the wolf exists in an uncanny and deconstructible rather than stably oppositional relation to the figure of the sovereign.[5]) That lupus is an auto-immune condition may be far from irrelevant here, not least when it comes to the question of expulsion from the Freudian inner circle of those that helped to found it. Lupus and lupus phobia might indeed spread in unstable, auto-immunitary ways from the back-street hospital to the very home and hearth of psychoanalysis, or vice versa. The auto-immune breakdown entailed by lupus involves, of course, disfigurement of one's face, the face that one shows to the world, a disfigurement that in a certain sense comes from outside infection (the purported risk of tuberculosis being heightened by unpasteurised milk, for instance), but that in another respect is also self-inflicted (namely, through auto-immunitary failure). The process of such disfigurement may describe what happened to the public face (not to mention the private relationships) of Freud's Vienna Circle, as much as that of the lupus sufferers themselves.

At its high point, then, lupus was at once a very modern condition – indeed a symptom of modernity itself as it stood at the crossroads between mass society, urban pandemonium, and rife infection and disease, on the one hand, and the birth of the clinic, medical breakthrough, public health and sanitation,[6] technological innovation and legal, organisational and administrative discipline on the other – and yet it was also something that found its origin and identity in supposedly ancient fears that seemed as yet unallayed: horror of vampirism, for instance, to which it was connected in medieval times, terror of the shape-shifter, revulsion of the leper, or for that matter dread of the devouring wolf. Lupus phobia may well connect to a fear of the 'open' in multiple senses, uncertainly both very new and very old: fear of open spaces, of open sores, open caskets, open jaws. As this fearful 'open' takes its many-headed hold, therefore, the spread of lupus (phobia) cannot be neatly confined so as to permit its isolation as the mere 'object' of a certain clinical or psychoanalytic practice, dispassionately considering its findings from the detached position granted by an authoritative scientific modernity. Instead, what we are calling 'lupus' – itself a convenient catch-all term for a number of distinct ailments across which the word somewhat messily spreads[7] – echoes the very story we might tell about the onset (and indeed fragmentation) of psychoanalysis. One might say, in fact, that lupus's historic arc mirrors the early history of psychoanalysis itself. The socio-cultural dimensions and psychic stakes of lupus – represented through the multiple prisms of gender, class, sexuality, the metropolis, modern cultural memory, and so on – resonate powerfully, because so ambivalently, with psychoanalysis's complex interests and tensions as they play themselves out. If the approach I am outlining seems, perhaps despite itself, to 'read' lupus somewhat too psychoanalytically, that is to say from the perspective of post-Freudian types of analysis, then I would suggest that, nevertheless, it simultaneously opens psychoanalysis to the 'other' of its own concerns.

Of course, by the time of *The Case of Miss R.*, Adler's break with Freudian psychoanalysis was long established, and indeed in the text itself he rarely misses the opportunity to contest certain modes of psychological explanation associated with his one-time master. The analytic legitimacy of the Oedipus complex is frequently challenged, for instance, and the child's struggle for superiority in the family setting is often denied any sexual interpretation. In this sense, to trace out any connection between the lupus motif and the question of psychoanalysis really comes down to another question of the domestic disputes within the psychoanalytic 'family'. It is interesting in this respect that Adler's interpretation of the anxiety neuroses of an overly indulged daughter unfailingly hinges on her attempts to assert superiority over those around her (efforts which, he acknowledges, derive from an actual deficit of such superior feelings). As one reads *The Case of Miss R.*, it is difficult not to be struck by the pomposity of Adler's criticisms of the girl's attempts at self-elevation, especially when one considers that the entire text is constructed out of his virtuoso performances in front of a captive audience of fans. If, according to Adler's reading, the badly spoilt Miss R. never misses an opportunity to place herself centre-stage, one senses a certain amount of projection on his part. In her quest to achieve superiority, Miss R.'s tendency towards boastfulness and condescension is hardly absent from Adler's own snobbery, for instance in his remarks about popular theatre (71). The strong whiff of arrogance that pervades the text, especially when one considers its performative conditions (Adler being able to decipher the case instantaneously, and on the spot), suggests that the tussle between deep feelings of inferiority, on the one hand, and the wish for ultimate superiority, on the other, is hardly confined to the analysand. It is perhaps no wonder that Miss R. has a personality type of interest to Adler, although despite the holistic or connective claims of Individual Psychology he never reflects on that personality type as anything other than a distinct 'object' of impartial psychological analysis.

In an earlier part of the text, a further possible explanation for Miss R.'s lupus phobia presents itself, although tellingly Adler is slow on the uptake. Miss R. writes: 'My face often became deeply flushed from the effort I made to repress my thoughts' (31). If the effort of self-repression, or self-cover-up, causes Miss R. to colour up with an embarrassment she cannot fully hide, the fear of lupus may arise from a certain projection or displacement of these feelings onto a reviled or repulsive 'other'. (An 'other' upon whom all eyes must turn for rather different reasons, such that the lupus sufferer as a figure of *unwanted* attention permits a certain kind of disavowal.) Such projection may not be Miss R.'s alone, however. For isn't Adler embarrassed to hog centre-stage so ostentatiously while pontificating about Miss R.'s attempts to steal the limelight? Such embarrassment, if it exists, is as much repressed in the text as the obvious connection between lupus phobia and the deeply flushed face of Miss R. Perhaps revealingly, Adler rather suddenly closes the chapter in which this fragment appears, by dismissing Miss R.'s self-reflections as 'useless puttering' (31). In a later chapter, meanwhile, Adler offers some reflections of his own about those men who expose themselves to women in the street, branding such 'exhibitionists' out-and-out 'cowards' (146). Indeed, what else are we to make of insufferable show-offs who, in Adler's own terms, 'extract a cheap triumph from their seeming power to force another human being into a wretched situation' (147) – namely, that of making a captive other degradingly beholden to oneself? One might think that Adler's moral indignation at flashers is something of a cheap cover-up. For, as he works his way through passages of Miss R.'s diary, each segment of extemporised interpretation is little more than a quick flash of Adler's prodigious mind, not least as it weighs itself against that of Dr Freud. (Although perhaps the entire performance is less a matter of besting psychoanalysis as such, than it is an expression of Adler's desire to go one better than Freud when it comes to commanding centre-stage.) Further on in the text, Adler writes that Miss R.'s neurosis begins at the point when she 'fills her time . . . by occupying herself constantly with the matter of superiority in her own circle' (173) – neurosis being the condition in which, as we are told a few sentences later, one is simultaneously 'ambitious, but discouraged' (175). Such neurosis leads to all manner of avoidance techniques in respect of the original problem, one piled upon the other, a veritable 'refuse heap' which becomes in turn the very 'mountain' that the neurotic aspires foolhardily to climb in his 'lust for power' (175–6). It is in such contexts, I would argue, that lupus phobia – with its complex origins in competitive egotistical drives, the desire to press others into service, as well as disavowal or embarrassed repression – leads us back to the family fall-outs of psychoanalysis (as itself, perhaps, the very analysis of fragile communality).

Miss R., then, increasingly rejects authentic social situations or social interaction ('the real demands of communal life', as Adler puts it (177)), in favour either of increasing detachment and isolation, or highly contrived relationships constructed purely on her own terms. But, as Adler himself asks, what happens 'when a girl like this attempts to avoid the sun?' (181) – sunlight, as we now know, being a recognised treatment for skin conditions. Given that much of the case study reflects on Miss R.'s deliberations over whether she would prefer to be a boy rather than a girl (the chapter in which this scene is presented, 'The Masculine Protest', concerns this very desire to convert femininity into masculinity,[8] and perhaps even to take all identity in a paternal direction), one wonders whether, in terms of the various correspondences we are tracing out across this text, Adler himself feels deprived of the sun, i.e., Freud himself? This would imply a chain of father figures, running from the Viennese tailor who Miss R. seeks to control as much as emulate, to Adler as a kind of paternal substitute tending to the child's needs in a way that presumably the parents are incapable of, to Freud as ultimate patriarch who Adler nonetheless wishes to match in a similar way that the daughter wants to rival her dad. The idea of the patriarch Freud as a 'sun' is not just fortuitous. In 1911, the very year of the split with Adler, Freud was preparing his text on Schreber, which included explicit criticisms of Adler's attempts to analyse psychic operations in terms of social relations. A break was becoming inevitable, and Freud was flexing his authorita-tive muscles. In that text, which discusses Schreber's delusional boast that he could stare directly at the sun without risk of dazzlement, Freud asserts the sun as a sublimated symbol of the father. But Schreber is deluded, of course. The sun is indeed as potentially blinding as it is warming or healing. Miss R. herself writes: 'I thought it out thus, that the sun had taken away some of my power of sight, and that I would have to go blind' (182). Here, Adler speaks of withdrawal from the sun in terms of Miss R.'s attempts to ensure she is 'cut off' from 'the problem which she seeks to avoid' (182). That a dazzling sun provokes such retreat and such blindness at one and the same time strengthens the impression that Adler may be talking as much about the analyst as about his patient.[9] Of Miss R.'s potentially insightful remark, however, Adler says merely that she 'would have been able to do nothing with such insight; it would not have helped her system'. It is possible to interpret such dismissiveness by suggesting that, like Miss R., Adler himself recoils from this insight, preferring wounded retreat and escape as 'the solution of life's problems' (182). Perhaps, in terms of all the associations we are following here, the fact that sunlight may alleviate the condition in question as much as encourage its repression is an idea that is simply unbearable to Adler.

Miss R.'s solution to such thwarted insight involves, once again, displacement. She tries to exert superiority by forcing others ('Olga or some other friend') to stare directly at the sun, hoping for some debilitating damage to their eyesight. Adler calls this, with some understatement, 'her unsocial trait' (183). At a stroke, risk of one's own blindness is converted into domination over others as precisely an effect of the inability to cope with 'the real demands of communal life', as Adler previously puts it. Moreover, these others are tricked into compliance ("'I don't know what is in my eye, I can't look at the sun, can you?'" (183)), mistaking hidden disdain for comradery.[10] Once again, it is as if Adler's own story – indeed, the story of the text's own manner of composition (I can't write this directly, while speaking; can you take notes?) – intrudes revealingly on that of his subject. Others can be dazzled, I no longer wish to be (and vice versa). Yet, still, intense fear of the sun – heliophobia, one might say – results in desperate suicidal feelings on Miss R.'s part. Ironically, that which comes to be considered an apt treatment for an auto-immune disease is here the very source of self-destructive impulses. It is as if we are in the midst of a hyper-auto-immunity whereby that which may alleviate or repair is thoroughly contaminated by that which aggravates the immune disorder (the sun causing suicidal feelings). Despite every effort at displacement or disavowal, then, something deeply moribund persists in such dealings with the 'sun'.

It is this heliophobia that drives Miss R. into retreat, keeping her off the streets for fear not just of sunstroke or sunburn but of a lightning bolt from the sky. In other words, heliophobia leads to a certain agoraphobia. Adler links Miss R.'s increasingly hermetic lifestyle with her private reading, which is devoted to an autodidactic kind of sexual education. Hiding away from the sun, it seems, only encourages the desire for sexual explanations − those that, elsewhere in the text, Adler refutes in his dismissive attitude to Freudian psychoanalysis. There are enough allusions to the self-harm caused by masturbation in this text (not least, on the part of Miss R.'s own father), that the risk of weakening eyesight accompanying such thorough scrutiny of secret books cannot go unnoticed. Here, a particular kind of illumination vies with terrible eyestrain. This is not only Miss R.'s predicament, of course (she herself fears that blindness may be contagious), in the sense that Adler's own case study wants to expose and disavow the Freudian 'text' − replete as it is with sexual explanation − at one and the same time. To countenance it if only to reject it. If the blinding eyestrain that results from ill-fated countenancing hints at juvenile masturbation as much as it recalls features of the Freud-Adler split, we might think that by straining at the Freudian 'text' Adler's own exhibition-ism risks becoming somewhat onanistic. (Here, it is interesting to note that, amid all the inconsistent features and effects of the Miss R. case history, Adler does strive to expunge Freud as 'object' in a way that echoes the auto-eroticism of the dreamer whose dreams with a dental stimulus lead to objectless release.)

In the pages forming the run-up to the chapter on lupus phobia, then, all manner of phobias suddenly present themselves.

Heliophobia provokes agoraphobia (and there is much in the pages of this book about prostitutes visible in high-up windows and on the street[11]), but it also prompts the dreadful idea that one's eyes might be 'knocked out' (it is interesting that this comes so soon after the remarks about eyestrain), which in turn aggravates fears with a dental focus, as Miss R. worries that her teeth may break or crumble at any moment. A lengthy scene follows concerning the anxiety associated with 'knocking out' or pulling teeth, during which Miss R. in fact swallows one of her own teeth in the dentist's chair (such stubborn auto-affection, for want of a better term, recalls the masturbation explanation of dreams of teeth-pulling found in Freud). One cannot fail to detect the potential for a nod or three in Freud's direction.[12] The case would seem to encourage Adler to prepare himself for the ensuing discussion of phobia in its own right by marshalling the psychological resources at hand. But they are totally unacknowledged. The lupus phobia arises from the next in this series of phobic connections. Miss R. writes:

> I was just returning from school. I had accompanied a friend and wanted to cross the street. A man approached us from the other side. He had a cloth around his face. I thought at first he had a toothache. When he came nearer I noticed that his whole face was eaten away. There was no nose, no lips, only a number of red holes. I felt as if someone had struck me. I was seized with such dread of this man that in order not to retrace his footsteps I turned around and made a detour home. (194)

Here, as the cloth gapes about the face, the play of veiling and unveiling, blindness and insight, returns once more like the repressed, and we are confronted by the disfigurement caused by wounds that just won't heal. Phobia spreads like lupus – the scene is agoraphobic and ondontophobic as much as lupus phobic, and derives its terrible power from all the preceding phobias that threaten to crowd in upon it. The heliophobia that leads to the thought of a lightning strike, for instance, may well lie behind the impression of being 'struck'. Various eating phobias alluded to earlier also possibly come home to roost in the image of a face nearly eaten away, albeit one that presumably has inordinate difficulty in eating. The dreadful visage of the lupus sufferer is foreshadowed by the 'angry face' (190) of the dentist that in the preceding chapter so terrifies the young Miss R. It rears its head, too, in the strange description of the father who 'continually slapped his face in his sleep' (221), with all of the shameful overtones of nocturnal masturbation (such night-time self-slapping, of course, risks 'knocking out' a tooth).[13] The needle Miss R. uses to scrape shameful tartar from her teeth while nobody can see recalls the tailor's lonely and lowly profession, and perhaps it is even the case that the 'perforated' (212), pin-cushion face of the lupus sufferer projects feelings of shame at the father's trade (perhaps even shame of the father or family shame more generally). Later in the lupus chapter, Adler suggests that Miss R. would not 'take up dressmaking because that is a subordinate profession', while during her time studying at a business school the fear that her father's trade will become known causes her 'blushing all over', not to mention a constant sense of being 'on pins and needles' (225–6). The latter, in con-junction with Miss R.'s reddened checks, once more connect her lupus phobia to family shame (one that the psychoanalytic family itself can hardly dispense with). Each phobia is contamin-ated or infected by the other.

Amid this collection of phobias and phobic connections, however, Adler tells us at the very beginning of the lupus chapter that 'the last thing she collected in her effort to rid herself of reality was a man with a rash' (195). Lupus may be decisive in prompting near-absolute recoil from 'the real demands of communal life', but nevertheless retreat into the home also sparks a desire to confess this episode to the father. Whether or not such talk is curative, it expresses renewed confidence in the family and its paternal head, as Adler himself surmises. But Miss R.'s motives are once more deceptive, in that what she really hopes to do is reappropriate the father and the family setting for her own ends, in order to come out on top.[14] If it is dubious whether the outside world will accord her a 'favourable, central place', then a return of sorts to the 'bosom of her family' offers the better chance of hogging the limelight (196). Miss R. must reinvent the family in her own image, and tellingly it is phobia that makes this possible (just as, for psychoanalysis itself, phobia compensates for a lapse in the paternal function, restoring the father's authority as the cue to forestall the subject's drift towards psychotic breakdown). Again, one wonders whether we might as well be talking about Adler himself (surrounded by his acolytes, dazzling them with his brilliant analyses of phobia), as about his patient.

Back home, fatherly reassurances aim to persuade Miss R. that lupus is not infectious, though her doubts persist and indeed grow. Confidence in the father is fragile and perhaps short-lived (he can only offer only a little consolation 'from time to time', which, as Adler observes, 'means almost nothing' (213)). The positive potential of lupus phobia in helping to realise the girl's strategic aims is, therefore, obviously limited. It can rebound on her at any moment, causing sudden upsurges of anxiety neurosis. Dread of lupus threatens to overwhelm the functional purposes of lupus phobia, as if – as Adler himself puts it – 'she can use her lupus phobia to escape the solution to any problem' (199).

Lupus, in other words, compounds the very problems for which it is also potentially the solution. The auto-immunitary character of lupus phobia, like lupus itself, thus threatens to spread. Miss R. imagines that the whole town is rife with lupus: '"Where," I asked myself, "is there a place on earth where there is no lupus? Where is there a spot where no lupus sufferer has left bacteria behind him?" The whole world appeared to me infected' (200).

Adler, the outcast progeny, comments: 'You see here the gesture of exclusion of the spoiled child' (200). Quite.[15] Miss R. sees the terrors of lupus as reserved for her, and for her alone. Nobody else suffers so. To her mind, it is a special kind of punishment. Her 'relentless misfortune' is 'diabolic' (206), although at the same time she is uniquely pure, uncontaminated, superior, 'sacred' or saint-like in fact (211). The family is her only resource, but it is not to be trusted (201–2). She resorts to an impossibly exacting regime of hygiene, trying to purge herself of any trace or taint of lupus – the purge, as we know, always coming close and closer to home (until, at last, the girl's own hands, scrubbed to the bone with potassium permanganate, become 'terribly rough, as hard as leather and full of cracks' (213), just like the faces of lupus victims themselves). Nonetheless, lupus phobia continues to manifest itself as a fear of the streets, of the vagaries of the outside world ('I clung to the belief that the soles of my shoes were infected by having stepped on the same pavement on which the man with lupus had walked' (203)). The terrible dilemma for Miss R. is that her washing compulsion is aimed simultaneously at fear of the dirty street-beggar who suffers from lupus, and fear of infection at the hands of her own family (domestic items 'had been infected by the infected hands of my family', for instance the bread that is cut by unwashed hands, the hands of a mother that clean the apartment floor or of a parent that handles money that may have passed through a sufferer's hands (204)). Thus it is impossible to decide which is the more dangerous place, the world outside the family, or the world within it (thus, Miss R.'s contaminated shoes, so she believes, come to infect the floor of the family apartment, as the contagion spreads inwards). Here, in being unable to decide whether it is more dangerous on the inside or the outside, Miss R.'s predicament is, of course, Adler's own. The story of lupus (and indeed lupus phobia) as the self-destructive result of a hyperactive and dysfunctional immune system is, in other words, near-identical to that of psychoanalysis.

As the lupus chapter of the case study draws to a close, Miss R. is found carelessly dropping her pocket mirror on the floor. (She becomes more and more mirror-obsessed, and more and more superstitious about broken mirrors.) That which is used to inspect the face makes contact with potentially infected ground. Unsurprisingly, the mirror – like the facial skin of lupus victims – cracks. Miss R. resorts to her sense of diabolical misfortune – she predicts years of bad luck – which ironically confirms something of her sense of identity, even though she is now rendered somewhat incapable of seeing her own reflection. Blindness and insight vie uneasily once more. The lupus contagion that causes cracks to appear almost everywhere yet again encourages Miss R. 'to escape the solution to any problem', to reprise Adler's own terms, or at any rate to find a certain solution in the avoidance of any solution. Despite all her efforts at hygiene and purity, she is simply blighted. At this point Adler, using words that might be turned upon himself, remarks: 'It is comprehensible that every one who does not believe in himself has to believe in something else, whatever it may be' (230). The cracked mirror nonetheless causes new depths of depression for Miss R., and sparks renewed attempts at displaced abjection, Miss R. contriving to break the pocket mirrors of several of those around her, rendering them, too, unable to properly contemplate their own faces except in cracked form, and trapping them in her own luckless state. Miss R. then recalls a childhood memory, 'collecting memories again to support her neurotic behaviour': 'that as a small child I was once afraid of a mirror. I was passing a glassware store and looked into one of the mirrors on display. From it a horribly swollen face stared back at me' (231).

Is Miss R.'s case history itself a similar kind of mirror into which Adler himself stares aghast, disbelievingly? In his commentary, he triumphantly identifies the significance of the scene – 'Again the swollen face!' – but is incapable of further analysis. As Miss R.'s tale continues, it turns out that the mirror in question is of a special kind, in that it is designed to distort all that it reflects, rendering partially unrecognisable every reflection, although making each one all the more compelling for its uncanny or monstrous distortions. Miss R.'s narrative wanders associatively in the direction of another memory, that of a petroleum lamp at home which 'had a reflector to make the light shine more brightly' (or in other words to manipulate or distort it). If the light therapy used to treat lupus is recalled here, nonetheless Miss R. finds this device bothersome and disturbing. On no account will she touch it. The source of potential healing, it would seem, once more transmutes into a possible source of contamination. Were she to touch it, another mirror might crack, incurring yet more bad luck (despite the fact that, as had long since been discovered, to be 'touched' by such light may be curative). Indeed, Miss R. fears that this mirror may break *on account of* 'the intense heat of the petroleum flame' – a strange reversal indeed of the positive effect of light therapy on cracked facial skin. She takes her seat – elsewhere likened to a throne – as far away from the light as possible. If Adler himself once more springs to mind, it is interesting to note that even this solution is not enough for Miss R. She pleads with the father 'to take the reflector off the lamp' (232), to break the spell as it were. Whether his mastery in such matters is indispensable, or whether, spoilt child that she is, Miss R. simply avails herself of his services, still the outcome is far from satisfactory. For, it being done, Miss R. worries about what they – the family – will do with this seemingly jinxed object. Mother wants it thrown in the trash, plain and simple, where Miss R. fears it will shatter, unseen, into pieces. Mother therefore offers to give it away to others. Despite all we know of Miss R.'s own gifts, this solution is also far from a reassuring one, presaging the spreading of yet more bad luck. (On other occasions, of course, she wishes for just such a thing, although equally she is also prone to considering herself uniquely unlucky.) Finally, the mirror is stored 'in a wooden box in the cellar', interred like a dead thing in the bowels of the home, a little like the vampire with whom lupus was connected in medieval times. If Adler interprets all of this in terms of the attempt to avoid bad luck (albeit by acknowledging the inevitability of one's bad luck) and thus to control one's fate, the returning 'repressed' of such vampiric burial seems equally fated. And not just for Miss R.

Notes

1 Alfred Adler, *The Case of Miss R.: The Interpretation of a Life Story*, trans. Eleanore and Friedrich Jensen (New York: Greenberg Publisher, 1929). Page references will be given in the body of the chapter.
2 The cultural phenomenon of certain individuals crossing state borders in search of 'raw' milk (notably in the US) becomes interesting here, to

the extent that it provides another context for thinking about lactaphobia and lactaphilia in terms of illicit border crossings and betrayals, of federal territory but also of the body, the family, the species, of the healthy/sick opposition, the raw/cooked distinction, and so forth. All of this might be interpreted with the concept of auto-immunity in mind. The idea that milk is at once the most natural and unnatural, the most familiar and alien, of liquid substances thereby gives rise to multiple strands of analysis.

3 Miss R. in fact makes this very same connection, mistaking lupus for a disease of biblical proportions (216).

4 Adler's departure happened in 1911. The Wolf Man case study was published in 1918, although it was written in 1914, the year that Jung left the group, a further and perhaps yet more devastating exit. One wonders, then, if the lupine references running across more than one psychoanalytic text have something to do with this history of banishment and exclusion (but also fearful return), especially since such ideas are an integral part of the 'wolf' motif across centuries of cultural practice and memory. (I do not have the time or space here to do adequate justice to recent analyses of the wolf motif, but as I mention subsequently, I would refer the reader to Agamben's *Homer Sacer* texts, where the wolf is identified with the outlaw, or Derrida's *The Beast and the Sovereign*, in which man's sovereignty is constructed in an uncanny relationship to the fearful wolf.) In this sense, the 'Wolf Man' may be as much about Adler and/or Jung (and, therefore, Freud himself) as Sergei Pankejeff, the original subject. Once again, the question of auto-immunity would seem to rear its ugly head. Or, as Freud famously says in *Civilization and its Discontents*, *Homo homini lupus* (man is wolf to man), and thus 'man' eats or devours himself as the (non- or lupine) man he truly is.

5 See Giorgio Agamben's *Homo Sacer* series, beginning with *Homo Sacer: Sovereign Power and Bare Life* (Stanford: Stanford University Press, 1998), and Jacques Derrida, *The Beast and the Sovereign* Vol. I (Chicago: Chicago University Press, 2009) and *The Beast and the Sovereign* Vol. II (Chicago: Chicago University Press, 2011).

6 The last chapter of the Miss R. case study details her fears and superstitions about gutter drains. Rumour has it that girls who step on such drains will never marry. This particular fear of hers extends into a phobic cartography, manifesting itself in the superstitious avoidance of certain tram lines, forbidden streets, no-go coffee houses, and so forth. Her entire psyche becomes a veritable map of potential infection, in other words.

7 This is why 'lupus' is in an important sense nothing other than fear of lupus, or lupus phobia. Or, to put it differently, given that Miss R. fears

handling a coin that may have come into contact with 'a drop of pus' (215–16) and then scratching her own eye so as to infect it, lupus is indeed in the eye of the beholder. 'Finally', she says, 'I fancied that the mere thought of contact with lupus might produce the disease' (216).

8   We might ask, who really dreams of the young girl becoming a boy? Miss R. herself, or Adler in the sense that the young girl's case may facilitate projection of his own anxiety neurosis?

9   It may be interesting to note that in the penultimate chapter of the case study Adler effectively disavows any blindness on his part, and projects it elsewhere, by accusing his own critics of being 'blinded by rage' in their belief that he totally dispenses with questions of sexuality in his own psychological approach (237).

10 In Adler's chapter on lupus phobia, Miss R. is to be found secretly rubbing sugar lumps on the supposedly contaminated soles of her shoes before delightedly feeding them to a sweet-toothed other. In fact she tries several different ways to infect her friends. Is this, in effect, what Adler is doing in holding forth before his own self-assembled congregation?

11 Adler speculates on the child's desire to make or have money, which provokes some degree of prostitute-envy, in terms of money's capacity to equalise relations (i.e., the child imagines that money is a neutral form of exchange-value capable of delivering equality, even though one might have thought that prostitution would as much unsettle as confirm such a conviction).

12 In some ways the entire case study could be read as a text crying out for a Freudian interpretation that is deliberately refused.

13 This scene connects to a feeling of family shame in the further sense that the tailor, as the case study makes clear, plies his trade late into the night. We might also note that it is interesting to find, near the end of the narrative, Miss R. seeking employment in a dentist's surgery, fascinated as she is to see what 'pulling teeth' actually looks like.

14 In connection with this, Adler details how Miss R. tries a host of different sleeping arrangements with various family members, bed-swapping night by night as a way of attempting to exert control and to establish pecking order within the home. Adler would doubtless feel his own interpretation of this behaviour to be at odds with Freudian sexual theory.

15 At another point, again perhaps revealingly, Adler states that 'pampered children leave places to which they have been long accustomed very reluctantly' (222).

Index

dialectic, xii, 17, 23–4, 26, 28,
31, 36n3, 37n9, 46, 51–3, 55,
57, 72n12, 122–4
dogmatism, 8, 185, 188, 190,
212

economy, 42, 47, 59–60, 71n7,
74–6, 80, 96n1, 106, 111–12,
204, 223, 225, 228
ego, ix–x, xxiv, 34, 40, 82, 99n9,
152, 155, 181n9, 201–2, 208,
243
Eisenhower, President Dwight
D., xiv, 75–80, 98n3
emancipation, 43–4, 51–2,
56, 65, 71n7, 72n9, 72n12,
73n18
Empedocles, 164
equality/inequality, 47, 49, 62,
64–5, 73n18, 220
ethics, xxii, 30, 45, 51, 54, 65–6,
122–4, 226–8, 230, 234n10,
234n12
Europe, viii, xxii, 28, 30, 35, 42,
71n2, 71n4, 73n15, 83, 132,
228, 234n15, 237, 239

Fanon, Frantz, xi–xii, 23–4,
26–36, 36n1, 36n3–n6,
36n9
fascism, xiii, 10–11, 13–14, 19,
39, 53
Foucault, Michel, 36n5, 50
freedom, xi, 23, 25–6, 56, 62,
64, 122, 200, 229, 234n15,
235n16

Freud, Anna, 152, 181n9
Freud, Sigmund, vii–ix, xiii–xv,
xviii–xx, xxiii–xxiv, 1–2,
16, 39–40, 82–96, 98n6–n9,
100–1, 133–40, 149n9–n10,
145–59, 161, 163, 166,
177–80, 180n1, 180n3–n4,
181n5–n6, 183n15–n16,
184n17, 203–4, 210, 215–17,
225–6, 232n2, 234n9, 236,
239–41, 243–4, 246–7,
254n4, 255n12, 255n14

Genet, Jean, xiv, 102–7, 109,
112, 122, 124, 125n1
Goya, Francisco, 119–20
Guattari, Felix, 56–7, 154

Hegel, G. W. F., xi–xii, xv, 3–4,
9–10, 12, 19, 20n7, 23–8,
31, 34–5, 36n2, 37n5, 37n9,
46, 52–5, 102–3, 120, 122–4,
125n1, 165
Heidegger, Martin, 3–4, 8,
131–2, 210, 214n11, 235n16
Hobbes, Thomas, 40, 45–6
Hume, David, xxi, 194–5,
198–9, 202, 208
Husserl, Edmund, 4, 235n16
hysteria, xv–xvi, 20n7, 85, 88,
133–41, 142n9–n10, 146,
148, 213n8, 218–19, 221,
232n1

Jew, 10–11, 13–14, 121–2,
234n15

revolution, xiii, 29, 44–5, 47, 49,
50–2, 56, 58, 63, 70, 71n7,
153, 200, 212n2
rights, xiii, 43, 62–70, 73n15,
73n16

Sartre, Jean-Paul, 4
Schapiro, Meyer, 132
science, xiv, xxi, 16–19, 74, 78,
95, 96n1, 186–7, 193–4, 199,
206, 212n2
Sophocles, 54, 61
sovereignty, 39–41, 52, 100, 239,
254n4–n5
Stanislavski, Konstantin, 222–3
sublime, 46, 113–20, 171–2,
175
symbolic, ix, 10, 142n10, 160,
183n16, 184n17, 206–7

totalitarianism, 11–14, 19, 64, 66
transcendent(al), 3, 27, 30, 55,
106–7, 124, 172, 187, 211,
212n2, 227
trauma, 65, 146–8
Trump, Donald, xvi

unconscious, ix, 15, 31, 78, 83,
86–7, 89–90, 94, 110, 211,
218, 226–8, 230
University, xv–xvi, 5–6, 78,
126–31, 133–6, 138, 140–1,
141n1, 141n6, 142n8, 142n10

Valéry, Paul, 166
Van Gogh, Vincent, 128, 131
Vidler, Anthony, 180n2–n3,
232n1–n2
Vienna Circle, xxiv, 234n9, 239
violence, xi–xiv, xvi, 28–9,
38–9, 41–61, 65–6, 69–70,
70n1–n2, 71n6–n7, 72n10,
72n12, 107, 120–1, 182n12,
203, 229; see also antiviolence;
counterviolence; nonviolence

Weber, Samuel, 126, 128, 181n8,
232n5, 233n7
wolf, xxiv, 238–40, 254n4

Žižek, Slavoj, xi, xiv, 9–15, 19,
20n7, 81–2, 98n5
Zurich School, 84, 93